Additional Praise for
Fraud Fighter: My Fables and Foibles

Wells' memoir is fantastic; the crime fighting is thrilling, but also the story of Dr. Wells' life and careers is an entertaining read as it vacillates between slightly notorious to downright legendary. Although the book is primarily a story of the motivations and achievements of one man, it has profound lessons for all—not the least of which is that crime fighters have fun and win in the end.

> Sherron Watkins, who helped uncover the Enron fraud
> and is one of the trio of whistleblowers named
> *Time Magazine*'s 2002 Persons of the Year

Fasten your seat belt and get set for a wild ride as you take an amazing trip through the life adventures of Joseph Wells. This is a story that only he could tell. You will laugh, cry, feel immense pride, suffer through disappointment, and perhaps even engage in a bit of self-denial when you realize that the "fraudster" exists in each and every one of us. When all is said and done, my hunch is that you will be more than a little envious of Dr. Wells' incredible life and accomplishments.

> R. Frank Abel, Past President, Maryland Chapter of the
> Association of Certified Fraud Examiners

Wow. Just wow. It took an enormous amount of personal integrity for Dr. Wells to put these words out there for us to see. And throughout it all, he kept his humor and grace. *Fraud Fighter* is, at turns, instructive, funny, and vulnerable. We are indebted to Wells for sharing so much of himself.

> Janet M. McHard, President, McHard/Accounting/
> Consulting/LLC

It takes a larger-than-life character to bust characters who would be larger than life. Dr. Wells is one of the good guys, a character with character.

> Mark Alimena, Partner, Financial Services, JH Cohn LLP

Will Rogers never met Ross Perot, yet Dr. Wells did. He also met Rudy Guliani and many other famous people. Funny and poignant, Fraud Fighter is classic Wells. Looking into himself, he finds a source of strength—he knows the window provided into his life will become a mirror, reflecting into our own.

> Joel T. Bartow, Director, Program Integrity, Express Scripts

What a great story of personal strife, tragedy, triumph, and love. I saw a lot of myself in Joseph Wells and both liked and disliked what I saw. To me, his story is a testament to the frailty of life and what perseverance and dedication can accomplish regardless of our beginnings. No one is perfect; we are all human and life is filled with good and bad. But Dr. Wells' "good" won out over the bad, and his legacy will live on in one of his greatest gifts to society—the Association of Certified Fraud Examiners. A great read!

Cecil Brasher, Director of Auditing, Union Pacific Corporation

Being an educator and always looking for readings for my *Principles of Fraud Examination* classroom, the chance to read Dr. Wells' autobiography was an opportunity I simply couldn't pass up. From the little I knew of the man, I sensed he had led a colorful life. I had no idea the poverty he overcame—yet what he has accomplished! *Fraud Fighter: My Fables and Foibles* is at times hysterical, unsettling, gloomy, shocking, and illuminating, and makes you a part of the investigative team. It will now become one of my course requirements, as reading it is a great way to gain a historical perspective of both the ACFE organization and its founder.

Linda G. Chase, Associate Professor, Baldwin Wallace College

A terrific read! Joseph Wells takes us on his remarkable and adventurous life journey from childhood, the military, investigating fraud in the public and private sectors, to the beginnings and growth of the Association of Certified Fraud Examiners. It's all here, the good, the bad, and the ugly.

Ray Cosgrove, IBM Special Investigator (Retired)

After reading Joseph Wells' book, I understood what a great personality he embodies. A real man and devoted husband, an FBI agent, a musician, a perceptive entrepreneur who appreciates people—not as employees but as human beings and friends—an anti-fraud motivator and creator, an excellent educator and writer; and more. All this is Joseph T. Wells. This book could be a great screenplay for a movie watched by millions.

Dr. Dimiter P. Dinev, Founder and Chairman, The
Association for Counteraction to Economic Fraud

As with many publications written by Joseph Wells, his autobiography, *Fraud Fighter*, is entertaining but also a learning experience. He details many of his attributes in his story for many to recognize as necessary for their own success as fraud examiners: ambition, foresight, compassion, and dedication to the fight against fraud.

George P. Farragher, Managing Director, Forensic
Financial Services, BBP Partners, LLP

Joseph Wells is known for his entertaining and enlightening writing and presentations. Now, through his autobiography, he continues to instruct us with compelling and poignant anecdotes of his own life experiences. His revelations teach us it is not where you begin life's journey, but how you finish.

Elvis B. Foster, President, Elvis B. Foster, PC

Joseph Wells can be compared to Aldous Huxley as a leader of modern thought, an intellectual who explores visual communications and sight related theories—but on a different work platform: fraud fighting. As Huxley once said: "Facts do not cease to exist just because they are ignored." It will be impossible for the reader to ignore the facts in Dr. Wells' fascinating life.

Jerome R. Gardner, Dallas County Fraud Auditor

A magnificent journey of a great man's quest for meaning, the history of his humble beginnings and his tumultuous history. Joseph Wells exposes his childhood, human failings, and professional accomplishments, including his creation of the ACFE—a gift to all who fight white-collar crime.

Grace B. Ghezzi, Vice President, Benefit Consulting Group, Inc.

Dr. Wells' autobiography should be an inspiration to all of us that an individual—any individual—can rise above personal adversity and make a real difference in this world. *Fraud Fighter: My Fables and Foibles* exposes Wells' human side in a way that resonates with the reader. This book is not just for anti-fraud professionals; it is a must read for anyone!

Michael D. Hansen, Internal Audit Manager, Public Employees Retirement Association of New Mexico

I idolize Dr. Wells for his work and contribution to the anti-fraud profession. *Fraud Fighter* is a brave undertaking, not only full of fraud fighting adventures but filled with human mistakes and failures which make the book all the more interesting. These did not change my opinion of this man; the admiration continues to grow. I thank him for sharing his story.

Beth Jaballas, Supervising Auditor, California State Compensation Insurance Fund

When I was editor-in-chief of the *Journal of Accountancy,* Dr. Wells was our readers' favorite author; he is a natural-born storyteller. Whether talking about himself, his FBI days, or his fraud cases, he will make you blush, sneer, smile, or even laugh out loud. You wouldn't expect less from a man whose life story could be Matt Damon's next blockbuster movie.

Colleen Katz, Editor-in-Chief (retired), *Journal of Accountancy*

It takes incredible bravery to put your complete life story in black and white for others to read. It takes enormous talent to write that story in your own words and make it compelling. Dr. Wells has both, as readers of his autobiography will undoubtedly agree. The tale of how he became one of the world's foremost anti-fraud experts is full of unexpected twists and turns that you just have to read for yourself.

Melissa Klein Aguilar, business journalist

The innumerable quotes, quips, case histories—even the occasional song lyrics—provide an enjoyable read by a fantastic writer into the life and accomplishments of an expectedly complex (and unexpectedly humble) Joseph T. Wells.

George Kyriakodis, Business Tax Officer, Upper Moreland Township

Dr. Wells is the most prolific author in the anti-fraud profession, and by reading this book, you'll also learn that he is the best, by far. This awe-inspiring autobiography includes incredible tales that take the reader through a full range of emotions that will not only teach you about Wells but about life. Reading *Fraud Fighter* kept me up all night!

Richard White, Adjunct Professor, Utica College

This story is a true and authentic look at the life of one of the great fraud fighters. It is a rare glimpse deep into the mind of the man who created the largest anti-fraud association in the world, how he did it, and why. But it is more. Dr. Wells candidly discusses his own demons and how he fought them, and won.

Tracy L. Coenen, Forensic Accountant, Sequence Inc. Forensic Accounting

Dr. Wells' autobiography provides a unique insight into the life and experiences that shaped the man who revolutionized the anti-fraud profession. His upbringing and struggles are not unique. However, what is different is his uncanny way of dealing with adversity and the ability to take advantage of those opportunities presented to him. After reading the book, there will be no doubt in your mind that Wells is a memorable character who was surely put on this earth to do exactly what he is doing: fighting fraud.

Bert F. Lacativo, Partner, Forensic Services,
PricewaterhouseCoopers LLP

This man is a master storyteller. Reading his book is like sitting with a friend over drinks. Dr. Wells may have had more to do with preventing fraud and catching fraudsters than anyone in history—and on top of that, he has had a wonderfully colorful life.

Kenneth C. McCrory, Principal and Founder, McCrory & McDowell LLC

This is not your normal rags-to-riches story. Dr. Wells gives open and honest insight into how it really does take one to know one. And once he unleashed the "fraudster" within him, the world of fraud prevention and detection was at his feet. This is an amazing tale that has it all—sex, drugs, rock & roll, and fraud!

David W. Nicastro, SVP Business Development, GlobalOptions, Inc.

Reading *Fraud Fighter* is a journey inside the head of a fascinating man. Dr. Wells has done a lot with his life, and is an inspiration to us. He allows us to see the duality that is inside everyone—some good and some bad—but in his case, always striving for goodness. The generosity that has always been his hallmark is played out in this literary gift. Few would have the courage to share as he has.

Marilyn B. Peterson, U.S. Government Agency

In this book, Dr. Wells makes no attempt to justify or rationalize what he may have done wrong; after all, he's human. His story is one of a man who rose above his environment and flaws by harnessing the energy of his passion in pursuit of his vision to leave this world a better place. Few men ever achieve their noblest dreams as Wells has.

James C. Sell, James C. Sell, PC

This is the colorful life story of the colorful character who founded the world's largest anti-fraud organization; chock full of entertaining war stories from a lifetime of slaying fraud and his own personal dragons. Only Joseph Wells could have created this intoxicating brew of sex, drugs, rock & roll, and, yes, accounting! Take a sip and you, too, will be addicted.

Michael S. Spindler, Executive Director, Litigation & Forensics,
Capstone Advisory Group, LLC

As anti-fraud professionals, it is easy to fall into a trap of believing we are better people than the lying cheats we investigate. What Dr. Wells' story does, with all his unapologetic self-revelation, is help us understand that we are not superior. We're just people, fraudulent and flawed. The difference is somewhere along the line we made better choices and somehow managed to associate ourselves with individuals of character and vision.

Kevin Sisemore, Internal Audit Manager, University of Colorado

An inspiring reflection on the paths one travels through life and how destiny can ultimately triumph—provided one knows the importance of fraud and how it can both positively and negatively alter one's course in life. This book is a profound portrayal of how decisions control successes and destiny. A must-read for anyone who ever thought one's past dictates one's future.

Peter E. Tobin, LTC U.S Army (Retired) and Audit Manager
(Chief Audit Executive), Perkins Coie LLP

Joseph Wells' reflections show us all that we are human. Reality is stranger than fiction in his hilarious account of an exciting life. The little frauds we commit each day are a faint echo of the headlines we read today. Accomplishments are measured by the individual, but readers can share vicariously in Wells' successes.

Robert M. Torok, Managing Director, RSM McGladrey

Dr. Wells' vision led to the birth of a new profession at precisely the time it was most needed. While it is easy to laud such an accomplished man, Wells' book allows the reader to step inside. With candor and contriteness he opens his heart, showing not only the accomplishments and accolades, but errors, misgivings, and personal failings that make him human. By letting us see him, warts and all, Wells stands taller. By showing us his own path through the desert, he encourages us all to find our way.

Jonathan E. Turner, Managing Director, Wilson & Turner, Inc.

A racy, riveting read about the life of a man whom many consider the father of the modern-day fraud investigator. Dr. Wells had to write this book; anyone in the field of fraud prevention has to read it.

John Fisher Weber, District Attorney Investigator

Fraud investigators have become the last line of defense for the common man, as each day the newspapers scream and the Internet buzzes about another criminal enterprise that would make John Dillinger proud. Joseph Wells pioneered this new breed of superhero, and his honesty and humble frankness about his upbringing make him all the more compelling as the hero of this tale. Anyone who ever wished they could be a fly on the wall while some of the most ambitious criminal schemes in the history of mankind were created, uncovered, and eventually blown up will find this book very hard to put down.

Lori A. Wigler, Partner, Mellen, Smith & Pivoz, PLC

Joseph Wells is one of the pivotal leaders of the anti-fraud movement throughout the world. *Fraud Fighter: My Fables and Foibles* is insightful, energetic, and full of real-life personal nuggets that show his passion and dedication in creating and nurturing the premier anti-fraud organization.

Ron Hagenbaugh, Ronald L. Hagenbaugh, CPA

Fraud Fighter

My Fables and Foibles

Joseph T. Wells

To Juan
Best wishes,

J. Wells
06/11

WILEY

John Wiley & Sons, Inc.

Published by John Wiley & Sons, Inc., Hoboken, New Jersey.
Published simultaneously in Canada.

For general information on our other products and services or for technical support, please
contact our Customer Care Department within the United States at (800) 762-2974, outside
the United States at (317) 572-3993 or fax (317) 572-4002.

Wiley also publishes its books in a variety of electronic formats. Some content that appears in
print may not be available in electronic books. For more information about Wiley products,
visit our web site at www.wiley.com.

Library of Congress Cataloging-in-Publication Data

Wells, Joseph T.
  Fraud fighter: my fables and foibles / Joseph T. Wells.
      p. cm.
  Includes index.
  ISBN 978-0-470-61070-1 (hardback); ISBN 978-0-470-63675-6 (ebk);
  ISBN 978-0-470-63676-3 (ebk); ISBN 978-0-470-63677-0 (ebk)
    1. Fraud—United States—Case studies.   2. Fraud investigation—United States—
Case studies.   3. Wells, Joseph T.   4. Auditors—United States—Biography.   I. Title.
HV6695.W43 2011
363.25'963092—dc22 [B]

                                                                          2011007558

Printed in the United States of America.
10   9   8   7   6 . 5   4   3   2   1

To the people who have helped make me a better person.
You know who you are.

Contents

Prologue

For reasons that I don't clearly understand, I love to write. My 19th published book is between these pages. But this is — by far — my most difficult undertaking because it is so personal. Naturally, discussing my fables was much easier than admitting to my foibles. Yes, we're human; we have all made mistakes. However, putting them on paper to be immortalized in print brings it to a whole different level. If you don't believe me, try it yourself.

Everyone lies. Everyone. We do so for two basic reasons: to receive rewards or to avoid punishment (or a combination of both). Although lying is not endemic to the human species, we learn it very early in life. Fraud, though, is a lie with a special twist — it is committed to deprive an innocent victim of money or property.

If you are a fraud fighter, your job is to talk to liars, cheats and thieves. As a result, honesty takes on special significance.

It doesn't mean that a fraud fighter like me hasn't lied. But it does mean you will admit your transgressions, regret them and vow to do better the next time. A fraudster wouldn't do that.

In the following pages, you will learn how I ended up in the anti-fraud field. And you'll find out that — like with many of you — much of it happened by accident; by fate; perhaps by pre-destiny; and yes, by occasionally being dishonest. This is not a story of someone pure and blameless but of a man who made many mistakes along the way to his calling.

My story (like yours) has a beginning and middle, but not yet an end. To quote William Shakespeare in *Julius Caesar*, "The evil that men do lives after them; the good is oft interred with their bones." So let it be with me. Or, to quote someone almost as famous (Popeye), "I yam what I yam."

Joseph T. Wells
Austin, Texas
May 2011

Part One

THE APPRENTICE

Part One

THE APPRENTICE

Chapter 1

Learning the Ropes

Are some people born as fraud fighters? Maybe, maybe not. I wasn't. Before finding my niche, I tried other lines of work. But I'll begin my story at the time I entered law enforcement and started learning about fraud detection and prevention. Later, you'll hear more about the personal and professional experiences that partly made me who I am.

Although I was born and raised in Oklahoma, I left there after high school and rarely went back. Later, through a fortuitous set of circumstances that I will describe, I ended up as a real-life, gun-toting FBI agent. In 1972, I graduated from the FBI Academy in Quantico, Virginia. My initial assignment was to El Paso, Texas, where the FBI's second smallest divisional office is located.

Ten years earlier, fresh out of high school, I had enlisted in the Navy and served ashore and at sea in the United Kingdom.

So I was aware you could just about fit England and Scotland in between Dallas and El Paso. During a day and a half behind the steering wheel, however, I learned the hard way that Texas is nearly four times as big as Oklahoma.

Halfway across Texas, I passed through Midland, home to El Paso's satellite office. I didn't know it at the time, but I'd return there later for a grueling, month-long, no-break stakeout. Whether my visits to Midland were long or short, I never got used to the 600-mile round trip between those two small offices. There were few towns in between. El Paso, after all, is in the desert and Midland is at the edge of the Great Plains.

The empty landscape wasn't the only thing on my mind, though. As a newly minted special agent, my primary goals were to learn the ins and outs of the El Paso office's culture and, with guidance, to convert the Academy's basic training into the everyday skills I needed to succeed in this particular field environment.

At first, I rode around with different agents, watching what they did and how they went about it. One day a local bank called the FBI office to report that one of their tellers had confessed to embezzling a few hundred dollars from her cash drawer. My first case!

I hurried over and spoke with their security officer, a retired cop. Even though we'd never met, I could tell he was bored with his job.

"In there," he said, motioning with his thumb. "She was caught in a surprise cash count, and confessed to 'borrowing' money out of her teller drawer."

I went in to the small conference room where the teller sat alone, red-faced and teary-eyed.

The first words out of her mouth were "I'm so sorry. I didn't steal this money; I was just short and borrowed some cash out of my drawer until payday. But the bank didn't believe me when I told them I was going to pay it back."

4

I put up my hand to interrupt her. "Miss, before you go any further, I'm required by law to advise you of your constitutional rights. First, you have the right to remain silent. Second, anything you say from this point might be used against you in court. You have the right to a lawyer before questioning. If you cannot afford one, the courts will appoint someone to represent you. If you decide to answer questions, you may stop at any time. Do you understand your rights?" I asked.

She nodded and blew her nose.

"Do you wish to have a lawyer?" I said.

"Should I?" she asked, seeming frightened.

"*You* have to make that decision," I said. "So, do you want a lawyer?"

She thought for a long moment then shook her head no.

I continued. "Do you want to tell me what happened?"

She nodded, and told me a sad story. Many times over the years the same basic facts would be repeated to me. The young woman was a single mom who didn't get regular child support. The bank paid her very little; she'd been on her current job for a couple of years, struggling mightily to make ends meet. She had borrowed money from friends and family but wasn't able to fully repay them, so she was reluctant to ask again. The embezzler's child was in first grade and needed some supplies. Additionally, she had gotten a disconnect notice from the electric company for nonpayment. The poor woman was facing darkness in her small apartment but, even more, she had trouble admitting to her daughter that she didn't have the money to get those much-needed supplies.

Because she worked in front of a drawer full of money every day, the temptation just got to be too much. She borrowed just what she needed — a few hundred dollars. When payday rolled around, she couldn't pay it back; her rent was due. A couple of weeks later, the young lady took a few hundred more. She said she didn't know how she was going to pay this money back, but she insisted it was just a loan; she said she was raised with better values than to steal.

Once her confession was complete, she broke down and cried like a baby. I too could feel tears welling up. There was a long silence while I composed myself.

Then I said, "Miss, let me step out and make a call to the government lawyers. I'll see if we can resolve this mess."

The United States Attorney's offices handle both civil and criminal complaints. The former typically involve cases where the government has sued someone and has obtained a judgment that they are attempting to collect. In El Paso, there were only two Assistant U.S. Attorneys who handled criminal matters. During my first couple of weeks in the division, I'd been introduced to Manuel "Manny" Marquez, so I telephoned him.

"Manny, I have a case here where a bank teller has just confessed to me that she'd taken the bank's money." I don't recall now how much it was, but certainly less than $1,000. "The interesting thing about this case," I continued, "is that she really didn't steal the money. She made herself a loan, and was going to return it on payday. But a surprise cash count showed her short by several hundred dollars. She told the bank officials that she intended to pay it back but they didn't believe her. Well, I certainly do."

I didn't expect Manny's reaction: He burst into laughter. "Agent Wells, how many embezzlement cases have you actually investigated?"

"Counting this, the total is one," I replied defensively.

Marquez laughed again, almost choking. "I thought so," he said. "Joe, I've never heard of a bank embezzler who didn't say he or she was borrowing the money. They actually convince themselves of that. But if you or I borrow money, we have to sign a note. If she's done that, release her. If not, arrest her on an information, and book her into federal custody."

As I learned at the FBI Academy, there are two ways to charge an individual with a crime. The first is an *information*, where the arresting official fills out a form setting forth the facts to which he or she has been a witness. In this case, it was the young lady's confession and the cash count sheet from the bank showing she was short. Those charged on informations are typically accused of simple or misdemeanor offenses. The other way to charge someone is to present the case to a grand jury, which may return an indictment. If it does so, the same grand jury can issue an arrest warrant for the person to be taken into custody. As a matter of procedure, the FBI prefers grand jury indictments because a number of people are listening to the government's side of the case; it's not the opinion of just one agent.

The Bureau is very particular when it comes to arrests; you must handcuff the person whether or not you feel that he or she is dangerous. That's because some people go totally berserk when taken into custody. With great reluctance, I told the woman to place her hands behind her back.

She gave me a quizzical look.

"I'm sorry, Miss, but the government prosecutor has told me that I must arrest you, and that means you have to be handcuffed."

She burst into tears again. "You're going to lead me out of here in handcuffs? But everyone will see me!"

When I simply nodded, she shrieked.

Actually, two agents should have been on this arrest. Nevertheless the office had decided that I could handle one female by myself. She came along without further resistance, but it could have easily turned out otherwise.

I made a mental note: When there is a possibility that someone could be arrested, always take another agent just in case there is trouble.

While I was driving her to the detention facility, she peppered me with questions in between her sobs: How long will I be in jail?

What happens to me next? Who will take care of my child? Will she know about what happened to her mom?

I didn't have most of the answers, and my better judgment told me to simply shut up. Once I turned her over to her jailers, my job would have normally been over; most of the time the FBI doesn't have a further role unless it is necessary to testify at grand jury or the trial. But since I was new on the job, I decided to go to her initial appearance before the magistrate. That is where a defendant is formally charged and bond, if any, is set.

When a first offender is nonviolent and not an escape risk, it's likely the judge will let him or her go on their own recognizance if the amount of money at issue is not particularly large. Unfortunately, her initial appearance (also called an arraignment) was in front of Judge Ernest Allen Guinn (1905–1974).

Guinn ruled from the bench like a pharaoh. He had a full head of white hair with a matching full Western mustache, all in stark contrast to his black robe. Later, I'd see him in a couple of other appearances and noticed a curious habit: He never looked directly at the defendant, but rather slightly off-center to his or her side. It's now easy to understand why: Shortly before his death in 1974, Guinn was written up in a *Playboy* magazine article entitled "The Ten Meanest Men in America."

And this distinguished-looking gentleman was indeed mean. The shaking defendant stood before him while Manny Marquez gave a little blurb about the case. The woman was represented by a public defender who didn't have anything to say.

Then Guinn looked off-center at her and said, "You are remanded into the custody of the federal government. Bond is set at $50,000."

Manny shook his head ever so slightly and audibly exhaled. Then the judge stood up while the rest of us got to our feet. Guinn left without another word.

Marquez whispered to me afterward, "What a prick. In any other district, this woman would have been turned loose until her plea." Manny didn't feel good; I didn't feel good; and certainly this young mother didn't feel good. Because she didn't have the 10 percent or so of the total bond required, she sat in jail.

Later she pled guilty and was sentenced by Judge Guinn to a year in prison. Her offense was technically a felony because the amounts involved were over $100. Still, jailing a first offender in a nonviolent crime for the money involved here was almost unheard of. I didn't go to the sentencing because I couldn't shake the shame I felt. The justice system had changed her life forever.

On-the-Job Training

I wasn't the only rookie in the El Paso office. Four others had arrived within the last few months. As said in the Navy since the days of sail, we were "learning the ropes" – developing the basic skills of our profession. The special agent in charge (SAC) was Don Selman and the assistant special agent in charge (ASAC) was Thomas D. Westbank. Next to the Butte, Montana, division, El Paso was the smallest, with fewer than 50 agents. When J. Edgar Hoover was alive, these two divisions were where the fuckups were sent rather than being fired first. At least that was what I was told in new agents' class when I received my orders.

It made me wonder: Why was I the only agent in my class sent there? Certainly I'd not messed up. Indeed, I'd graduated near the top of my group through a combination of hard work and luck. Rookie agents fully expected to perform assignments that our more senior colleagues would not want. I was no exception. Because El Paso shared a border with Juarez, Mexico, the new guys were called regularly in the middle of the night to take to jail some federal fugitive who had been stopped by Customs or

Border Patrol. Our sole duty was to take the prisoner into custody and transport him (I don't recall any women) to jail in El Paso to turn over to the U.S. Marshals for further action. All of the rookie agents quickly tired of this duty, but none of us complained.

On almost my first day in the office, I was taught how to commit time fraud. Virtually every agent participated in this activity, which was so common that it had its own name — "banging the books." On top of their normal salaries, FBI agents were paid an extra 25 percent of base pay for what was called *administratively uncontrollable overtime* (AUO). In order to receive the pay, agents had to average an hour and 49 minutes of overtime per day. If your average fell below this for a two-week pay period, your AUO money was cut off altogether; for example, if you averaged only an hour a day for a pay period, you got nothing. At the office agents were required to sign in each morning and out each evening on a form called the "Number One Register." Each agent signed in chronological order: 6:10 AM; 7:00 AM; 7:30 AM. As a veteran agent explained to me, "Here's how it works, Joe. Suppose you're the first one in for the day, and you get to the office at 7:30. You want to sign in as of 5:30 AM so that the guy that comes behind you can sign in at 5:35 AM, and the next one at 5:40 AM. If you actually did sign in as of 7:30 — when you really got here — the other guys would lynch you because they'd have to sign in after that and would lose their AUO."

At first, I was incredulous: Fraud against the government was a federal offense, and we investigated such violations. When I mentioned this to the agent who had instructed me how to bang the books, he replied, "Joe, if you've told a lot of lies in the past, you'll never get into the FBI. But once you're in, you're going to have to tell a few lies to stay in." End of discussion. So yes, for the entire time I was in the FBI, every agent I knew banged the books every workday. Over the years, this doubtless amounted to hundreds of millions of taxpayer dollars.

Because of the size of the division, there were only two squads: the SAC's and the ASAC's. A squad was typically 15 to 30 agents. I was assigned to Westbank, the ASAC. Behind his back, we called him "Squatty Body." It was an apt nickname; he was short and pudgy. But his most distinguishing feature was his red hair. By my best guesstimate, he had about a half-dozen hairs on his head — each seeming thirty feet long. I imagined that in the morning, before he came to work, Squatty Body would carefully wind each of those hairs to and fro to cover his obvious baldness. Then, according to my theory, he would douse his head with marine varnish so that none of them would move. His quiffing fooled no one; we knew he was nearly bald. Squatty was not a mean person, but he had a completely inflated view of himself. In the words of one agent: "If you could buy him for what he's actually worth and sell him for what he thinks he's worth, you'd make a fortune."

One of my first assignments in El Paso was to assist in the upcoming annual inspection. Each field division of the Bureau was inspected once a year by headquarters, which would send out a team from Washington for a week or two. The size of the inspection team was governed by the size of the office; in the case of El Paso, that consisted of two guys. The FBI had a complicated system of advancement. The pinnacle was to become an SAC. That meant you had a fiefdom and held power over the lives of every agent and clerk within your geographical boundaries. Your directives were just about absolute.

To become an SAC, one had to endure many transfers: first as an agent for an indeterminate period of years; then as a field supervisor on a squad; followed by an assignment as a headquarters supervisor; back to the field as an ASAC; then a tour on the inspection team; and, finally, the plum job of being an SAC. So, the inspector position was a senior one, and your performance as one determined whether you would get your own office.

The SAC and the inspectors had a somewhat odd relationship. As a part of the bureaucratic game, the inspector could give the office a clean bill of health. But then someone upstairs would assume that the inspector was not doing his duty. If the inspector felt the office was a complete mess, that would mean much more paperwork and the SAC might lose his job. Or he might not, in which case he would try to make sure that the inspector didn't get the coveted office. But I was concerned with little of that. Most of the inspection involved files and procedures. However, it was necessary that the office be spotless, and that's where I came in.

The office baseboards were dirty. But the El Paso division chose not to buy a gallon of paint; it may have cost ten bucks — and then there would be forms to fill out. It was less hassle and less out-of-pocket expense to get someone (namely me, the junior man) to spend the better part of two days on his hands and knees giving the baseboards a good scrubbing. As a side benefit, there was the lesson in humility that I learned. Squatty was so impressed with the zeal with which I scrubbed that he wrote a memo for my personnel file, stating that I had gone above and beyond the call of duty on an "inspection project" not further defined. It certainly sounded more important than what I actually had done.

Although rookies were prohibited from riding around together in FBI cars, that happened more times than I'd like to admit. On one such occasion in El Paso, there was a warrant out for an escaped federal prisoner. All agents in headquarters had been furnished a photo of him. Sure enough, the office got a call stating that the bad guy was at a certain address. When the message was broadcast over our Bureau radios, Al Stanley and I were in the area and radioed back that we would take a first look. It was our impression that the fugitive would be inside the house. But on a drive-by, we spotted him sitting outside, alone. Al and I concocted a hasty plan. In a situation such as this, there should have been at least six agents on the arrest, but we were too new on the job to know that, and were in a hurry to make the bust. We decided to park around the corner. Al would start walking at one end of the block, and I would do the same from the opposite end. Then we'd meet in front of the fugitive and, without warning, jump him. This fellow really, really didn't want to be arrested and cuffed, so quite the melee ensued. Al ended up with a bloodied chin, and I had knots all over my head from the blows struck. But finally we handcuffed him, got him into the back of the FBI car, and drove away.

The so-called fugitive screamed at the top of his lungs, "What are you doing to me? I haven't done anything wrong! Let me out!" Then he started kicking at the back window.

Al was driving. I looked at the fugitive's photo and then back at our detainee. Uh-oh. We had the wrong guy. I told Al to pull over to the curb, and we got out to talk it over.

When it became clear we'd arrested the wrong person, I said, "Shit! What are we going to do now, Al? The office is going to be tear-ass that two rookies are riding together, and this is probably going to get us a letter of censure."

After rubbing his injured chin and thinking for a moment, Al said, "I've got a plan." He opened the back door, and helped the arrestee out to the street. Al then made the sign of the cross in a way that looked totally official and said, "I hereby pronounce you unarrested." When I unlocked the handcuffs, the poor guy took off like a stripe-assed ape. Al and I got back in the Bureau car, and proceeded slowly to the office, terrified that the "unarrestee" would call and complain. But he didn't. We had dodged a bullet on that one.

Speaking of bullets, another rookie and I had just gone for an early-morning coffee on a different occasion when a call came on our radio that there was a bank robbery in progress. It was on I-10 at the exit we were nearing. I was driving this time, and we arrived at the bank just as a car in the parking lot was trying to peel out. The driver saw us and cranked off a couple of shots, one of which hit our windshield. He must have figured we were law enforcement because of our cheap four-door sedan with black-wall tires. In a split-second decision, I floored the gas pedal and broadsided the getaway car, shattering the driver's side window. Then the robber started firing again. How we avoided being hit I will never know. But the robber wasn't so lucky. My partner, Marv Michelson, and I emptied our revolvers, striking the guy in the face and shoulder. Almost immediately, patrol cars from the El Paso Police Department were on the scene. The robber was still conscious and tried to flee from the passenger's side, but the police quickly had him in custody.

Marv and I then noticed a man lying near the back entrance to the small branch bank. When we got closer, we could see him face down in a river of blood. We rushed to his side hoping to render first aid, but it was too late. There were two clean bullet holes in his back from a .45 caliber pistol — a huge handgun. When we flipped him over, Marv and I almost slipped in the blood. While the entry wounds were relatively small, the exit wounds in his chest were big enough to put your fist in. The deceased was the branch manager who had arrived, as was his custom, a half hour before the bank was opened for the day. No one exactly could figure out why the shooting took place, but after the banker had been hit twice, his adrenaline enabled him to run to a service station next door and shout out that he had been shot. He then turned back to the bank and collapsed by the rear entrance. A trail of blood marked his path. The robber was convicted, sentenced to death, and eventually executed.

Being an FBI agent is generally not a dangerous job. Unlike police and state troopers, the Bureau is not part of the front line of defense. As of this writing, fewer than 50 FBI agents have been killed in the line of duty. Most go through their entire careers without firing a shot, although they practice and qualify on firearms repeatedly throughout their service. In my case, although I would go on to later draw my weapon a number of times, this was the only time I fired it in an actual situation, and it occurred early in my career.

Because I'd totaled an FBI car and shot someone, there were many forms to be filled out. The paperwork seemed endless. For example, the heart of any investigation was conducting interviews. For each one you completed, there was a form to fill out: the FD-302. Although the contents were largely narrative, there was a place on the form for who conducted the interview and when, as well as a field for the date the form was typed up. I probably filled out several thousand 302s, and it made me what I call "form-averse." Since I have now been self-employed for three decades, people who work for me know to fill out the forms and get me to sign them.

My Second Marriage

About a year before I was assigned to El Paso, I was working in Lynchburg, Virginia, where I met a young lady named Dawn McGivens. Both divorced from our first spouses, she and I were immediately attracted to each other and began dating. Soon afterward, I successfully applied for admittance to the FBI Academy, an experience I'll describe in greater detail in Chapter 2, where I'll also speak of my earlier marriage, which had lasted only six months.

While at the Academy, I spent my weekends in Lynchburg with Dawn and her daughter, Beth. Although Dawn and I spoke of marriage, I was not ready to commit. I didn't know where I was going after the Academy, and I finally broke off our relationship about the time I got transfer orders to El Paso.

Three months after I arrived in Texas, I called Dawn. By the time the conversation had ended, we'd decided to get married.

The wedding was small. Later it would seem fateful that we had married on April Fools' Day. I flew from El Paso to Lynchburg for the ceremony. Beth stayed with friends — her birth dad had abandoned her — while Dawn and I drove her Volkswagen Beetle to Texas. Dawn and I started our honeymoon/cross-country journey, and she called her sister from Shreveport, Louisiana. Suddenly, a strange expression came over her face, and she dropped the phone. When I picked it up, her sister told me their mother had suffered a fatal heart attack two days previously; the FBI had been searching everywhere for us. The following morning, we drove through blinding rain to Dallas, the nearest town of any size, and caught a flight back to Bluefield, West Virginia, for the funeral. I can't think of a bigger buzzkill than having your new wife's mother drop dead on your honeymoon, but that's what happened. After the services, we flew back to Dallas and resumed our trip to El Paso. Romantic it was not.

My relationship with Dawn was tumultuous from the start. Looking back, much of it had to do with her having to make a radical change in her lifestyle. She had been a teacher in a quiet town, and now had to relocate at the whim of the FBI. Because Beth was outgoing and made friends easily, she adjusted better and enjoyed her new surroundings. After the move, we rented a comfortable apartment in El Paso for the three of us.

Because of Beth, I decided to quit smoking. It was a sudden decision and lasted for about four years. I had gone to the grocery store and among other items, I'd bought a new carton of cigarettes. When I got to the car, the urge to quit smoking overcame me. I placed the fresh carton under the wheel of the car and ran over it as I left the parking lot.

However, I merely traded one addiction for another when I started running and became hooked on the endorphins it produced. At first, it was difficult for me to even run a quarter mile. But I kept at it. Within six months, I was running 60 to 80 miles a week. The weight melted off of me. When there was little to do at the office, I'd go home, change into my running gear, and go to the desert surrounding El Paso. There I'd do at least 10 miles, sometimes 15. During my runs, I'd plan activities for the next day, solve my cases and even the world's problems, and think about my marriage. Running helped relieve the frustration I felt about being in another marriage destined to fail.

Fred G. Robin III

Since El Paso, my first FBI assignment location, had a reputation as a "disciplinary office," a few fuckups were transferred there. Fred G. Robin III stood at the top of the list. He was incompetent but, more than that, he was dangerous and had little or no judgment. Rumor had it that Robin was previously assigned to North Dakota, where he chased a fugitive to an outhouse in the middle of nowhere. Since there was only one exit, all Fred had to do was to wait for the bad guy. But that wasn't fast enough — Robin reputedly started shooting through the outhouse door, seriously wounding the escapee. That resulted in his transfer to El Paso. Fred G. Robin III had more hang-ups than a row of hat racks. He never would have made the cut as an agent except for the one thing he had going for him: Robby, as he liked to be called, was distantly related to J. Edgar Hoover. Experienced agents avoided him like the plague. He therefore tended to prey on young, inexperienced guys — like me — who had yet to fig-ure him out.

One day shortly after I arrived in El Paso, I was riding with him on I-10 when we were getting ready to exit. Just then a teenage boy with a typical lead foot cut in front of us to get off the freeway first. Robby was furious and started snorting, which he did without fail when nervous, mad or stressed. He plugged the car's blue light into the cigarette lighter, and stuck it on the

17

roof. (FBI cars had a built-in siren but since we weren't cops, no red light.) With the siren wailing and the blue light flashing, he chased down the offending driver. Even with my inexperience I knew the FBI didn't issue traffic citations, so I wondered what was going on. I was about to find out; as soon as both cars stopped, Robby bailed out of his driver's seat, ran up to the kid's car and cursed him unmercifully while shaking his fist. I simply slunk down in the passenger's seat, embarrassed.

Stakeout in Midland

The El Paso Division of the FBI had one resident agency (i.e., satellite office). It was in Midland, Texas, a small oil town of fewer than 40,000 people, about 300 miles east of El Paso. Because traffic between the two locations was so sparse (and also because FBI agents were unlikely to get speeding tickets), the drive usually took us less than three hours. One of our men learned from an informant that a car dealer in Midland was running an illegal sports gambling operation. A case such as this normally requires a wiretap, technically known as an interception of communications. The warrants for such a matter are a paperwork nightmare and must be authorized by the Justice Department in Washington. But the agent in charge of the case, Armando Gonzalez, jumped through all of the hoops and finally got his wiretap approved. Then the real work began.

At the time, regulations required that all telephones coming under the wiretap be monitored continuously by agents and that all pertinent conversations be recorded. If a call wasn't relevant to the gambling operation, the agent had to stop the recording and not listen to what was being said. To the best of my recollection, we were monitoring four lines, which meant that four agents had to man the recording equipment. That could have been done from El Paso, but at the time long-distance telephone service was expensive. So the office rented a small, World War II—era house in a rundown Midland neighborhood, and assigned eight agents to man it. The home had only two bedrooms and one bath. One bedroom was devoted to tables loaded with large reel-to-reel tape machines and the other was for sleeping.

To avoid detection, we arrived in the middle of the night in two cars, and then hid one. Our instructions were that only one agent could leave, once a day, to get food and other supplies. That privilege was bestowed on Armando by Armando. Wiretaps were approved only for 30 days at a time. Thank God — while we were there, I never set foot outside. It was the longest month of my life. Stuffing eight guys in a 1,000-square-foot house was akin to jamming ten pounds of potatoes into a five-pound bag; it was terribly crowded. We worked in shifts around the clock; four guys were always on duty while the remainder slept in sleeping bags in the other bedroom. This case occurred in the dead middle of a West Texas winter. The wind howled, the temperature was in the teens, and the leaky house was built before insulation was common. Most of us shivered all of the time. And someone was constantly stinking up the bathroom.

Even though the phones had to be monitored continuously, the telephone traffic died down after office hours. So in the evenings, we'd break out the booze. At least that's the way it began. I wasn't much of a drinker at the time — that would come later in my life. But I'd try to stay even with my cohorts even though I was a rank amateur. Pretty much every night I'd drink myself to sleep only to wake with a pounding headache and a hangover. For most of the first week, only the agents not working would drink in the evening. Naturally that changed. The second week, the happy hour moved forward from around six in the evening to three in the afternoon. By the third week, we were drinking at noon. And for at least the last seven days, we started in the morning and drank until we went to bed. In one instance

I was so drunk that I passed out at the recording machine with earphones dangling from my head. When I came to, one of the married gamblers was talking to his girlfriend in a conversation that was clearly irrelevant to the operation. While we fraudulently listened in to telephone calls of this sort, we didn't keep a record of them. In this situation, I simply went back and erased that portion of the tape.

Finally, we went back to El Paso loaded with tapes. Sure enough, there was a gambling operation that was run out of the car dealership, but it was not as extensive as we'd hoped. We had gobs of evidence about what was going on. The judge hearing our initial complaint wanted the FBI to identify its informant. But that wasn't gonna happen; as a matter of policy and for good reasons, the Bureau never named its informants. Snitches frequently were found at the bottom of a river, wearing cement boots. The FBI wouldn't pursue a case that required revealing its sources. And that's what happened here; all that work went down the drain.

An Ethical Lapse

In El Paso, I investigated a fair number of bank embezzlements. Most of them were straightforward enough, but one stumped me. At a bank, $10,000 in cash disappeared from the head teller's drawer. There were perhaps 30 employees, and I interviewed every one of them. No good suspects emerged, but a couple of people warranted a polygraph exam. The lie detector is a very controversial piece of equipment. The results cannot be used to prosecute someone; because they're unreliable, they can't even be introduced in court. But they can give you direction in an investigation. An FBI polygraph examiner put two or three people who worked at the bank on his magic box. Upon conclusion, he said emphatically, "Wendell Jarrell is your man." There was no doubt in his mind. But try as I might, I couldn't get Wendell to confess. I therefore leaked the results of the lie detector to the bank, which found an excuse to fire him. Not long after that, he got another job, and I fraudulently leaked the information to his new employer, who also fired him. Then I repeated the process one more time. The problem? Wendell didn't do it; I found that out over a year later — after I had been transferred from El Paso.

An El Paso agent phoned me then and asked, "Joe, do you remember that mysterious disappearance of $10,000?" Indeed I did. "We solved it," he said. "You are not going to believe what happened. We got a lead in another bank case that had striking similarities. The difference is that one of the tellers remembered that a toddler opened a closed door to the teller area and walked in. He had been trained by his brother, age 14, to grab the first handful of money he saw and walk out with it. It seems that the older brother and his two friends had stolen from at least six banks using the same method." The agent was right, I couldn't believe it. And I felt terrible at what I'd done. I had violated the rules and harmed an innocent person. There was a valuable lesson for me in this: If you can't win playing by the rules, you don't deserve to win. Fraudulently, I would violate the rules again later.

The Suicides

One sunny spring afternoon in 1973, I was walking up the short steps on my way into the Federal Building in El Paso, returning from a day's work. To my left, I saw a blur then heard a crack and a thud. Looking over, I saw an attractive young woman in a red-and-white pinafore dress lying on the grass, still clutching her purse in one hand. Her head was turned at an odd angle, almost backward on her neck. I heard a slight gurgle, and watched as she took her last breath. She had dived headlong out of a third-floor restroom's window. Several other people and I rushed to her side, but I knew it was too late; she was already dead. I didn't find out why someone so innocent-looking would take her own life. And other than my mother's death, which occurred many years later, this was the only time I have seen anyone die in front of me. It's something that you never forget.

Around the same time, I read in the paper that some fellow swan-dived out of a building in El Paso and landed in a huge exhaust fan. They didn't find him until several days later when the building's air conditioner wouldn't work. Everyone gets depressed, perhaps even despondent; but I've never contemplated killing myself. We'll all be dead soon enough.

Robin's Rump Roast Rip-off

Fred G. Robin III had picked up some information from one of his sources at Fort Bliss that civilian employees at the base commissary were selling store food out the back door. Robin swung into action; it could be a really big scheme, he proclaimed. Shortly before Christmas, he talked the office into loaning him half a dozen agents to set up surveillance on the commissary. We closed ourselves off in two adjacent buildings that had a perfect view of the back door. In order to catch these heinous thieves, we had brought along binoculars and even cameras with long-distance lenses. We were set, arriving early and staying late. I was put in charge of the surveillance log. Each time some- one walked in, out, or around the back of the store, they were photographed and I dutifully noted the time and their physical descriptions and activity (or lack of it) in the log. By late in the day, nothing eventful had happened, and we were all getting bored and itchy.

Finally, we hit pay dirt. We had buttoned up most of the equipment, and were ready to call it quits. But then one of the civilian employees at the commissary handed a large bag to a lone white male who put the probable loot in his car and drove away. We followed in a caravan of FBI vehicles. Once the crook was outside the gate, we pulled him over and several agents approached his vehicle. The guy was so shaken that he wet his pants. The contraband in the bag consisted of a roast, a frozen turkey and perhaps a dozen yams. He was arrested on the spot for petty theft and taken in for booking on a misdemeanor charge.

Later, we found out why our miscreant was so nervous. He was a retired colonel who had come back to work at the base as a civilian employee; they were commonly known as double-dippers because they were already collecting one retirement check and could be eligible for a second as a civilian. As might be expected, the former colonel was fired and lost his right to a second pension. He didn't serve any time, but that misstep cost him probably several hundred thousand dollars in retirement benefits. The civilian worker at the commissary was also fired. He was a fairly senior employee who also lost his potential retirement benefits. Often crime pays, but not this time.

On February 27, 1973, the little town of Wounded Knee, South Dakota, was seized by followers of the American Indian Movement (AIM) who opposed the appointment of Richard A. "Dick" Wilson as Oglala Sioux tribal chairman. The U.S. military and government agents surrounded the town that same day. The government brought in 15 armored personnel carriers, rifles, grenade launchers, flares, and over 100,000 rounds of ammunition. Oh, and FBI agents too. The siege lasted 71 days and three people were killed before both sides made peace.

The El Paso office "volunteered" Robby, thinking that any time he would spend away from the division would be good for everyone. Robin naively thought he had been handpicked. In fact, that was so, but not for the reason he believed. Robby considered it an honor to sleep in a tent in the bone-chilling South Dakota winter.

When I was transferred from El Paso, I put the outrageousness of Fred G. Robin III in my rearview mirror. Much later, I heard that he had been posted to Atlanta, where I'm almost certain his misadventures continued.

On to the Big Apple

When orders arrived, transferring me from El Paso to the New York office (NYO), I thought I would faint. I had some fun and worked on interesting cases in El Paso, and, except for my second troublesome marriage, I had good memories of my rookie duty station.

Until then, the largest place I'd lived in was Oklahoma City, while attending college. At the time the FBI reassigned me, it was customary for agents to remain in their first office for 12 to 18 months. There you could make rookie mistakes and go on to your next office, wiser and with a clean slate. Dawn had gotten a temporary teaching job at one of the local high schools in El Paso so we decided that she and Beth would stay behind until the end of the school year.

I left West Texas by myself in early 1974, during the biggest oil embargo in history. Gasoline was in short supply from coast to coast, and long lines at service stations were the rule, not the exception; many had no fuel at all. So I loaded my Volvo 164 with topped-off fuel cans that weighed so much the rear axle sagged. What an idiot — if someone had rear-ended me, I would've been one crispy critter.

As luck would have it, though, all I had to put up with was constant fumes from the gas cans. So, regardless of how cold it got, I kept one window cracked open at all times. En route to my new assignment in New York, a little more than 2,000 miles from El Paso, I spent a couple of nights in Oklahoma with my aging mother. Although we never got along particularly well, it was sad to see her get old.

Prior to leaving El Paso, I'd inquired with the NYO about temporary quarters. The news was disturbing. At that time, the maximum reimbursement for travel was $25 a day. That was allotted as $9 for lodging and $16 for food and other expenses. But even a fleabag in Manhattan was $50 a night. So the office arranged for me to stay at Mrs. Papazzian's rooming house in Astoria, Queens, just across the East River from Manhattan. I finally found my way there. An elderly lady, Mrs. Papazzian lived downstairs in her impeccably kept row house. Upstairs, four tiny bedrooms were served by one common bathroom and shower. I took the one remaining room. It would become my home for the next four months, and the place almost drove me nuts because of the boredom and confinement. There was no television, and my sanity was maintained by the fact that I had brought along my stereo receiver with a pair of headphones. I'd listen to music at nights until I drifted off to sleep. The three other fellows occupying rooms included another FBI agent who took me to the office to show me how to get there.

Next morning he and I walked to the elevated train station at Queensboro Plaza for the ride into Manhattan. In the middle of rush hour and in broad daylight, a man on the platform was urinating onto the tracks. I shouted to my companion, "Do you see that!?" He put his finger across his lips. "Just ignore it," he said quietly. "You're going to see a lot of strange things in this city."

The NYO was located at 201 East 69th Street in a converted warehouse. The nearest subway was about four blocks away at 68th Street and Lexington Avenue. As we trudged through the bitter cold to the office, my colleague explained that I would have to stop at the guard desk and that he would try to catch up with me later. Once inside the foyer, he went upstairs. The guards thoroughly inspected my credentials, made a couple of phone calls and told me to report to the office of the ASAC. At that time, one out of every seven FBI agents was assigned to New York and the office was spread out over 13 floors. Right before the elevator doors closed for my ride up, a giant of a man with graying temples stepped in. I introduced myself to him and shook his hand. He replied simply, "John Malone." He then proceeded to inspect me from head to toe, toe to head, and front to back — without saying a word. I didn't know who this guy was at the time, but there was no doubt that I was ready for inspection by anyone. My shoes shined like mirrors, I had on a crisp starched white shirt with a conservative tie and my finest (actually, only) dark-blue pinstriped suit.

I left the elevator at my stop. Before the doors closed, another agent on the floor spotted me getting out. "Holy crap!" he exclaimed. "You're new here, aren't you?" he inquired. I nodded. "You just rode up with Cementhead, who is in charge of the NYO," he gravely advised. "Don't ever let him know your name. The guy is a real prick." Uh-oh, I thought. Less than ten minutes on my new assignment, and I'd already screwed up. I hoped it wasn't an omen. It was not; in three years in New York, I didn't see Cementhead again.

I walked on to the ASAC's office. Later, I learned he too had a nickname: Hitler. Funny, I mused while waiting for him to get off the telephone, he didn't look like Hitler and didn't act like him. But he did have a German surname. I wondered what my fellow agents might call me behind my back.

"Hello, Okie," the ASAC said when he hung up the phone. I occurred to me that I already had a nickname; if I didn't before, I did now. "I've been looking over your background. Impressive for a rookie, Okie. You're going to be assigned to the Bribery and Political Corruption Squad." He obviously could spot the confused look on my face so he continued. "I'm aware you know nothing about bribery or political corruption. But I'm assigning you there because that squad has an empty desk." That decision ultimately determined what I would specialize in as an FBI agent. The ASAC grunted out of his chair and said, "Come on. I'll introduce you to your supervisor, Vinnie Daugherty." On the way, "Hitler" told me Vinnie was a drunk who would be retiring in about a year. "He won't give you any trouble," the ASAC advised. "Just do your job and you'll be fine."

Interestingly, the work of an FBI supervisor involved little supervision. He typically assigned cases to agents and stayed out of their way while they conducted investigations. Cases usually came from sources: referrals by an affected entity (such as a financial institution or another government agency); other FBI offices that requested a specific investigation within another geographical territory; a complaint from the public; or, in rare cases, directly from FBI headquarters.

The supervisor's other main responsibility was to sign out paperwork. By now, I was starting to appreciate just how much red tape was involved in doing my job. Cases from other offices, in the days before e-mail, arrived by regular mail unless there was an emergency. In those situations, they could arrive by teletype or even telephone. The latter had to be followed up with a written communication; nothing in the FBI was done on a strictly oral basis. Reports were either interim or final and were furnished to affected parties; another office; FBI headquarters; other federal, state or local agencies; and/or to the prosecutor. A private victim of a federal offense, strangely enough, wasn't advised of the case's outcome. That's because the United States of America was the ultimate victim, or so they said.

Vinnie's standard tactic was to leave for his mostly liquid lunch about 11:00 AM and return after 2:00 PM. Late in the afternoon, three sheets to the wind, Daugherty would sign out just about anything to FBIHQ, which received routine copies of all our reports. So if an agent had a complicated or controversial report, that's when he would give it to Vinnie.

Vinnie sat in the corner of the squad room with a small partition surrounding his desk. There was room for only one chair, so most people who had to see him stood. Supervisor Daugherty was thin and appeared to be much older than what he actually was. He had watery eyes and a red nose — a dead giveaway for someone who had spent too much time hitting the sauce.

After introducing me, the ASAC disappeared. The soft-spoken Daugherty gave me a perfunctory greeting, and told me that I was being assigned for training to Boyd Howell. Originally from Illinois farm country, Boyd had been stuck in New York for nearly 20 years and on the Bribery and Political Corruption Squad for 10. I couldn't have asked for anyone better to show me the ropes. Slight of build and older with a sprinkling of gray hair, Howell took me under his wing.

By my first summer in New York, Dawn and Beth had joined me. We rented a cottage in Kings Point, New York, just east of the Queens county line. The cottage was shabby but had a great location: down Steamboat Road about three blocks from the U.S. Merchant Marine Academy, on Long Island Sound.

I should have known more bad things were going to happen to my marriage in New York. I'd flown back to El Paso to make the trip east with Dawn, Beth, and her dog. We four were crowded in Dawn's Volkswagen Beetle, which she had bought before we were married. It was about 2:00 AM when Dawn first got her view of New York; Beth was asleep in the back seat. As I turned on to the Brooklyn-Queens Expressway, the traffic was still bumper to bumper. Dawn, who grew up in little Bluewell, West Virginia, burst into tears at the terrifying sight of it all. Being from a small town myself, I understood her awe of big-city life.

That first week, Dawn and Beth went into the city to see the Statue of Liberty. When they returned, Beth let her dog — which she'd had since early childhood — out of the house, and he was promptly run over and killed on Steamboat Road.

A Big Case Becomes Mine

Boyd was smack-dab in the middle of a rather complicated investigation involving allegations against Herman Simon Klegmeir, district director for the Immigration and Naturalization Service (INS) in Newark, New Jersey. For years, there had been rumors Klegmeir was on the take. The INS was divided into geographical districts that covered the entire country. Any foreigner coming into the United States was, in essence, under the authority of the local district director. Which district was determined by the alien's original port of entry or his final residence. New York and Newark were the largest INS districts in the United States, followed by Miami and Los Angeles.

All requests by foreigners to enter the United States were handled by the district director's office. He or she had ultimate decision-making power, but as a practical matter, the staff handled such things. Aliens coming into the States could enter on a visa, but the ultimate was for them to be issued a "green card" (by the way, I have no idea where that name came from; the cards weren't green), which gave them the right to stay in the United States for extended periods without being citizens.

The investigative theory was that Klegmeir was demanding bribes to issue green cards. Boyd had developed two INS agents who agreed to work in New York's Chinatown to see if they could gather more information. The underground in Chinatown was effectively controlled by five tongs, the Chinese equivalent of Mafia families. Over time, the two INS agents had developed a relationship with Benny Ong, a mainland Chinese native who was reputed to be the head of one of the tongs. Each time the INS guys met with Ong, they wore body recorders to capture the entire conversation. These meetings had to be transcribed, and that is where I came in. The steno pool was normally in charge of the transcriptions, but it had fallen months behind and the head stenographer had complained to Howell that the conversations were almost impossible to decipher. So Boyd loaded me up with a pile of tapes, and my job was to transcribe them word for word. It took a long time to do. I thought maybe I was going to pull my hair out; the meetings invariably occurred in a Chinese restaurant with much background noise – clinking glasses and the like. Adding to the difficulty was Ong's heavy Chinese accent.

After the agents had developed some rapport with Benny, he confirmed that he had also heard that Klegmeir was on the take. More specifically, rumors on Mott Street (one of the main thoroughfares in Chinatown) had it that Klegmeir was taking bribes from Stanley Yee, a wealthy Chinese restaurateur who owned at least a dozen eating establishments in New York. Yee was allegedly making the payoffs to obtain green cards for his workers, nearly all of whom came from mainland China. The problem for us was that Ong had no proof.

Around this time, Boyd Howell received a transfer to his dream location (known officially in FBI circles as his "office of preference"), Springfield, Illinois. It proved pointedly that it was easy to get assigned to the NYO and almost impossible to get out. From Boyd's point of view, he couldn't leave New York fast enough; he was thrilled to be returning to his native hunting ground. It was logical for Vinnie to reassign the Klegmeir matter to me as the case agent.

Even though Howell taught me a lot, we weren't the same kind of agent; he was more thoughtful, deliberate, and cautious. I was much younger and admittedly full of impatience. Boyd, in my estimation, had fooled around with this case a bit too long, and I was determined to bring it to a head. Howell worked undercover and in the shadows, but that wasn't my style.

One of my first moves was to discontinue the INS agents' meetings with Benny Ong. The intelligence had dropped off dramatically, and the meetings were a paperwork nightmare. It was not standard FBI practice to interview the principal subject of the investigation first. Had I approached Klegmeir right away, he would have only denied the allegations, and I wouldn't have had anything to confront him with. The FBI methodology was to start at the outer circle of culpability and work inward toward the main suspect. Or, as an agent told me once, "What we do in the Bureau is eat around the apple until the core drops out."

In lectures I've given on investigative techniques, a common question is "How do you keep the suspect from finding out he or she is being investigated?" The short answer is that you can't — at some point your target is going to know. But if you've secured physical evidence so it can't be tampered with, and interviewed enough witnesses to lock in their testimony, there's little the subject of the investigation can do to send the inquiry off track.

Since I had a specific lead — that Yee was paying off Klegmeir to get green cards for the former's workers — I presented the matter to Rudolph Giuliani, then an assistant United States' attorney, and his colleague, Ed Kuriansky, to seek grand jury subpoenas for Yee's workers' records. (Yes, that is the same Rudy Giuliani that would later go on to fame.) Rudy had developed a reputation as an agent's prosecutor. If you could convince him of a case's merits, he could be very aggressive. And he was this time. Subpoenas *duces tecum* (a Latin term that roughly translates to a demand for records only) were served for all of Yee's restaurants. This basically gave Yee two options: Cough up his paperwork, or sit in jail until he did. But Stanley didn't go down without a fight. His attorney argued furiously with Giuliani to no avail.

The records were an absolute nightmare because all of them were in Mandarin. I naturally couldn't make out a word, so we hired a Chinese interpreter who converted the payroll data to

English. Chinese people usually have three names, and the last name normally comes first. For example, "Yun Chin Bang," when converted to English, would be "Chin Bang Yun." The heart of FBI record keeping was its index system. All names of key individuals — suspects, co-conspirators, witnesses — were indexed in the Bureau files. The first step in just about any case was to search the index to see if the person's name was already there. At that time, there were no computers and no FBI-wide index. So if you suspected that someone in New York had been involved in a case in Los Angeles, you would ask LA to hand-check its index. At best, it was a time-consuming, haphazard system. (Now, because of computerization, a nationwide search can be conducted almost instantaneously.)

Since I was unsure of the exact method to sequence the Chinese names, the clerks had to conduct a six-way search on each name (i.e., the complete list of variations with a first, middle and last name). It nearly drove me and the clerks batty. But all was for naught; our files reflected nothing. I then turned over the list of several hundred names to my INS counterpart, Sol Solzberg, asking him to search their records. I liked Sol very much even though he was an odd sort. Not too long after I was assigned to New York, we agreed to meet for the first time at a convenient breakfast place.

Right away he said to me, "Obviously you're not from New York."

"Why?" I asked.

"I saw you standing on the corner," Solzberg said. "Two things: First, you waited for the traffic light to turn green before you crossed. Second, you didn't look down for dog poop before proceeding. Us natives would have done it differently."

Sol was not a criminal investigator. In his early fifties and overweight, he had never married and still lived with his mother. Solzberg was thrilled at the prospect of chasing bad guys, and got the search done right away. The results were informative: About a dozen of Yee's workers turned up, all with a common element. They had entered the Port of New York originally on visas, and then at various times had sent in letters stating that they had "moved" to New Jersey. A further search of Newark's records showed they had all been issued green cards by none other than Herman Simon Klegmeir himself.

I asked Solzberg how common it was for a district director to sign off on green card applications personally.

"In the 30 years I've been with INS, I've never heard of it happening," Sol replied.

Until now. Once Klegmeir approved the green cards, all of these workers, at varying times, sent letters to the Newark and New York districts of the INS stating that they had "moved" back to New York and asked that their files be transferred. Of further interest was the fact that in their applications, all were recommended by Stanley Yee.

What had happened was as obvious as the nose on your face. None of these people had moved from New York; it was all a ruse to get their files transferred to Newark so Klegmeir could approve the green cards. With this knowledge, I attempted to interview Yee. It came as no surprise when he declined. I went back to Rudy's office with my new information.

"You're on to something, Joe," Giuliani said. "Let's put Yee in front of the grand jury."

It was just what I was hoping for. To apply some additional pressure, Sol had managed to conjure up a few technical violations of INS regulations on the part of Yee. Stanley was long a natural-ized U.S. citizen, so these infractions couldn't be used to deport him. But it was still something that Rudy or Ed could ask about in the grand jury.

When it was his time to testify, Yee denied everything: making payoffs, having Klegmeir as a silent partner in Stanley's

Chinese restaurants, even the technical violations. Again, no surprises there, but we had to follow procedure. He barely admitted that Klegmeir had eaten at Yee's establishments. We also got hold of Yee's banking information, which showed us nothing other than he was quite wealthy.

It was now time for Klegmeir's turn in the barrel. Ed Kuriansky pulled him before the grand jury and grilled him for an hour or so. Herman admitted nothing except for casually knowing Stanley Yee. Whatever technical infractions of INS regulations occurred he blamed entirely on Stanley. His explanation about why he personally approved green cards for the Chinese immigrants was that he routinely did this. Klegmeir denied any favoritism at all toward Yee. The only useful information was the location of the suspect's bank accounts (or at least the ones he admitted to). We subpoenaed them from his financial institutions.

You would think that no one receiving ill-gotten gains such as bribes would stash the loot in his own bank accounts under his true name. Even so, over the years I investigated fraud, it happened repeatedly. But not in the case of Herman Simon Klegmeir; his banking records reflected no suspicious activity at all. His stonewalling us was no great surprise.

I still had about a dozen Chinese immigrants to interview. Thus far, I'd been reluctant to do so for two reasons. First, the language barrier presented great problems. FBI agent George Proctor from the Newark office assisted me in the interviews, but he didn't speak Chinese either. So we had to use an interpreter, which greatly slowed us down. The second reason for my reluctance had to do with the Chinese culture. The immigrants were scared to death of the police. Most shook like a leaf when we questioned them, and it was difficult — usually impossible — to get candid answers.

The interviews would have been worthless except that we got bank account information from all of them. So back I went to Rudy's office, requesting even more subpoenas. Giuliani was getting impatient, and so was I. So far, thousands of man-hours had been expended with no real results. Kuriansky handled some of the paperwork. When I explained to him what was happening, he gave me the 12 or so subpoenas I needed.

The bank records showed a very unusual pattern. Not one of these immigrants had a checking account, but all of them had savings. The deposits coming in were obviously from their meager earnings. It was in the withdrawals that we hit pay dirt. In every case, each immigrant had taken out exactly $10,000 in cash — about a week or so before their green cards were approved by Klegmeir. The implication was clear: The immigrants were paying Klegmeir, undoubtedly through Yee. Whether Stanley was adding more cash to those amounts, I didn't know. If he was, that was not reflected in his bank accounts.

I was excited to set up a meeting with Rudy to tell him the news. When I went into his cramped office, he placed a quick call to Kuriansky and asked him to join us. Giuliani's desk was strewn with papers, and it was obvious from his demeanor that he was hassled with other cases. Nonetheless, he listened carefully to what I had uncovered. As I spoke, Rudy put his fingers together and brought them under his chin.

When I finished, the prosecutor was silent. He then looked at Ed but didn't say anything. Both nodded to each other almost imperceptibly. They brought their eyes back to me and Ed spoke for the both of them. "Joe," he said. "You've worked very hard on this case. You've left no stone unturned. We agree with you that Klegmeir is on the take from Yee. But unless he hands up Klegmeir or until you can put money in Herman's pocket, you don't have anything. And you know that."

I looked at Rudy. At this time, Giuliani still had a full head of hair, but you could tell it was not going to last. And he always looked like he could use a good meal. While I was mulling over what to say, I silently asked myself: Does Rudy have one blue suit and one white shirt, or does he have a hundred? I'd never seen him in anything else. Giuliani broke the silence.

"Joe, I agree with Ed. You've worked your butt off on this case. Maybe you can find a way to apply more pressure to Yee. He's the key. However, if that doesn't work, we're going to have to recommend you close the case," he said in a measured voice.

I knew they were right but it was still a bitter pill. The disappointment must have been obvious on my face.

As I stood up, Rudy got out of his chair, patted me gently on the shoulder, and said, "Sorry, Joe."

When I left, which was in the middle of the afternoon, I stepped into the bright, cool sun of downtown Manhattan. I felt as though I'd been kicked in the chest, so I started walking slowly uptown at a leisurely pace. It was a good way for me to blow off steam and think about what my next step might entail. The walk was therapeutic.

By the time I arrived at the NYO, I was calmed down and I had a plan. Put pressure on Yee, Rudy and Ed had suggested. I was going to do exactly that. Had I called ahead for an appointment with Stanley, his lawyer would have told Yee not to consent. Instead, a few days later I made several phone calls to find out where the Chinese restaurateur was at that exact moment. He was at one of his restaurants in Midtown. So I gathered up several key documents and headed out. Yee was surprised to see me and from the look on his face, he wasn't happy I'd shown up. I asked to speak to him privately in his tiny office.

"Mr. Yee," I started, "we know that you have perjured yourself before the federal grand jury about Mr. Klegmeir." Stanley said nothing. "When we prove that, you could go to prison." Still nothing. "But we are not after you, we are after Klegmeir. If you cooperate, I am going to recommend to the government's attorneys that you not be prosecuted." Again, Yee was silent. "We know that your workers have paid Herman bribes through you to obtain green cards. That is a very serious offense. All of these people could be deported when we prove our case. You don't want that; they will not be welcomed back to mainland China and will probably be jailed or might even be executed. Believe me, we will prove this case — with or without you," I bluffed. "Mr. Yee, you can make it easier for us and you'll be rewarded for that by possibly avoiding prosecution." An FBI agent doesn't have the authority to convey immunity, I explained; that can be done only by the government's lawyers. "But they frequently take my recommendations, and I am willing to speak up for you if you tell me the truth."

Yee didn't say anything for a while. I remained quiet too, so what I told him would sink in.

Finally, in broken English, he said, "I no rat on my friend."

"Stanley," I countered, "this could help you avoid a prison term and probably save your restaurants."

Yee shook his head and repeated, "I no rat on my friend."

"Mr. Yee, does this mean you would go to jail for Mr. Klegmeir?" I asked.

"Yes," he said without hesitation, "I no rat on my friend."

I thought for a bit and then pulled out my big gun: a transcript of Klegmeir's testimony before the federal grand jury. Giuliani or Kuriansky would not have wanted to be involved in my tactics; grand jury testimony was technically secret, although it was frequently leaked even by prosecutors.

"Mr. Yee, if Klegmeir is your friend, why would he say these things about you to the grand jury?" In his testimony, the INS district director denied receiving any money from Yee. But when asked about all of the administrative violations, Klegmeir blamed everything on Stanley. Yee could read English much better than he could speak it. He took his time looking at the sections I had pre-marked, and he carefully examined the front page, which clearly reflected that the document was a transcript from the federal grand jury. He said nothing but uttered a few audible grunts.

I couldn't resist. "So this is your 'friend,'" I said. "With 'friends' like this, you don't need any enemies."

Yee was silent and handed me back the transcript. You could tell by the look on his face that he was shaken. Stanley said, "I say nothing more now."

I left, but had the feeling I would be hearing from him. A week or so later, I got a call from an attorney who said he represented Mr. Yee. He wanted a meeting with the prosecutors and me. I arranged it. The attorney, Ed, Rudy and I met in a conference room. I had no prior experience being involved in a plea deal so the entire procedure was new to me. It became readily apparent that Yee's attorney had been around the block a few times.

Stanley's lawyer said, "Hypothetically, my client can hand Mr. Klegmeir to you on a silver plate. What can you do for Mr. Yee in return?"

Ed said, "Hypothetically, if your client can do that, perhaps the government can grant him immunity to prosecution on bribery charges, plus agree not to pursue his perjury to the grand jury."

I silently wondered about all of this "hypothetically" stuff. Later I learned that it was an intricate dance that attorneys engage in to discover each other's position without actually committing themselves.

Yee's lawyer, thankfully, did not mention the leaked grand jury testimony to Ed or Rudy. After he left, Rudy asked, "How did you get Yee to come around?"

"Well," I said, "I didn't beat or threaten him."

"So how did you do it?" Ed asked.

"You don't want to know," I answered.

Giuliani's and Kuriansky's eyebrows shot up simultaneously, but they didn't press the question.

When Stanley finally appeared before the grand jury again, I got a call from the prosecutors, who said that Yee had come clean, fully implicating Klegmeir. Yee even knew where the money was stashed — in a bank in Tel Aviv, under Herman's own name. Since Israel didn't fall under U.S. bank secrecy laws, I was able to confirm through our international contacts that Klegmeir did indeed have an account with a balance exceeding $250,000. That's hard to amass on the salary of a public servant. He probably hid the cash under his mattress until he got enough to make the trip in person so he could deposit the money.

The grand jury subsequently indicted Herman Simon Klegmeir. Shortly before his trial, Klegmeir appeared quietly in Federal Court and pled guilty to one count of bribery. He was required to disgorge all of his ill-gotten money, and he drew a prison sentence of a couple of years. Case closed.

Although I could have been proud that justice was served, I was actually ashamed for what I'd done in leaking the grand jury transcript; my own little fraud. It was a valuable lesson that I'd vowed to learn before but had fraudulently violated again: If you can't play by the rules, you don't deserve to win. And I didn't deserve to win this one.

After spending about six months in our rented cottage in Kings Point, Dawn and I bought a townhouse in the only place we could afford: central New Jersey, nearly a two-hour one-way commute to my office in the city. The place was called Twin Rivers, and it was a planned community. Some enterprising real estate investors had bought up several hundred acres of fallow potato fields and built 2,500 townhomes there over a period of a few years.

Twin Rivers had its own schools, post office, supermarket and sundry conveniences. It was just a mile or so off the Jersey

Turnpike. Buses took commuters like me to the Port Authority Bus Terminal on the West Side of Manhattan – a 70-minute trip. From there, I'd take three escalators down to street level and then two more down to the subway. Then I would walk underground for a few blocks, where I took the cross-town subway shuttle from Times Square to Grand Central. I'd take more escalators underground to get to the uptown subway, which I would take to 68th Street and Lexington Avenue. Then I'd endure a four-block walk to the office — no matter what the weather. In the evenings, the commute would be reversed. By the time I got to the office, I was exhausted; to arrive at about 8:00 AM, I'd leave Twin Rivers on the 6:07 bus. In the afternoons, if I left the office at 5:00 or so, it would be at least 7:30 PM before I would walk in my front door.

Dawn, however, had quickly scored a job with the pharmaceutical giant Johnson & Johnson at its headquarters in East Brunswick, New Jersey — about a ten-minute easy commute from our home by car. Beth enrolled in junior high school at Twin Rivers and was making friends. But we were barely making ends meet. We had only Dawn's un-air-conditioned Beetle for transportation, and money was so tight that we rationed ourselves to meat a maximum of three times a week. It was an unpleasant reminder of my childhood poverty, which I'll now step back in time to describe.

Chapter 2

My Earliest Years

It's my impression that most people's childhood memories are pleasant; mine aren't. I was born June 27, 1944, at Patterson Hospital in Duncan, Oklahoma. A small town of 20,000, located in the south-central part of the state, it was established on June 27, 1892 (exactly 52 years before my birth) by William Duncan, a Scotsman who set up an outpost on the Chisholm Trail, where nearly 10 million cattle were herded between Texas and Kansas in the late 1800s.

Duncan's claim to fame is twofold. First, it's the birthplace of Hollywood director Ron Howard, who also starred as "Opie" on the legendary *Andy Griffith* television series. Second, it's the original home of Halliburton. At this writing, Halliburton has earned a bad reputation for supposed corruption in Iraq and as the alleged beneficiary of illicit bounty from former Vice President Dick Cheney, Halliburton's onetime chief executive.

Its original name was Halliburton Oil Well Cementing Company. Founder Erle P. Halliburton wasn't from my hometown, but he picked Duncan early in the twentieth century because of its proximity to the oil fields in Stephens County, which described itself as the "Buckle on the Oil Belt." I grew up with the constant click of oil well pumps sucking black gold out of the ground. Drilling rigs dotted the red clay landscape, which yields only one crop: cotton.

Speaking of cotton, that was my dad's nickname because of his blond hair. "Cotton's" true name was Coyle Averett Wells, but no one called him that. He was born in western Arkansas on July 17, 1906. He and his dad moved to Oklahoma when my father was young. I didn't know my paternal grandmother; she died giving birth to my dad. I was named for his father, Joseph Terrell Wells, and for my maternal grandfather, William Thomas Driggers. Joseph Terrell Wells was of Welsh ancestry; my mother, Vola, was a combination of Caucasian, Comanche Indian and Black Dutch, also known as Melungeon. My mother was the youngest of nine children. She had a sister who died in infancy and was left with eight older brothers. Virtually all of them quit school young and worked their entire lives in the oil fields. Vola Driggers Wells (later, McMasters) was born on October 28, 1910. She lived and died within a 25-mile radius of Duncan.

My Dysfunctional Youth

Therapists would later tell me I can't remember much of my younger days because they were so unpleasant. I do recall some happy times when I was five or six years old. But by the time I was seven or eight, my dad's drinking had the better of him. Until it got him fired, he worked at the Sun-Ray Oil Refinery, about five miles out of town. He was medically ineligible to serve in World War II as a result of losing the trigger finger on his right hand to an oilfield accident before I was born.

My most vivid childhood memories are of the fights between my parents. I'd lie in bed at night while they screamed at each other. On several occasions, my mom threw dishes at my dad, and they shattered against the wall.

Cotton and Vola separated several times. In one instance, when I was about six, my dad told me he was going out for a pack of cigarettes. In reality, it was another separation but he didn't say that. I looked for him for weeks, thinking he had abandoned me. Traumatic events can have a lasting effect. In my case, they gave me a lifelong fear of abandonment. Even today, when my wife goes to the store, a small voice inside me says she won't come back.

My most unpleasant memory was of a night when my dad came in dead drunk, and passed out face-down in bed. My mother was so furious that she beat him with the buckle end of one of his belts. Blood soaked through his shirt; he was unconscious. I rushed into the bedroom crying, and tried to stop her. She was so enraged that she turned the belt on me, whipping me as hard as she could. I stayed out of school for a few days until the bruising and bleeding had partially healed. Vola Wells was not a cruel person, but she had a bad temper. She didn't apologize for the fit she threw, and I never forgave her. This incident would forever change the way I felt about my own mother.

We lived at 709 Elm Street in a two-bedroom, one-bath house. It was a couple of blocks from the railroad; certainly not the nicest area in town but good enough. My sister, Sue, and I had twin beds in one room while my parents slept in the other. I didn't know Sue (her full given name was Jimmie Sue) very well. She was nine years older than me, and we had little in common. At age 16 or 17, she got pregnant by an airman stationed at Sheppard Air Force Base in Wichita Falls, Texas — about an hour away.

This brief union produced Terry Young, the oldest of my nieces and nephews. Sue moved out of our house, and I saw little of her from then on. She'd eventually bear four children by different men. By the end of her life, Sue was a hopeless alcoholic.

Living on Less

After my father lost his job, Cotton and Vola split permanently, and he took off for parts unknown. I'd sit at the kitchen table and cry for hours, pining away for him. In my child's mind, this was my mother's fault; she had chased away my dad. At the time I completely ignored that he was a drunk who'd gotten fired from his job, leaving no way to support his family.

Shortly after he left, we lost our home; even our furniture was repossessed. Having nowhere to go, we stayed for a short time with my Uncle Cecil, who lived in Comanche, 10 miles to the south.

I got my first job — shining shoes on Saturdays at a local barber shop. I'd hitchhike from Comanche to Duncan and back again after work. Often, I'd have to walk a long way from where I was dropped off. But other times, a driver would go out of his way to take me directly to the shop.

Most of my pay went to Vola, who gave it to Uncle Cecil for food. We stayed in Comanche for a month or two, until my mother could save up enough from ironing and cleaning for us to move back to Duncan. Her father, Grandpa Will, helped however he could but he was poor too. We were all poor. Getting welfare was out of the question. I don't know if it existed, but all my relatives were dead set against handouts.

Just before school started in the seventh grade, my mother found an elderly woman willing to share her home in exchange for upkeep. We didn't live there more than a month. We were expected to provide our own food, but this senile lady was convinced we were stealing hers.

My mother and I didn't have any furniture, and could pack everything we owned in a couple of bags. Vola had never worked outside of the home, and had no education to speak of. She was therefore doomed to menial jobs. When we had nothing to eat, we would either do without or get a free meal from one of her brothers; five of them lived in or around Comanche.

After leaving the elderly lady's home, we lived for years in a series of dilapidated apartments and houses. Since my mother normally paid rent by the week, we'd often move after a couple of weeks because she couldn't stand the place.

In one apartment, the gas-fired water heater was located in the closet. Naturally enough, on an evening when my mother was away, the closet caught fire and burned every stitch of clothing we had except what was on our backs. Also lost in the blaze were most of our family photographs. Times were tough; we relied on her church to give us hand-me-down clothes. Vola didn't drive, so we got around by walking or mooching rides. It was especially difficult when we had the money to buy groceries: I would carry two bags for several blocks and so would she.

The saving grace for me was music. It was then, and has been since. Although Mother and I didn't have a television, we did have a radio. I would listen to it for hours, and dream of going to a live concert. But stars didn't tour Duncan, and traveling to Oklahoma City or Dallas was out of the question. So I simply listened, and wished I was with them. What a wonderful escape it proved to be. People who know me well are aware of how much I love music; it is in my very soul.

Not a Fashion Maven

Memories dim, but I clearly remember being in the seventh grade — probably the roughest time in my early youth. It was about 1957, when kids in my junior high school were very fashion-conscious. In Mrs. Gibson's class, I sat in front of a pretty girl named Linda Langley. She was very uppity, and almost never spoke to me.

But one day she hissed, "Are those the only two shirts you have?" As a matter of fact, they were, thanks to the closet fire and poverty. I'd wear one, wash it by hand, hang it up to dry and wear the other the next day.

I was so embarrassed by Linda's outburst that I made two vows: First, that one day I'd have ample clothes — only of the finest quality; now I do. Second, that I'd always be pressed and shined; and I am. People tell me I have an eye for clothing. If so, it's because I've carefully studied the subject. Mind you, I don't have lots of clothes, but I have enough. And they fit; my suits and dress shirts are handmade.

The eighth grade was somewhat of a watershed year; in Mr. Lowery's class I learned how to construct a grammatically correct sentence. We were taught verbs, adverbs, nouns, pre-positions, dangling participles and how to diagram a sentence. Mr. Lowery taught by a sure-fire technique. If you didn't get what he was teaching, he'd march you before the class and bust your butt with a special paddle made for him by one of his prior student-victims. Talk about motivation; he knew what it was. Through a variation of the same method, he also greatly discour-aged talking. Students caught were sent to the front of the class where they would trade licks with the paddle.

Once, my classmate George Schaeffer and I violated Mr. Lowery's principle, and suffered the consequences. On our way up to the teacher's desk we conspired to go easy on each other. I hit George first, as gently as I could.

Mr. Lowery then said, "That's not the way to do it, Joe. Let me show you how; bend over." He then laid one into me that made my eyes water. But since crying was unmanly, I shed no tears. God, it smarted.

Lowery then told George, "Do it right, or I'll be forced to show you too." Schaeffer took the hint and with his hands shaking in unison with my body, popped me with three licks. I was bruised and sore, and sat for the next few days with only the greatest difficulty. But this dark cloud had a silver lining: I definitely learned how to write a grammatically correct sentence.

Oklahoma History, also a required subject in the eighth grade, was taught by Quanah Cox. He was the grandson of the last great Comanche war chief, Quanah Parker (1850–1911), who never lost a battle to a white man. Chief Parker's mother was a white woman captured as an infant during a battle in 1834, and raised by the Indians. Parker was distinctive for being born with one brown eye and one blue. Grandson Quanah Cox, although light-skinned, had obvious American Indian features, notably high cheekbones.

I learned from Mr. Cox to listen carefully, and to do my homework before class. To ensure you were listening, he'd look directly at you and call out another student's name. If you answered, and the other student didn't, Mr. Cox would embarrass you both by pointing out that neither was paying attention. And to make sure you read your assignment before class, he'd ask questions whose answers would be obvious to anyone who had done the homework. Students who didn't know the answers would be called to the front of the classroom, and paddled. There are good arguments against corporal punishment. But in those days it was common, and for me, it worked like a charm. I still remember the "Five Civilized Tribes": Cherokee, Chickasaw, Choctaw, Seminole, and Creek.

Dirt Poor in the Land of Poor Dirt

By the time I reached the tenth grade, my mother had gotten a job cleaning Mack Oil Company's offices from 5:00 PM to midnight. Prior to that, she had worked anywhere she could, taking in ironing, cleaning houses, cooking — whatever it took. She was thrilled to get the position. For the first time in years she had steady income, even if it was modest.

I continued to work odd jobs. One summer, when I was 14 or so, a local fireman, A.D. Green, hired me to work in his car lot. The operation was small and strictly low-overhead — no phone, office, or bathroom. A.D. was the only salesman, and his schedule at the fire department was 24 hours on-duty, then 24 off. That dictated my hours: every other day except Sunday. My duties were to clean and dust the cars and refer any walk-ins to A.D.'s telephone number. He didn't have a chair for me, so I'd sit in the cars — trying to ignore the blazing heat.

On one occasion, A.D. asked me to move several cars to different locations on the lot. I told him I didn't know how to drive. But A.D. said not to worry. "The ones I'm asking you to move have automatic transmissions. Be careful, and you'll be all right."

I tried. The first car was parked between two others. A 14-year-old boy behind the wheel for the first time doesn't know how to judge distance or back up. So when I put the car in reverse, I scraped the vehicle to my right. It freaked me out so badly that when I put the car in forward, I ran into the auto on my left. Result: three wrecked cars. A.D. was very upset, and fired me on the spot. And that was the end of my automobile babysitting career.

Looking beyond High School

About this time, I began to think about what I'd do if and when I graduated from high school. Vola, with her limited vision, never even suggested college. She was a glass-half-empty kind of person, but I didn't recognize it at the time. My mother sincerely believed that people who set their goals too high would fail and be disappointed.

"We'll never be rich or like people who are," she'd say. My problem was that I actually bought into this idea. I wasn't motivated by money; I just wanted to get out of Duncan as soon as possible.

But Vola had other ideas. "Get yourself a good job at Halliburton and you'll be set for life," she advised. This confused my young mind — I didn't want to work for Halliburton, and I wanted to go far away. But I didn't know how.

Since I was a mediocre student at best, it seemed right to take vocational education classes and forget the college prep stuff. So I enrolled in Machine Shop, a class taught by Mr. Brown, a kind and patient man. I was a student of his from tenth grade until I graduated. Machine Shop taught lathing and welding. I wasn't very good at the former but excelled at the latter. This marked the first time I can recall that I actually had talent at something.

Welding students learned to fuse metals together by arc welding (with a torch using a generator-supplied electric arc) and by acetylene welding (with a flammable-gas-fed torch). The object of both methods was to join the metals in a beautiful welded line or "bead." If the torch — electric or acetylene — was too hot, it would burn through the two metals being joined; too cool, and the weld wouldn't hold. Different metals welded dissimilarly because of their thickness and composition. The right combination could be produced only through much practice and a flair for the art.

Later, machines did much of the welding, cheaper and flawlessly. At the time, I didn't realize this and how it would limit my advancement. But I was troubled by the prospect of spending eight hours a day behind a mask like that worn by Gort the alien robot in the classic movie, *The Day the Earth Stood Still*. Now that I know myself better, it's obvious I wouldn't have enjoyed a career of staring at a welding bead.

High School

For most of high school, I was a nothing. Not popular, not in the right clique, not an athlete; just a young boy trying to put one foot in front of the other. I had no time whatsoever to participate in extracurricular activities. If I had clothes or spending money, it was only because I had worked for them. As a result, I greatly resented my mother, whom I always blamed for running my dad off. Of course, it was not entirely her fault; but because it took me years to recognize and accept that, Vola and I argued constantly. I couldn't understand why other kids had nice clothes and access to a car, while I had neither. I spent entirely too much time pondering, "Why me?" In retrospect, I see it as a complete waste of emotion.

My menial jobs continued. There were so many that I remember only two more of them well: first, being a dishwasher at the Hillcrest Café. After a day at school, I'd have my hands deep in soapy water until the restaurant closed. I cleaned all the dinner dishes, pots, pans and utensils. Often, when I'd finished washing everything, someone would come in just before closing time and order a meal. Then I'd have to repeat the process, much to my chagrin.

Mother still worked nights at Mack Oil Company; so it helped that I'd get an evening meal for free at the Hillcrest. But a few months after I began work, the place closed, throwing me out of a job once again. Then luck turned my way. I was hired as a janitor for the Stephens County Health Center, a job I held until I graduated from high school. I'd go in after the office closed for the day, and spend a couple of hours cleaning up. It was an easy slot, and my supervision was almost nonexistent. When I wasn't in the mood to clean (which was most of the time), I'd just hit the high spots and save the serious cleaning for later. The health center had a small library where I discovered several books on female anatomy — complete with graphic photos. Hey, I was a young testosterone-filled boy, and this was totally new territory for me. Let's just say that I became an avid student of this subject matter for too long, and my cleaning chores suffered as a result.

In Machine Shop class I met Larry Wilson, who would turn out to be my lifetime friend. Called "Red" because of his hair, Larry probably resented the name. But he never said so to me or, as far as I know, to anyone else. Red saw something in me that I didn't; he always predicted I'd turn out to be something. Now, when we talk, he tells me how smart he was to recognize that.

Red is a year older than me, so before I was eligible for a driver's license, he'd tote me just about everywhere in his souped-up 1954 Olds. Many a day during the freezing winters, he'd pick me up in front of our duplex at 1016 Pine Street, and drive me to school. Red didn't go to college, and he never left Duncan. He recently retired from 36 years at Halliburton. For me, it would have been a fate worse than death. But for him, it was the right thing to do.

My First Girlfriend

Though I had no wheels, I took Driver's Ed as a junior. I got my license and fell in love for the first time — with a girl I met in class. Her name was Linda Vanort. It was hard for me to believe my luck; she was pretty and popular and came from a great family. Everyone called her Linda Van. Her dad, Ernie, owned the local lumberyard.

Linda said she loved me. We were inseparable for the rest of the school year. When school was out until August, she went away to be a counselor at summer camp like she always did. And just before she left, Linda broke up with me, saying it wouldn't be fair to tie me down. It nearly tore my heart to pieces.

During the time we were together, we found any excuse possible to make out. Although she offered her virginity to me several times, I declined. Premarital sex was greatly frowned upon then, and I was intent on "saving her" until we were married. I found out later that premarital sex was actually very common. People did it, and simply said they hadn't.

It was difficult for us to date, however. I didn't have a car and when we went somewhere, Linda's parents took us — to my great embarrassment — or we would double-date with someone who had access to an automobile. Then I bought my first car, a 1947 Chevrolet coupe I nicknamed the "Blue Goose." It cost me all of $75 and had exactly the quality I was looking for: It ran.

But the Blue Goose certainly wasn't much to look at. Although the body was relatively dent-free, the car probably hadn't been painted since it left the factory. Automobiles made in 1947 didn't have acrylic paint; there was no such thing. The result was that after 15 years, the color of the enamel on the car had turned from a medium blue to chalk. No manner of polishing or waxing could remove this film. So in a fit of inspiration or frustration, I brush-painted a large dark blue question mark on one door. Satisfied with the look, I then painted the same thing on the other door. My handiwork was an instant hit in the parking lot of Duncan High School.

My other major improvement to the Blue Goose was to clean the felt headliner with a small whisk broom. It was either that or spend a dime at the local car wash to use their vacuum, something I could ill afford; with gas at 29.9 cents a gallon, I needed to save all my scarce money for fuel. When I finished cleaning the headliner, I noticed through the dust in my eyes that the whisk broom had made small tears in it. But Linda had a novel and economical solution: She cut little patches from brightly colored and patterned fabric, which I glued to the headliner. What a sight. Even before the term was in common use, I'd "pimped my ride."

The Blue Goose served me well through high school, never having a moment's mechanical difficulty. Though the tires were nearly bald, I didn't care; I was just thrilled to have something to drive. When I graduated, I sold the car for $100 — a tidy $25 profit.

A Seed of Hope Grows

Toward the middle of my junior year, the situation with my mother had become untenable. We argued almost constantly, and many times it degenerated into a shouting match. Once Vola told me that she "hated me," and I returned her remark in kind.

But I was close to my friend Raymond and his family. They invited me to move in with them in exchange for cleaning and ironing. I jumped at the chance, and didn't live with Vola again, although we continued to speak infrequently. One of my teachers, Bill Dean, had an elderly sister who had a home across the street from Raymond. When Bill and his wife, Margaret, visited his sister, it was common for me to cross the street and talk to them. They had no biological children but had adopted Tina as an infant. She was six years younger than I. We got along great. One day, out of the blue, Bill and Margaret asked me to move in with them.

I stayed at the Deans until I graduated from high school. It completely changed my life. There's no telling where I would have been or how I'd have turned out otherwise. The family was the most loving, caring, and supportive I'd ever met. For the first time, I had a tight-knit group of people who really believed in me, and urged me to do my best. They also planted a seed in my brain: Maybe I could be anything I put my mind to. What a concept.

Tina and I became very close. We still are to this day; she's like the sister I always wanted. I was good for her because I was close to her age, and she could tell me secrets she wouldn't tell even her mom and dad — mostly about the fact that she was starting to like boys. Tina even insisted on practicing her kissing technique on me before she actually needed it. But there was nothing even remotely sexual involved. Tina was a disciplined student, and I learned from that. The following year I posted my best grades ever in high school, thanks to her and the support I'd received from her parents. I stayed close to Bill and Margaret for the rest of their lives. Bill died in 1994; Margaret, in 2001.

The Best-Looking Girl in High School

Not too long after the beginning of my senior year, rumors were circulating that Linda Vanort had "put out" for Bill Mirabel, a tall, strapping fellow student with blond hair. I was devastated, and couldn't believe it. When I confronted Linda in the school parking lot, she admitted with some pride to having sex with Bill. This crushed me; after all, I'd squelched my testosterone to "save" her for our marriage.

"Why, Linda, why?" I asked quietly with tears in my eyes. She was as gentle as possible when she replied, "Because you wouldn't do it with me." Then the girl I loved walked away. I stood there alone, crying. Then I got into the Blue Goose and sat behind the wheel crying some more. Although we didn't date again, our paths would cross years later.

For a couple of months after Linda, I sort-of dated Rita Blake, a brown-eyed beauty in one of my classes. She truly touched my heart, and even decades later I've never forgotten how wonderful she made me feel. We sort-of dated because our encounters were limited to the drive-in theater, where she could see me clandestinely to avoid her on-again, off-again boyfriend. But alas, he won out; at the height of our romance, Rita announced to me that she was getting engaged to him. Lucky for me, I didn't have much time to mourn because the best-looking girl at Duncan High School had set her sights on yours truly.

Jeanette McDuff was labeled "Most Beautiful" in our high school yearbook, which devoted an entire page to her photograph. It was easy to see why; she was statuesque with a great figure. Blessed with gorgeous dark eyes, matching shoulder-length hair and a come-hither smile, Miss McDuff was one of the most popular girls in school. A teenage legion of eager boys pursued her, but she couldn't be bothered with them.

A couple of weeks after we first met, in American History class, she invited me to accompany her to a school event. I nearly fainted — me? I picked up Jeanette at her home in the Blue Goose — after showering two or three times and taking a razor to the peach fuzz on my face. Doug Pruitt — whom I knew vaguely from school — was there to squire Jeanette's sister, Grace, to the same event. Little did I know then that Doug and I would become lifelong friends.

I don't remember what the occasion was, but some of the most popular kids in school were there. I wasn't one of them. It was hard for me to not at least know the other students; there were 239 in our graduating class. But knowing them and hanging out with them were two different things. Jeanette was a confident young woman, and knew what she wanted. Somewhere in the middle of the party, she decided that her classmates should know that she was with me so she held my hand. Later that evening, Jeanette slipped her arm in mine. I was thrilled and proud to be seen with her. When I took her home, I walked her to her door to say goodnight.

When I was turning to leave, she said, "Aren't you forgetting something?" For a moment, I was confused, but she cleared that up immediately. "I want you to kiss me goodnight," Jeanette said levelly, looking me in the eyes. I wasn't waiting to wake up from this dream or for her to change her mind. We kissed, and she went inside.

Over the next few days, I wondered if we had a shared future. Then a classmate approached me and said, "I understand you and Jeanette are going together. You lucky dog!" During the early 1960s, "going together" had special meaning: You were dating someone exclusively. I sought out Jeanette, and told her what I'd heard. With a twinkle in her dazzling eyes, she asked, "Do you want to go together?"

I immediately replied, "Yes . . . yes!" She didn't hesitate. "I do too. It's settled then; we're going together."

I felt better than if I'd won the lottery. Because of Jeanette, my popularity shot up at once. Suddenly I was a cool guy, and took full advantage of it. But for the life of me, I couldn't understand what she saw in yours truly. In one of our make-out sessions in the Blue Goose, she explained it to me. "Joe, I know you're poor. But you're kind, intelligent, and make me laugh all the time. Plus, you're good-looking. What more could a girl ask for?" I felt ten feet tall.

Jeanette had given me confidence, and it has lasted a lifetime. After all, if Jeanette McDuff could love me, others could too. She and I dated until we got out of high school. Jeanette then entered Oklahoma State University. Later we lost touch, but she'll always have a special place in my heart.

Meanwhile, I had figured out how to escape from Duncan. And I didn't do it halfway, either; I went down to the sea in ships.

Off to the Navy

In 1962, the military draft was still very much a reality. If you didn't seek a college deferment, chances were you'd be drafted — into the Army. I decided to enlist in the Navy for two disparate reasons. First, I'd been in the Boy Scouts for a time and had slept on the ground during campouts; it wasn't for me. Second, I'd seen the musical *Anchors Aweigh* starring Frank Sinatra and Gene

Kelly. It had a happy ending but, more important, I loved the uniforms and the thought of traveling the world. About a month before graduation, James Cook from high school and I visited the Navy recruiter and enlisted on the "buddy program," which meant that you were guaranteed to at least go through recruit training together, if not get the same assignment after that. James and I didn't know each other well, but both of us would at least face the unknown with someone we were acquainted with. We enlisted before finishing high school but departed on June 12, 1962 — about two weeks after graduation.

My first-ever airplane flight was from Oklahoma City to San Diego, via the now-defunct Trans World Airlines. We were met by a bus that transported us immediately to the Naval Training Center, next to Coronado Sound, an inlet from the Pacific Ocean. Before James and I left, the recruiter told us to bring only the clothes we would wear that day; they would be shipped back home, and everything else would be issued to us. Our first evening in boot camp was spent standing silently at parade rest; the recruiting officials had to tell us how to assume that position, with our feet spread and our hands behind our backs. Talking and moving weren't permitted.

After what seemed an eternity, we were divided into "companies" of about 80 men each. Ours was Company 306, and the people thrown into this group — from every corner of the United States — would be my roommates for the next nine weeks. Looking around me, I concluded that we were a motley crew. We were called to attention from parade rest, then loosely marched to a barber who sheared off all but a quarter inch of our hair. Next, we were issued four pairs of dungarees — two white, two blue — a pea coat, a seabag, white hats, underwear and socks. We also got a blanket, sheets, and a pillowcase. But before we put on our new uniforms, we had to hand-wash everything issued to us. The Navy had a saying: "A new article is a dirty article." I'd never thought about it before, but our recruit company commander, Chief Gunner's Mate L.P. Meitenger, pointed out that we didn't know where the new clothing had been: probably dragged on the floor, made by people with dirty hands, etc.

Over the next few months we got much practice in the art of washing clothes on large concrete washing tables just outside our barracks. These tables had been shaped in the form of a very shallow V so that the water could seep toward the center, where holes allowed it to drain to the ground. We were each issued a scrub brush and a bottle of Wisk liquid detergent. Although the powers that be purposely did not issue bleach, our whites (and especially our white hats) were expected to be spotless. So we openly stole salt from the chow hall to scrub the sweatbands of our hats. When the wash was complete, we had to hang our clothes a special way. For some reason, the Navy didn't give out clothespins; it issued short pieces of thin rope called "clothes stops." You tied the ends of your uniforms to one end of the clothes stop, looped them around a clothesline and secured everything with a square knot. Navy tradition required every sailor to know a lot about tying knots, and we practiced this art a lot, though we seldom used it after boot camp.

When we finally got dressed in our newly washed clothing, we all looked alike. That is exactly what the Navy wanted — to remove any hint of a caste system. It worked. You didn't know if the guys you were with were millionaires or paupers. In my case, the uniforms were a great idea. It totally hid that I was so poor. Recruits started at the magnanimous sum of $78 a month, which was more than adequate in boot camp. Other than cigarettes and toiletries, there was nothing to spend money on.

Several recruit officers were appointed for each company by the recruit company commander. The principal ones were the recruit chief petty officer (RCPO), assistant recruit chief petty officer (ACPO) and the master-at-arms (MAA). The latter was in charge of making assignments for the almost-continuous barracks inspections we endured. Because of my experience as a janitor in high school, I was chosen as the MAA. This was a good news-bad news situation. I didn't actually have to clean but if anything wasn't up to snuff, I would catch hell for it. I took the job seriously, and our barracks was considered to be the most shipshape. Chief Meitenger told us something early on that stuck with me: "Do what you're told to do when you're told to do it and do it to the best of your ability and you'll succeed in the Navy." It made perfect sense.

After about three weeks in recruit training, the chief decided to make some changes in his petty officer appointments. Our RCPO was a guy named Shuman, and he was picked because he had a college degree. But he was a dolt and universally disliked by his fellow recruits. So Chief Meitenger decided to jump me over the ACPO to become the new RCPO and Shuman was busted out of the recruit officer ranks altogether. I hadn't understood how many privileges the recruit chief petty officer enjoyed until I got the position. In essence, I was in charge of 80 men when Meitenger wasn't there; my wish was their command. Although I tried not to abuse my authority, it was heady indeed. I think I succeeded in boot camp because I was on a level playing field.

One thing I remember vividly about recruit training was the abundance of real milk. When I was growing up with Vola, it was a luxury. To save money, she bought powdered milk, a foul-tasting concoction, and mixed it with a bit of the real thing. I wasn't fooled; it was awful. In the chow hall I was stunned when I saw you could have all the real milk you wanted from a self-serve dispenser. Sometimes I'd have a half-dozen glasses with a meal. At the time, milk was advertised as "nature's most nearly perfect drink." Only 30 years later would it be decided that milk was full of fat and therefore bad for you. Still, today it is my favorite beverage, although I greatly limit my intake.

Before I graduated from boot camp, I wrote to my dad. It had been years since I'd seen him, and we talked very infrequently. But I got his address in California, where he had moved. He'd finally gotten a steady job working in a bicycle repair shop. I invited him to my boot camp graduation and, to my great surprise, he showed up. It was quite the ceremony, with recruits mustered by company in neat rows. As recruit chief petty officer, I marched at the head of Company 306, carrying a sword. A band played and we marched in columns by a reviewing stand filled with high-ranking officers and dignitaries. About 20 companies — roughly 1,500 men — graduated that day, watched also by thousands of other recruits at earlier stages of training.

It was customary to recognize the top recruit in the group with the American Spirit Honor Medal. I can't describe how stunned I was when they called my name over the loudspeaker, and I was ordered to report up front. Cotton Wells had been tipped off about the honor; I hadn't. So he was in the receiving line when the bronze award — about the size of a silver dollar — was handed to me. If he had been more proud of me in the past, I can't remember it. Little did I know it was the last time I would see my father alive.

Live Wires

During boot camp, a battery of intelligence tests determined what we'd each do in the Navy. In my case, it was decided — for me — that I would be an electronics technician (ET). After San Diego, my next stop was San Francisco, or, more precisely, Treasure Island, a Navy training facility in San Francisco Bay. Man-made for the Golden Gate International Exposition in 1939, Treasure Island abuts Yerba Buena, a natural outcropping attached to the Bay Bridge, which links San Francisco to Oakland.

I'd taken the bus to San Francisco and was deposited at the Key Terminal, where all buses connected. After some searching,

I learned there was direct service to Treasure Island, and that it would depart in an hour. With time to kill, I climbed onto a shoe shine stand, thinking it wouldn't hurt to arrive at the base "squared away," a Navy term for neat. Next to me also getting a shine was a middle-aged gentleman in a suit and tie.

He struck up a conversation, asking me where my home was and where I was headed. When I told him I was going to Treasure Island, he said, "I'll be happy to take you there. It's a nice day and I drive a convertible." Gee, what a nice guy, I thought. These people in San Francisco are very friendly. I was about to find out just how friendly this guy was. He'd chatted during the trip but, in the middle of the bridge, without warning, he put his hand on my crotch and smiled broadly. It took me a fraction of a second to realize my newfound "friend" was gay. When that sank in, I nearly jumped out of his moving car.

"Look," I stammered, "I don't do that kind of thing. Please let me out." I don't know where I would've gone had he deposited me on the Bay Bridge, but the fellow quickly retracted his hand, and apologized profusely.

"I'm very sorry," he said. "You're attractive to me and I thought you might enjoy me pleasuring you. There is no reason for you to be frightened; I won't hurt you."

He insisted on driving me on to the front gate of the Naval Training Center. I grabbed my seabag, and couldn't get out of his convertible fast enough.

Electronics school lasted nearly a year. For that entire time I was bombarded — eight hours a day — with formulas for voltage, current, amperes, watts, electrons, servo mechanisms, power amplifiers, transistors, vacuum tubes and a plethora of concepts that I've managed to forget. We were tested like clockwork every two weeks. This was supposedly the most difficult school in the Navy, and I believed it. If a sailor flunked an exam, he was placed back in the next class, which was two weeks behind the one he was in. Should he be unlucky enough to fail the same exam again, he was washed out of school and sent to the fleet — usually in the Deck Force. That unfortunate group was assigned to maintain the ship. It was a crummy job: scraping rust and painting over it; refinishing decks; pumping water out of the bilge; cleaning up cooking utensils after meals. That's what motivated most of us to stay in school. I finally graduated 59th out of a class of 63, and had barely a passing average. But I avoided the Deck Force — at least for the time.

The Worst Kind of News

In November 1962, I was asleep in my bunk at the barracks on Treasure Island when I was shaken awake by a young lieutenant; I remember his gold braid. Unless something's wrong, officers don't wake enlisted men in the middle of the night.

"Seaman Wells?" he asked quietly, so as not to disturb my mates.

I nodded.

"Please slip your clothes on, and meet me in the watch's office."

I did so without saying a word.

"Seaman Wells," the lieutenant said, "I'm sorry to inform you that your father was killed last evening in an automobile accident."

I stared blankly at him.

"Your father's remains are at a funeral home in Kansas, where the accident occurred," he said gently. "They're waiting for you to call them and make arrangements. Here's their telephone number," he said, handing me a piece of paper. "I've already authorized ten days' emergency leave for you. I'm afraid that's all I can do. You're on your own from here. I'm very sorry for your loss." He stood up and shook my hand, which was my signal to go. The lieutenant was visibly upset and uncomfortable. I walked out into the foggy night.

I didn't even have bus fare to Duncan, much less money to bury my father; he had no life insurance. First I called the funeral home. It would cost nearly $1,000 to transport him to Oklahoma for burial in their cheapest coffin. Otherwise, he would be interred in a pauper's grave in the small town near where he met his demise. The Kansas Highway Patrol said that he was killed instantly when, driving on the wrong side of the highway, he collided with a semitrailer loaded with oil drilling pipe. The officer I talked to said the conjecture was that he was either drunk or fell asleep at the wheel.

In addition to being distraught, I was very broke. It was two weeks before payday, and I was making a bit over $100 a month. There was the problem of the burial, hopefully in Duncan. First, I turned to the Red Cross. This fine agency — which I later learned to dislike — wouldn't give me the money or even loan it to me; I wasn't earning enough to suit them. And the Navy had no method for advancing me on my paycheck. So, out of desperation, I called Bill and Margaret, collect. I'd already used the few remaining dollars I had to call the funeral home and the authorities in Kansas from a pay phone. The Deans wired me the money to come home, and I worked out a deal with the funeral home for me to pay them by the month for the cost of my dad's cheap casket and to transport him by train to Duncan. For the next two years, I struggled mightily to pay off the funeral bill, but I finally did.

My last phone call before leaving San Francisco was to my mother. Although Vola and Coyle had been divorced for years, I thought she should know. In turn, she called my sister, Sue, who had married a soldier and was living in Alaska. We both arrived in Duncan about the same time. It took me two days to get there by bus, and she flew. Sue stayed with my mother and I slept at the Deans'. I'd not seen my sister in several years and she was a mental wreck, crying constantly and hysterically.

"The last I heard from him," she sobbed, "was when he called me long distance collect and wanted me to wire him some money. I turned him down. But the last time you saw him you were a hero," she said accusingly.

I then recalled him visiting me in San Diego less than six months ago. I was in Duncan only four days for the funeral. The day before my dad was buried, Sue and I went to the funeral home. His casket was closed, and she started beating her fists on the coffin screaming, "That's not my daddy in there! I want to see!" The funeral director and I tried to discourage her, for naught. He then opened the casket for a couple of seconds. It was Coyle, all right. But the left side of his head was missing and the wound had been covered with gauze. I threw up in my handker-chief while Sue shrieked. The memory will be with me for good.

That evening, Sue and I visited with Aunt Lilly, Coyle's half sister, who lived off Highway 81 between Duncan and Comanche. Sue was acting strange — in addition to being distraught. Several people were at Aunt Lilly's. We hadn't been there very long when I noticed Sue was gone. We looked around the house to no avail. I'd driven over in the Deans' car, and it was still parked outside; she was just gone. Not knowing what to do, I drove up the highway toward Duncan. In less than a mile I spotted her running straight up the center stripe as fast as she could go, crying all the time. After much pleading by me, she got into the car and we returned to Aunt Lilly's. But Sue was incoherent. I'm not sure if she was drunk or just out of it. For the first time I realized how messed up she was in the head.

My dad's funeral the following day was anticlimactic; my sister was like a zombie and my mother was stoic, not uttering a word. There couldn't have been more than a dozen people there. Coyle Averett Wells was buried in the Comanche cemetery, and it would be years before I could afford to get him a headstone. I returned to San Francisco the next day.

My sister didn't recover from her alcohol and mental problems. About ten years later, she was arrested on one of her many drunk driving charges. She hanged herself in jail with her blouse — dead at the age of 40, leaving behind four young children. I was mad at her for at least 20 years. As far as I was concerned, she took the coward's way out.

After struggling for nearly a year to get through electronics school, I finally received orders to report to the United States Naval Communications Station (NavComSta for short) in Londonderry, Northern Ireland. Until then, I hadn't even known the place existed. There was one complication: It would be some time before the transfer was effective, so I was to serve aboard ship in the interim.

At Sea, Off Scotland

My sea duty was aboard the *USS Boyd*, a Fletcher-class destroyer that had been commissioned in 1942. With 11 battle stars from World War II and another 5 from the Korean conflict, the *Boyd* was one of the oldest destroyers still left in the fleet. It had been named for Joseph Boyd, who took part in Steven Decatur's expedition into Tripoli harbor during the first Barbary War. She still carried many scars, including those from the famous invasions of Okinawa and Iwo Jima. Her hull number was DD-544 (the "DD" stood for destroyer). The *Boyd* had been decommissioned in 1947, and re-commissioned in 1950 for the Korean War. The U.S. government donated the Boyd to the Turkish navy in 1969. Twelve years later, Turkey melted the proud old lady down for scrap.

While I was stationed on the *Boyd*, she patrolled the North Atlantic. I worked on the ship's communications equipment, and was probably the worst electronics technician ever. Luckily, though, every sailor performed a wide variety of tasks. At sea, there are no Saturdays, Sundays, or holidays. All of the work is done in shifts, usually four hours, which are called "watches." These run the gamut from kitchen patrol (KP) to repairing damage, hanging over the side with a bucket of gray paint, a chipping hammer and a container of red lead (a rust inhibitor); to manning the wheel.

During a 60-knot gale about 100 miles off the east coast of Scotland, I was unfortunate enough to be on the bridge, actually steering the ship. In the days before GPS and more sophisticated navigation, ships found their way around the ocean with compasses and sextants; I knew how to operate neither. In a storm, however, the object was not to get to your destination; it was to keep the vessel perpendicular to the waves. Should you get parallel to them, chances are the ship would roll over, and everyone aboard would drown.

The only way that a young, inexperienced teenager would steer is under the supervision of a senior enlisted man. In my case, it was First Class Boatswain's Mate O'Connor. Boatswain's mates are as salty as sailors come; they spend most of their careers at sea, and have seen everything the angry oceans can deliver. Like many lifelong sailors, O'Connor was drunk except when at work. He was a good 30 pounds overweight, with a boozer's telltale red nose. "Boats," as all boatswain's mates are called, had the habit of beginning and ending every sentence with a bull-frog-like croak.

I was at the helm nearly four straight hours, fighting the wheel to keep us upright. It was exhausting and totally terrifying. Each time a 30-foot wall of water would break over the bow, it would crash against the glass on the bridge. I kept waiting for that glass to crack, but somehow it didn't. And with each wave, the ship's forecastle would dive underwater, and we'd be pitched into complete darkness. Then the vessel would creak, groan, and pop.

I could envision the headlines: "Due to Incompetent Helmsman, Two Hundred Sailors Lost at Sea in Storm."

I've been afraid before and since, but not like this. I thought the vessel would breach (that is, sink) at any second. If there is a God, I wondered, why would he let me die this way, in the freezing ocean? What had I done wrong? After all, I'd been a pretty good boy and had been laid only once in my life. I was about to wet my pants from fright. It was all I could do just to stand upright.

But Boats was standing calmly to my left and to the rear of me with his hands clasped behind his back. Out of the corner of my eye, I saw that he definitely had a pair of sea legs. No matter which way the ship pitched, his gyroscopic balance kept him straight. I was determined not to let him know how scared I was, so I started making small talk about the recent holidays, hoping he wouldn't detect I was frightened nearly out of my wits.

"Boats," I shouted over the din, "what did you get for Christmas?"

He answered back loudly, "(Croak) well, all I got was a new shirt and a piece of ass and both of them were way, way too big (croak)."

That truly broke the tension. I started laughing so hard that I let go of the helm and grabbed a handrail to keep my balance. The ship's wheel spun rapidly, but I quickly recovered and straightened the ship. From then on, I was never afraid at sea again. And to this day, when someone asks me what I got for Christmas, I'm almost always tempted to repeat that memorable line.

In my six months on the *Boyd*, I learned just how tough it was being a sailor. You were with your mates in cramped quarters 24/7. But it was there I got some of my best lessons in getting along with others, and lying well enough to keep the peace. There was really no other choice; you couldn't walk away from an argument and never see that person again. With 200 men aboard, you pretty much saw everyone every day.

We didn't leave the British Isles. Most of the time, we practiced maneuvers with our English colleagues in some of the roughest waters in the world. The North Irish Sea is particularly violent. Most sailors get seasick only once, and then become more or less immune to it. I too was seasick only once. But it lasted about a month, and I vomited nearly every day.

The things I remember the most are the great coffee — it was so strong you could just about float a horseshoe in it — and the terrific, piping-hot food, if you could keep it down. I also recalled being cold nearly always; the North Atlantic isn't known for its tropical clime. But in bad weather I depended on my trusty Navy-issue pea coat. Fifty years later it's still my warmest piece of clothing and I wear it every winter.

Duty Ashore in Ireland

The *Boyd*, after I'd been aboard for about six months, deposited me in Glasgow. I waited two days for transport to Londonderry. During my brief stay in Glasgow, I spent most of my time in a coffee shop and a dancehall with recorded music. At both places, I continually heard the song "Please, Please Me" by an English band I'd never heard of — The Beatles. This was in the fall of 1963, about a year before the Fab Four hit the United States and changed the face of rock 'n roll music. Later in 1963, I sent my old girlfriend Jeanette McDuff a 45 RPM Beatles record. She played it for her sorority friends at Oklahoma State University; they concluded this new band wouldn't make it in America.

From Glasgow, I took an overnight ferry to Belfast, on the northeast tip of Northern Ireland. Then I boarded a train for Londonderry. The scenery was unforgettable: green, rolling hills that lead up to high cliffs overlooking the North Irish Sea. Londonderry, or Derry, its original name and the one preferred by the locals, is the second-oldest continuously inhabited place in Ireland, tracing its roots to the sixth century. It is also the second-largest city in Northern Ireland, with a population currently around 100,000. The town sits at the mouth of the river Foyle and empties into the North Irish Sea.

Northern Ireland, with the exception of Derry, is predominately Protestant while the remainder of the island is overwhelmingly Catholic. The United Kingdom and Ireland share a long, bloody history of disputes over religion and taxation. In 1921, the British annexed Northern Ireland, also known as Ulster, as a part of the British Empire. Ireland, which the locals called "the free state," remained an independent country.

As the U.K.'s westernmost port, Derry played an important role in the Battle of the Atlantic during World War II. The Royal Navy, the Royal Canadian Navy, and the U.S. military established a presence there. At the end of the war, the United States remained, and eventually converted its operations there to a communications station. In the days before satellite transmissions, the only way to get a radio signal from the United States to Europe was by hopscotching it across the Atlantic. The transmissions would go from eastern America to Newfoundland to Thule, Greenland to Reykjavik, Iceland to Derry to southern England to The Netherlands and then on to other parts of Europe. The signals, known as single sideband, were decrypted and recrypted at each stop.

NavComSta Londonderry was manned by roughly 100 Navy personnel and half that number of local civilian employees. The latter did the dirty work, such as base maintenance and cooking. The sailors were assigned to one of three sites: transmitters, receivers, or cryptography.

Each site was covered 24/7. The work schedule was a bit odd — two nights from 4:00 PM to midnight, then two day shifts from 8:00 AM to 4:00 PM, followed by two graveyard shifts from midnight to 8:00 AM. Afterward, we'd get 80 hours off and then start the cycle again.

About half of my tour in Londonderry, which lasted for nearly two years, was at the transmitter site, and the rest was at receivers. Because I didn't have a cryptographic clearance, I didn't work in crypto at all. Roughly a third of the sailors were electronics technicians, a third were radio operators and the rest were support personnel such as clerks and yeomen.

My job exclusively was to repair communications equipment. For every piece of gear we had on line, there were at least two backups. So if a transmitter quit, you'd switch to one that was working and fix the broken one. This was before printed circuits and microchips, so everything worked on vacuum tubes.

The complexity of electronics was beyond my grasp. If something broke while I was on duty, and I couldn't fix it by replacing a vacuum tube, I'd just wait for the next shift and let the competent technicians there have a go at it. Somehow I got through my entire tour in Londonderry without my mates figuring out just exactly how electronically ignorant I was. Had it not been for my friends Paul Cafasso and John Hart, who always covered for me, I might have been exposed.

Single Navy men in Londonderry lived in a barracks. This one was the most deluxe I'd seen: four guys to a single room with bunk beds. Where you slept depended on your seniority in the room. I started off with a top bunk but worked my way down. One of the things I liked most about the Navy was the camaraderie — people of different backgrounds being thrown together and becoming friends. There were hardly any heated arguments and no fights that I can recall. Fighting was a serious offense, and those battles usually ended in a captain's mast — one step shy of a court martial.

I was friends with my three roommates but especially close to Marty Lowman. He was from the Delmarva Peninsula, where his father raised chickens. Marty had a great sense of humor. One of my early roommates, a guy named Pulley, was from Tennessee and played the guitar, sort of. Before he was transferred, he taught me three chords. I've been playing ever since; at one time I was probably good enough to turn pro, but that would have meant almost sure poverty, so I have always played just for fun.

My other close friend, but not a roommate, was Bill Perry, who came from North Carolina and smoked a pipe to appear sophisticated. Bill had managed to scrape together enough money to buy a two-seat English Sprite sports car. Because we had over three days off between workweeks, we toured every county in Ireland, many of them multiple times. Getting three guys in a two-seat car required some ingenuity. We constructed a third seat out of wood that fit over the hump between the two seats. Then we covered the wooden seat with a pillow. Bill always drove, and Marty and I rotated between the other two seats. It was crowded and mostly uncomfortable, but we were young and full of adventure. Ireland was indeed beautiful and green, averaging about 300 days a year of almost constant drizzle.

England was not nearly so wet, as I discovered on a six-day solitary vacation to London and Liverpool. Because British bands were in their prime, my goal was to hear as many of them as I could, and I did. Indeed, The Beatles were the only group I considered important that I didn't see perform live. But I did see them. During my London safari, I was coming up one day from the Underground (subway) at Piccadilly Circus. It was so crowded on the streets that I could hardly move. Shortly thereafter, the foursome arrived to give a performance and I saw them, amid deafening screams, bound out of their limo and race up the steps to the concert hall. In Liverpool, I visited the original Cavern Club, where they got their start. On that same trip, I also saw Eric Clapton, the Rolling Stones and many other bands before heading back to Ireland.

One of Derry's principal industries at the time was manufacturing shirts. There was little work for men, so they migrated to England for jobs. But the shirt factories were filled with girls. I was told that for every eligible man there were about ten women. On the weekends, singles would congregate in two or three different dance halls. The guys would stand on one side and the gals on the other. There were always more women than men, and the fact that we were Americans — rich by Irish standards — enabled us to have our pick of dance partners.

These places didn't offer liquor. But at the base, we had a Quonset hut that served as a bar and club. Guys would load a taxi or car with women, and bring them to the base. The problem for most men, which sailors all over the world would envy, was that there were too many women to choose from. But it was hard — although not impossible — to get laid; these lasses were usually brought up as strict Catholics, and premarital sex was greatly frowned upon. They wanted to get married, move to America and raise a family. Many of my fellow sailors tied the knot, some for love and some for loneliness. I dated one girl seriously, Mary Huchings. She worked in a shirt factory and was one of six children. Her father was in England working, and I don't believe I ever met him. But I did visit her many times in her mother's row house in the Bogside area of Derry, which later became infamous as the location for many of the bloody battles between the Irish Republican Army (IRA) and British soldiers during the 1970s.

At the time I was stationed in Derry, it had barely moved into the twentieth century. The homes were heated with peat or coal; there was little or no refrigeration; and few of the houses had telephones. People would typically go to the market each day and purchase what was to be consumed within the next 24 hours. Potatoes were an important part of their diet. The meat wasn't very good, and came in strange cuts. It wasn't like America, where meat was wrapped in neat cellophane packages. Outside Irish butcher shops, plucked chickens dangled by their necks and cuts of beef hung on hooks.

Mary's grand design was for us to get married. I was extremely lonely for the States and considered the possibility for a time. Ireland didn't perform what they called "mixed marriages" — a Catholic to a non-Catholic — so Mary convinced me to take instruction from a priest on how to become a Catholic. I went to perhaps three sessions before bailing out. I was soured on religion anyhow, so it was no big deal to me. But it was to Mary, and eventually it led to us breaking up. That was okay — I was only 20 years old and there were more fish in the sea.

Virtually everyone old enough remembers exactly where they were on November 22, 1963, when they learned that President John F. Kennedy had been shot. I was in the recreation room at the barracks in Londonderry, watching television with my mates. Because of the time difference between the United States and Europe, it was evening when the program we were watching was interrupted with the bad news.

At first, we didn't understand that he was dead, only that he had been shot. When the full truth became apparent, we and all Ireland stopped to mourn. Because Kennedy was of Irish ancestry, he was extremely popular there. The Guildhall in Londonderry was set up so that those who wished could sign a book of condolences that was later sent to the president's widow, Jacqueline. On each side of the book stood a sailor at parade rest. Londonderry was the only American military installation in Ireland, and people came from all over the small towns and villages to sign the book. The lines were huge, but orderly and quiet. And every age group was represented — small children barely old enough to write and old, decrepit people who could barely walk. Many arrived in wheelchairs. Sailors, including me, stood watch over the proceedings in four-hour shifts. Most people had tears in their eyes as they signed; many were sobbing, tears streaming down their cheeks. Originally the signing ceremony was to be two days. But the lines kept forming, and I recall that the Guildhall received visitors for over a week. I can't remember any public event in my life that was so moving.

On December 25, 1964, I woke up to my first (and only) white Christmas. Ireland was not typically cold, but neither was it warm. In July, for example, the average daily temperature was in the mid-60s. But on Christmas Eve in 1964, a freak storm had covered the ground with snow. It wasn't more than two or three inches, but enough to provide a white blanket. My roommates and I looked out our window and marveled at the sight. All of us had seen snow, just not me on Christmas Day. It was gone by late afternoon. Winter turned to spring and I left Ireland for Southampton, England, and returned to the United States by troop ship in May 1965. The following month I was honorably discharged at the Brooklyn Navy Yard. With no job on the horizon, I returned to Duncan, Oklahoma, and stayed with the Deans.

Back to Oklahoma

It was wonderful to see Bill, Margaret, and Tina again and to be back on American soil. To help pay my keep, I got a job pumping gas at a Phillips 66 service station. I hated it so badly that I considered reenlisting in the Navy, and went so far as to call the recruiters on the telephone. They offered me a $10,000 reenlistment bonus — a small fortune in those days — and three years' guaranteed shore duty at the American embassy in London if I'd sign up for a six-year hitch.

I was sorely tempted but fate intervened. I ran into my high school buddy Doug Pruitt, and he made me an offer I couldn't refuse. Doug was living in a duplex in Oklahoma City rent-free in exchange for rehabbing the property. He said that there was an extra bedroom in the duplex, and it was mine for the taking. Jobs, Doug said, were plentiful in Oklahoma City. I jumped at the chance and spent $800 of my meager savings on a 1961 Chevrolet Biscayne for transportation. When I moved in with Doug, I started looking through the classified ads for a job. I had two basic criteria: First, I didn't want anything to do with electronics, my field of training, because I was so bad at it. Second, I wanted an indoor job. Oklahoma City, smack dab in the middle of the Great Plains, had brutal summers and even worse winters. I wanted nothing to do with either.

Although I went on a variety of job interviews, my first offer was from a consumer loan company, Dial Finance, and I took it. Dial was a chain throughout the Midwest, headquartered in Des Moines, Iowa, and probably had 100 offices in total — three in Oklahoma City alone. Dial specialized in loans for amounts ranging from $300 to $2,500 to established blue-collar workers. The company had a management training program. The pinnacle for employees was to head one of Dial's offices.

All employees started the same way: collecting past-due debts. So it was with me. The procedure was similar for all delinquent loans. First, the borrower would receive a couple of notices by mail. That would be followed by a phone call, which is where I came in. We were trained to be nice but persistent and not to get off the phone until we had an exact date that a payment could be expected. If money didn't arrive, more calls would be made. If those were unsuccessful, a personal visit to the borrower — at work or at home — would follow. This was colloquially known as a chase. Thank goodness for federal laws that came later outlawing a lot of common debt collection techniques. But this was before then, when almost anything was allowed to collect money. I approached my position with characteristic zeal; it was perfect for that black corner of my heart.

On one occasion, I had to chase a borrower about 40 miles from our office. He lived down an unpaved country road, and before long, I was bogged down to my car's axles in sand.

It appeared somewhat hopeless until a nice man happened on scene in a pickup truck. He pulled my car out, and I thanked him.

Before going on my way, I asked, "Do you know where the Baldwin family lives?"

"I'm Baldwin," he replied, "and our house is just over yonder. Anything I can help you with?"

"I'm Joe Wells from Dial Finance," I said with a sheepish smile, "and I'm here to repossess your wife's sewing machine." And I did.

Within two years, I had been promoted ahead of schedule to assistant manager of the downtown branch, one of the largest in the chain. I was no longer collecting loans; I was making them. In another year, I probably would have had my own office and my future would have been secure — all at the ripe old age of 24.

Fooling Around

Not too long after I moved in with Doug, he told me that my high school flame, Linda Vanort, had married and moved to Oklahoma City. I rang her mother up in Duncan, and she gave me Linda's phone number. Almost instantly Linda and I were having a torrid affair, helped along by the fact that her husband was a salesman, and was gone for days at a time. I had learned a valuable lesson from high school when Linda offered herself to me and I turned her down: Don't reject a woman's advances. I made it my new creed.

Linda and her husband lived on the third floor of an apartment complex. Whenever he left, she'd call me, and I'd stay with her until he was scheduled to return. Late one evening, we were making mad, passionate love when we heard a click at the front door. Luckily, the safety chain was fastened. It was her husband, returning home early and unannounced.

There were only two ways out of the apartment: the door where he was standing and the window in their small bedroom. It was a three-story drop to the concrete parking lot; doubtless I would have broken a bone. So with lightning speed, I dragged myself and my clothing under the bed while she let her husband in. I felt certain that he would shower or go to the bathroom, and then I would make good on my escape. But after a few days on the road, her husband had only one thing on his mind — sex with his wife.

Linda tried nearly everything she could think of to dissuade him, but he was having none of that. Finally she relented, hoping to get it over quickly. They were directly above me in the bed, much to Linda's and my horror. And I was below, getting banged in the head by the wooden mattress supports.

What in the hell am I doing here? I wondered. Linda's husband eventually drifted off to sleep, and I belly-crawled, stark naked, to the front door, dragging my clothes behind me. Only after I stepped out of the apartment, and quietly closed the door behind me did I dare get dressed. Afterward, I had a long talk with myself: There was no reason for me to be involved with a married woman. So I ended it. Linda wanted to divorce her husband and marry me, but I was having none of that. If she couldn't be trusted to be faithful to her spouse, she couldn't be trusted to be faithful to me. How's that for a double standard?

My First Marriage

Doug Pruitt had joined the Army Reserve to avoid the draft. We only got a few months' free rent in the duplex when Doug had completed his rehab of the place and went away for six months to basic infantry training. I had to move and selected a one-room basement apartment in an old complex; it was all I could afford.

I soon met Carol Benjamin, an attractive brunette who was sharing an apartment on the second floor with another woman. Before long, Carol was spending more time in my small apartment than in her own place. Within a month she confessed to me that she was pregnant when we met but had no interest in marrying the guy. Carol came from a strict Catholic family where an abortion was out of the question. And this was not an era when being an unwed mother was socially acceptable. So Carol and her mother made arrangements for Carol to spend the last three months of her pregnancy in a home for unwed mothers supported by the church. Then the child would be placed for immediate adoption.

This was a very difficult time for Carol, and I supported her morally however I could. But it was difficult for me too. We were allowed only to exchange letters; no phone calls. The letters got more and more passionate, and by the time she was released, us getting married was a foregone conclusion. I wasn't sure if I really loved her or just felt sorry for her. But I would soon find out. Our three-day honeymoon was at a resort at Lake Eufaula, about a two-hour drive east of Oklahoma City. On the first night of our stay, I woke up in a cold sweat asking myself: What the hell have you done? We were together about six months. I've not seen or talked to her since.

Smart Enough

A couple of years into my Dial Finance career, I had a casual lunch with Don Gentry, a fellow veteran, that turned out to be a life-changing event. Don was going to college on the GI bill. I had sort of heard of it but knew none of the details.

"Basically, the government pays you to go to college," Don informed me.

"Wow," I replied, "it's too bad I'm not smart enough to do that."

Gentry laughed. "It has nothing to do with smarts. If you're a high school graduate and a veteran, you're eligible. You should look into it."

I took his advice and called the Veterans Administration. To my astonishment, they would pay me by the month as long as I was in college, and it was nearly enough to live on. Around the same time, I'd taken my beat-up Volkswagen (the motor in my 1961 Chevrolet Biscayne had blown up, and I had to get rid of it) into the dealer for work.

The dealer, Nick Gangas, was naturally trying to sell me a new VW, but I couldn't afford it. He asked me what I did for a living and I told him. Nick's eyes lit up. "I have an idea that may make you enough money to help buy yourself a new car," he said. I was all ears. "I opened this dealership about a year ago," he continued. "The accounts receivable from auto repairs are very high and very delinquent, and I have no one to collect the past-due debts. How would you like to do that on a commission basis? Collection agencies charge 50 percent of what they collect; I'd give you a third and set you up in your own office here. I have lots of space."

What luck, I thought. I could go to college on the GI bill, work my own part-time hours, and maybe even make more money than I am right now. Nick and I shook hands on it before I left that day.

College Man

While still working at Dial Finance, I spent evenings at Nick's on the phone collecting money. It was like shooting fish in a barrel; one of the main reasons that he wasn't collecting money is that his customers weren't being regularly billed. Nearly all of them said, "I've been waiting for a bill. If you'll send me one, I'll pay it right away." Within a couple of months, I was raking in the dough, and Nick was happy.

I quit my day job with Dial, and became a full-time student at Central State College (now the University of Central Oklahoma) in Edmond, a bedroom community about a half-hour north of Oklahoma City. My desire was to go to the University of Oklahoma in Norman, but it was more expensive and about an hour south of where I was living. My plan was to get basic courses at Edmond that would transfer to OU.

My first semester at Central State was terrifying. To get full GI Bill benefits, I had to take at least 14 semester hours; I signed up for 16, the normal course load. But I was at least four years older than my fellow freshmen, and had had no college prep courses in high school. My subjects were the basics. Because I felt so intimidated, I studied all of the time when I wasn't working; no girls for a change. To my great surprise, the studying paid off: my GPA was a 3.8! Maybe I wasn't so stupid after all.

The second semester as a freshman, I studied even harder — if that was possible. When my grades came in late that spring, I'd earned a 4.0. To keep the government money rolling in regularly, I went to summer school and repeated my perfect grade average. I started remembering again what Bill and Margaret had alluded to — almost anything was possible with the application of enough sweat.

By the beginning of my sophomore year, I started looking seriously at a math and physics major, and took as many of those classes as I could. Physics was easy for me; I actually understood it. Abstract math was more difficult, and not as easy for me. But I had an ambition I'd not discussed with many people: I wanted to be an astronomer. It probably came from the many nights during my youth — laying in the backyard and staring at the stars. I knew all of the major constellations in my sky by heart, and would spend hours pondering life on other planets. I was convinced then and now that there are other beings out there somewhere. This was a time before man had been to the moon — although there was talk of it. To me, the Martians would probably have to visit us first since we had no way of going to them — just yet.

But that wasn't the most important issue when I was a sophomore in college; I just wanted to peer through the strongest telescope in the world, which at the time was at Mt. Palomar in California. However, calculus was about to dash my dreams. I struggled mightily studying it, but by midterm in my spring semester, I was failing. I paid a visit to my counselor to discuss the dilemma and told him of my secret ambition to be a stargazer.

He listened carefully, and paused after I'd told my story. Then as nicely as he could word it he said, "Son, if you're having this much trouble with basic calculus, you'll never be an astronomer. And with a bachelor's degree in math and physics, about all you'll be qualified to do is teach high school science. To be an astronomer, you'll need a Ph.D. My advice to you is to change your major."

I was crushed. Within a week, the harsh reality had started to sink in. I talked to my instructor about allowing me to withdraw from class with a passing grade. Otherwise, the five-hour class would figure into my grade average as an F.

The professor was totally unmoved by my plight. "You get what you earn here," he said sternly. "You've earned an F so far. If you withdraw now, it will be with a failing grade."

He then handed me an IBM punch card for me to take to the registrar. In the blank line for my grade, he inserted "W/F" to indicate I had withdrawn while failing. On the way to the registrar's office, it occurred to me that the letters "F" and "P" were so similar that they were ripe for alteration. So I put a little hook on the "F" and turned in my card with a "W/P."

Yes, I fraudulently altered my grade to avoid severe damage to my average. And I wasn't caught. Since I committed that particular crime without being detected, I completed the semester — just one course shy of having the physics part of my anticipated double major. At the same time, I applied to and was accepted at the University of Oklahoma. I enrolled in the College of Business, thinking that at least I'd be able to get some sort of job besides half starving as a teacher.

The first semester of my junior year was mostly filled with business classes: marketing, management, accounting, economics and the like. I didn't particularly like accounting, but it was easy for me. The most complicated accounting math at the time was long division, and I knew I could do that.

Other majors didn't really provide the student with a specific skill; accounting did. Moreover, accountants were in demand and jobs were plentiful. It was considered the most difficult major in business, which therefore gave it some élan. So accounting it was. I thought that just because I majored in it didn't necessarily mean I'd do the work. While the accounting classes past the basics were small — no more than 30 students — core classes like management were ten times that size. In Management 101, we were seated alphabetically, which put me near the back of the amphitheater where the class was held. Next to me was Jack Whitestone, who would become my lifetime friend.

How I Came to Use Drugs and Became a Thief

I was in college during the Woodstock era, when kids burned their draft cards and rioted over the war in Vietnam. Since I was a veteran and didn't have to concern myself with that, I was instead interested in the "free love" aspect of the hippie lifestyle. I didn't get seriously involved with a woman during my last two years in college, but the sexual revolution was under way, and I tried to do my part to participate.

By 1969, I was probably one of the few students who had not smoked marijuana. Hell, even future Supreme Court nominees had gotten stoned. Jack Whitestone was about to help me lose my drug-free virginity. One sunny afternoon, Jack, his hippie girlfriend and I headed out to the lake. Jack had this old convertible and the top was down. I smelled a strange odor coming from the front of the car and Jack said, "Joe, have a toke on this weed. It's great."

I was absolutely terrified; mere possession of marijuana was a capital offense in Oklahoma at the time — at least on paper (although I am positive no one was ever executed). I refused to imbibe. However, when we got to the lake, Jack and Joanie were completely high and laughing. With prodding by them, I smoked a joint for the first time. When I first started feeling the effects, I asked myself how this could possibly be illegal. I was hooked. After that I spent as much time as I could puffing weed. Only then did I discover that pretty much everyone else was smoking the stuff too. I'd even get high and go to accounting class. Whatever the professor was saying at the time seemed eminently profound. I'd think, amortization — what a concept! Far out! Strangely, my grades didn't suffer.

The commute back and forth to Norman was taking its toll on my beat-up Volkswagen. Since I was working part-time at the dealership, they sold me a brand-spanking new Beetle at their cost of $2,300, which included air conditioning. I financed all I could, and my payments were a whopping $62 a month. But I rationalized that I was spending nearly that much keeping my old wreck operating.

Late in the fall of my junior year, I stopped by a men's clothing store at the mall to purchase something and to see one of my buddies who was working there. He told me that a couple of guys would be hired for the Christmas season, and that he would put in a good word for me if I wanted to apply. I did, and was hired; it didn't interfere with my job at the dealership.

The place was owned by an old geezer I'll call Mr. Zac. Every employee hated him. He was cheap beyond all reason, demanding, and bad-tempered. Each night when the store would close, Mr. Zac would eye us all suspiciously as we filed out, obviously worried that we'd stolen some of his precious merchandise. To get back at him, the workers would steal from the store. Once, even a huge display case came up missing, stolen and thrown away by his disgruntled employees. Mr. Zac never solved that mystery; the workers hung together, and just played dumb. I was above all of that — or so I thought. But then he did something that made me hate him too.

One afternoon, I was upstairs in the stock room getting some merchandise off the top shelf. The reach had pulled my shirttail out, and I was standing there tucking it in when Mr. Zac walked by. He didn't say anything, but when I returned to the sales floor, one of the guys told me that the old man wanted to see me at once. I walked in to his little cubbyhole office, and he told me to close the door. I was a bit mystified, but Mr. Zac got right to the point.

"What we you stuffing in your pants up in the storeroom?" he demanded.

"Just my shirttail," I stammered.

"I don't believe you," he said accusingly. "I think that you were stealing from me. There's only one way to settle this; drop your pants right now."

What he said didn't sink in at once, but when it did, I was incredulous. "Drop your pants right now, or you're fired."

I stood there in stunned silence, not knowing whether to comply or to do what I really wanted — smack the old bastard in the face. However, I thought, I needed the money, so eventually I unbuckled my belt and let my pants drop. He looked and grunted then gave me a dismissive wave when he saw for himself that I didn't have any of his stuff on my person. When I returned to the sales floor, though, I had a completely different mind-set. No longer was I interested in selling clothes; my only thoughts were of revenge. I did my best to try to steal him blind. I lifted outerwear, underwear, socks, shirts, pants — anything I could get away with, whether I needed it or not. Mr. Zac was never the wiser, and I left the job with an almost entirely new wardrobe. My first experience with employee theft, alas, was when I was the thief.

Later, I learned from *Theft by Employees*, a seminal study by sociologists Hollinger and Clark, that my reaction to Mr. Zac's treatment of me was typical human nature — something employers and fraud examiners should keep in mind.

The spring semester before I graduated from OU at the end of the summer was filled with interviews. I learned quickly that I would be a much-sought-after candidate. My grades were good — even great — and I was a veteran. Because so many young men were being drafted to go to Vietnam, my status was quite attractive to prospective employers. I had close to 20 job interviews and almost that many offers. It was a banner year for accounting graduates, and I was courted by all the Big Eight firms and several second-tier ones, and had prospects with several large corporations.

The Wonderful World of Auditing

Once all of my job interviews were completed in college, I had to decide which offer I'd accept. It was a nice problem to have. Eventually I took a position as an auditor trainee with Lybrand, Ross Bros. and Montgomery (LRB&M). It was one of the Big Eight accounting firms that would eventually become Coopers and Lybrand and then morph into PricewaterhouseCoopers.

The location of my choice was a bit unusual: Lynchburg, Virginia. Other than its name, it was an absolutely beautiful place. Located in the foothills of the Blue Ridge Mountains and on the banks of the James River, Lynchburg has a long and storied history. The city was named for James Lynch, who started a ferry service across the river in 1757. Thomas Jefferson had a property, Poplar Forest, nearby. Lynchburg has many old colleges that date to the early Deep South: Randolph-Macon Woman's College and Sweet Briar among them. It is also the home of Liberty University, founded by the late controversial televangelist Jerry Falwell.

I interviewed with LRB&M in the spring semester before graduating in the summer of 1970. The Lynchburg office was small, with fewer than 20 professionals. The whole setup was appealing. I'd be working for a Big Eight firm, getting the training that only a large organization could provide. But the office was small enough where I'd get to see audits from beginning to end. In the largest locations of CPA firms, junior auditors would be assigned one task — such as reconciling the cash accounts — and wouldn't be exposed to the big picture of the audit for several years. I was drawn to the small-town atmosphere and small-office environment.

When I returned to Norman from my job interview in Lynchburg, I had an offer in hand. All that was required was for me to graduate and move cross-country. I skipped the graduation exercises altogether because I was itchy to get to Lynchburg. But OU mailed me two certificates: my diploma and a certificate showing my admittance to Beta Gamma Sigma, the national scholastic fraternity for accounting students. I graduated fifth in my class at the University of Oklahoma — not bad for a Navy veteran who had started college a few years previously, unsure he was good enough to make it.

In truth, I surprised myself and nearly everyone who knew me. There wasn't anything fraudulent about my hard work in college, but I felt that if anyone discovered that this poor boy from Duncan had done this well so far, they'd believe I was a fraud. Hell, that was the way I felt about myself.

When I began work in Lynchburg, I found the job dismal. As a junior auditor, I worked with a variety of more experienced men (there were no women auditors at the time) on different jobs. Most of them could have been done by a trained monkey: adding columns of figures, reconciling checking accounts and observing inventory. Many days it was everything I could do to stay awake. But I remember two inventory observations in particular.

One was for a cement manufacturer in rural southwest Virginia. The company had large silos of material — sand, rock, and gypsum — as well as finished cement that had not yet been bagged and shipped. An auditor was not required to take inventory but rather to observe it being taken by company employees. In this situation, I had to climb atop 40-foot silos to watch a worker drop a weighted line down the hatch of the silo until it stopped. That told him the depth of the material he was inventorying. This occurred around the end of the calendar year — late December or early January. The weather was horrific: cold with blowing snow. I thought I'd freeze my ninnies off.

My other memorable inventory observation was inside at the C.B. Fleet Company. For the uninitiated, C.B. Fleet is the world's premier manufacturer of enemas; at the time, all were made in Lynchburg. C.B. Fleet was a client of LRB&M. One year I was selected to help observe inventory, which includes work-in-process. I recall being out on the assembly line during inventory observation watching enema nozzles spinning around on their manufacturing contraptions. I wryly thought to myself: So this is why I went to college — to watch enemas being counted!

A more serious audit assignment involved my examining the books of the local Red Cross. It received 100 percent of its funding from the United Way. A year prior to my audit, Red Cross had received supplemental funds to help families devastated by a major hurricane. United Way had earmarked this money — tens of thousands of dollars — as a clothing allowance for hurricane victims.

The instructions to the local Red Cross office were to award $200 for a total loss of clothing and $100 for a partial loss. I was auditing these disbursements when I came across a curious pattern. For a while, $200 disbursements were mixed with $100 ones, but then the $200 disbursements stopped altogether. At the end of the fiscal year, the balance remaining, perhaps $10,000, was transferred into the Red Cross operating account, and from there, the money was used to pay bonuses to the employees.

I questioned the local management about why the $200 disbursements were stopped.

"Well," the manager said, "we didn't have any naked people coming in to request money."

"What?" I asked, not understanding what he was saying.

"The rules were that we were to award $200 for a complete clothing loss and $100 for a partial. Everyone who came in here to request money was dressed in something, so that means there was not a total loss of clothes."

The guy wasn't even embarrassed by his own ludicrous logic. I reported this incident to the partner in charge, but he signed off on the audit anyhow. I washed my hands of the whole thing; what a fraud.

In addition to auditing being incredibly dull, the hours in public accounting were murderous, especially during "busy season" — the period between January and April when individual and partnership tax returns were done. The staff was expected to be at a client's site during the day and then come back to the office at night and on weekends to prepare returns. Eighty-hour weeks were common. I wasn't very experienced at conducting audits, but I hated doing tax returns. There was nothing logical about them; it was all about Tax Code regulations. For the most part, an auditor was required to memorize these arcane rules only to forget them when they changed, which was nearly every year.

My work schedule left little time for partying or socializing. However, I was asked by my office to accompany "Miss USA," Deborah Shelton, while she was in Lynchburg during a promotional tour. Originally from Virginia Beach, Debbie asked for my phone number before she left, and actually called me when her reign was over. We dated furiously for a bit, but the 200-mile distance between us spelled doom for a long-term relationship. She later went on to minor stardom with a semi-recurring role in the television series *Dallas*.

Nearly a year after moving to Lynchburg, I was very fortunate to find a dream place to live. It was less than ten minutes out of town, a cabin sitting high on the bluff over the James River. The property was on ten acres and completely surrounded by trees. It was beautiful and private. The cabin belonged to an elderly doctor whose tax work was done by LRB&M. That particular year I was assigned his returns. Somehow during one of our business meetings, he mentioned that he had a cabin, but he'd not gone there much since his wife had died several years earlier. The doctor didn't want to sell the place, but he asked if I'd like to stay there rent-free to provide security and to keep it in shape. The cabin, although it needed a good dusting and cleaning, was ideal for me. It was so private that I could have walked around naked — which I actually did a couple of times just to prove the point. But most of the time I spent outside was sitting in a chair looking out at the James. My time inside the cabin, when I wasn't sleeping, was devoted to listening to music. I relished the fact that I could play my stereo as loud as I wanted without bothering anyone.

On New Year's Eve in 1971, I hosted a party for about 20 people, mostly from the LRB&M office. That night I met Dawn; about two years later, she became my second wife.

Aiming to Become a G-Man

After 18 months of public accounting, I was convinced it was the wrong profession for me; I detested it. One of the older auditors, Dan Imhoff, hated it too. He had married young, fathered four kids, and frequently looked out the window, dreaming he was somewhere else. I'd already passed the CPA exam, but needed two years' experience before I could use the designation. I was at the point where I didn't care; this was not the kind of work I was going to do.

"Dan," I said one day, "I've just got to find something else. I can't stand auditing." He looked at me wistfully, and said, "Joe, if I were young and single like you and full of piss and vinegar, I'd go be an FBI agent."

"An FBI agent? What the hell is that all about?" I asked incredulously.

"I'm not really sure," he replied. "But I bet chicks would dig an FBI agent."

That's all I needed to hear; I called the recruiter that afternoon. When he learned I had passed the CPA exam, he encouraged me to apply for admission to the FBI Academy. The application process is arduous, and takes about six months to complete. Three months or so after filing my application, I started hearing from friends that the FBI was checking up on me.

One of my former buddies, Dennis Garston, said, "Joe, I told them everything."

"Everything, what?" I asked.

"You know, about smoking weed and all that stuff," Dennis replied.

I thought I was sunk. What I didn't know was that the applicant investigators were hearing this almost universally about other would-be agents. If the person checking you out decided you were otherwise a good guy, he wouldn't mention marijuana in his report. The reason is that, because of the FBI's strict no-drugs policy at the time, it would've had to quit hiring people; in the hippie era, nearly everyone had tried weed.

So I passed the background checks and came home one night to find a telegram under my door: I'd been selected as a special agent trainee and was to report to Washington on August 14, 1972, a Monday. The telegram was dated August 9. I called the local recruiter, and explained to him that the notice was too short; I was in the middle of some audits, and had clients that would have to be reassigned.

He said, "Joe, I'll call headquarters and ask them for a delay if that's what you really want. But the Bureau accepts only one of a hundred applicants. My advice is to be in Washington on Monday."

The next morning I informed the partner in charge of the LRB&M office, Ralph Burnett, of my dilemma. He was very gracious, and told me to go for it; I did. By Sunday afternoon, I had my clothes packed, and set out on the three-hour drive to Washington. I placed my minimal furniture in storage, and put my relationship with Dawn on hold for the time being.

On August 14, I showed up at FBI headquarters in my dark suit, conservative tie, and white shirt. Little did I know that this was the expected uniform of an FBI agent. About 40 other men were there, and we became classmates. We were sworn in promptly at 8:00 AM en masse. Then we took our seats in school-type desks for our initial orientation. I looked around me; we were dressed almost identically. J. Edgar Hoover had died slightly over three months ago, on May 7, but his ghost still walked the halls. Hoover had a certain image of what an agent would look like, and we were to keep up that front. I didn't know then that Hoover's dark spirit would haunt all of us for years to come.

We spent the morning filling out forms; would they never end? The answer was no; there seemed to be a form for everything you could think of and many you couldn't. During orientation, we looked at each other nervously.

I kept thinking: What am I doing here? Surely they'll find out that I'm not worthy; I've pulled off a fraud. Then a thought occurred to me that brought out the dark side of my humor: What does it tell you about an outfit that would actually issue live ammo to CPAs and lawyers? I started snickering to myself while trying to keep my head down. It didn't work — the instructor spied me and asked accusingly, "What's so funny? Perhaps you'd like to share it with the rest of the class."

I broke out into a full belly laugh. The instructor was not amused, and my fellow agent trainees looked at me quizzically. But the instructor didn't press the issue, and we went on to filling out more forms.

The FBI Academy

By mid-afternoon, we headed for Quantico, located in a special area of the Marine base about an hour south of Washington. Those of us who had brought cars drove; the remainder took a bus. The FBI facility was nearly brand new. I believe we were the third or fourth class of new agents who were trained there. The structure was magnificent. There were several buildings interconnected by glass-enclosed walkways. This made it possible to get to any part of the Academy without going outside. Two new agents were assigned to each room, and two connecting rooms shared a toilet and shower. Everything was built in — beds, desks, and lockers. We were assigned a roommate by alphabetical order; mine was Barry Williamson from Florida, previously an FBI clerk. We got along well but were not good friends.

There were three kinds of classes at the Academy: new agents, in service (short specialized courses for veteran agents) and the FBI National Academy. The latter was training for local police officers and lasted about 12 weeks. The selection process for police was rigorous and considered a precursor to entering upper management in most police departments.

New agents' training was 14 weeks long. We were more or less free to leave on weekends with the exception of the first one. Several of us went over to the Officers' Club on the Marine base on the first Saturday evening. I met a young attractive woman named Judith Madison, who was visiting a girlfriend married to a Marine. Judith and I danced and talked. She was in the process of getting a divorce, but it wasn't in the cards for us to date; I was being faithful to Dawn. Judith and her girlfriend asked for a tour of the Academy, and I arranged for one the following day. Judith would end up being my lifelong friend.

Fourteen weeks at Quantico was about all anyone could stand; it was like being in a glass bubble. The curriculum was difficult. Approximately half of our time was devoted to the classroom and the remainder was physical fitness and firearms training. The latter two were not easy for me. I was totally out of shape and had never fired a gun. Someone estimated that we fired 10,000 rounds of ammunition in practice, and I believe it. Just through sheer repetition, we all became more than adequate marksmen. Each agent trainee was issued a Smith & Wesson Model 19 six-shot revolver. It was blued steel, and had to be cleaned after each practice session. After graduating from new agents' training, most of us bought a different pistol. Mine was a Smith & Wesson Model 60 five-shot stainless steel revolver with a two-inch barrel. An agent's personal weapon was limited to those approved by the FBI. At that time, only revolvers were permitted; they were the most reliable weapons of all, and would fire even after being immersed in water or dragged through mud.

Although things have now changed, it was customary then to let the shooter score his own targets. Not surprisingly, cheating was rampant because a trainee could not graduate with a failing score on the firearms range; I certainly committed my share of target-scoring fraud. After training school, agents would be required to re-qualify on the shooting range eight times a year. There, too, agents were allowed to score their own targets and to report the same overstated results.

Although I was impatient to begin my first field assignment, I expected some of my duties would be monotonous. But I was willing to tolerate that as long as I also got to work on important cases. As I would learn later, tedious duties sometimes were unexpected sources of the challenging assignments I yearned for.

One good example is the kidnapping I solved in the New York office, not long after I broke up the Klegmeir INS bribery scheme. After El Paso, I was no longer an apprentice in my profession.

Part Two

JOURNEYMAN

Chapter 3

Busting More Crooks
in Gotham

C omplaint duty, they called it. To respond in emergencies,
the NYO assigned clerks and junior agents to answer the
office phones during non-business hours. The clerk did
most of the little work that was involved. An agent like me might
draw the assignment a couple of times a month. It was the clerks'
only job, but for agents, this was additional duty that earned us
time off during normal hours.

The graveyard shift was the least desirable; few of the
"emergencies" reported were legitimate. Instead, most calls were
from people who were paranoid, had seen unidentified flying
objects, or were just plain crazy. The office even had a "nut box"
index system for such people who telephoned regularly. Some
called so often the clerk didn't have to refer to the nut box.

My first night on complaint duty was uneventful but interesting and instructive. The clerk seemed to have a canned answer for just about every nut call.

Here's an example:

Caller: "Aliens are invading my brain!"
Clerk: "Wrap some aluminum foil around your head; it'll block the incoming signals."

And another:

Caller: "The FBI is tapping my phones!"
Clerk: "What makes you so important that the FBI would go to the trouble?"

It was all I could do to keep from laughing out loud each time a kook phoned. One of the regular kooks was Martha Mitchell, the wife of former U.S. Attorney General John N. Mitchell. She was as paranoid as they came, and would call the FBI at all hours of the night to complain about the Nixon administration. There were special instructions on how she was to be handled should she call — Mrs. Mitchell was permitted to rant and rave to her heart's content. The complaint personnel were to let her talk until she ran out of gas. Often that would take a long time. I had the unfortunate task of talking to her one night. Although I don't remember the conversation, I came away concluding that she belonged in a loony bin.

At about three o'clock one morning, a call came in. The clerk listened for a while, and then put the caller on hold.

"You better take this one," he told me.

On the line was a deputy from the Nassau County Sheriff's Office. They had picked up an apparent kidnap victim, left bound and gagged alongside the Long Island Expressway. The victim, Brian Parrwalter, was the son and heir of James Parrwalter, who had made a fortune manufacturing electrical equipment for the automotive industry.

Kidnapping became a federal offense not long after famed aviator Charles Lindbergh's infant son was abducted and later found dead. The law was worded in a way that, if a victim had been missing more than 24 hours, it was presumed he or she had been transported interstate. This gave the Bureau the jurisdiction it needed to investigate. Moreover, the FBI routinely assisted local police when interstate commerce, as it was called, was involved.

During his two days of captivity, the victim had no alternative but to relieve himself in his trousers. When he was brought to the NYO for debriefing that night, I was the sole agent on duty, and that task fell to me. Naturally, Parrwalter didn't want to go anywhere before cleaning himself up, and so the deputy had allowed him to shower and change clothes. That might have destroyed valuable evidence; I didn't really know.

Parrwalter was in his mid- to late twenties and handsome. He arrived for the debriefing visibly shaken, wearing a jacket and jeans. The deputy stayed with us but didn't ask many questions; clearly he saw this as an FBI case. For the next three hours I interviewed Parrwalter, asking him every question I could think of. Then I went over it again to make sure I hadn't overlooked anything.

There was precious little information to glean. The victim was in his father's circular driveway late at night at their mansion in Brookville, the toniest neighborhood in the toniest part of Nassau County. He was unloading a bag from the trunk of his car when someone he didn't see clubbed him on the back of the head, briefly knocking him out. He wasn't seriously injured but still had a bump on his noggin when he spoke to me.

Parrwalter remembered regaining consciousness, then being tied up, blindfolded and put in the back seat of a car. One person sat beside him, and the driver and one other passenger occupied the front seats. They said little, even though Parrwalter kept questioning them repeatedly about what was going on. He was driven for what he estimated to be about a half hour. It was obvious to him from the sounds and constant honking of car horns that he was in a densely populated area, perhaps Manhattan. The car stopped and Parrwalter was pulled out by two individuals, one on each side, and led up two flights of stairs. Someone then unlocked a door and shoved him inside what he thought was an apartment. From the echoic sounds around him, he concluded it was nearly empty.

The kidnappers immediately shoved Parrwalter into a closet, where he remained until his release. In addition to pulling a hood over his eyes, they gagged him with a cloth to keep him quiet. Every now and then his captors removed the gag and gave him water but no food. I could only imagine how helpless he felt.

His sole clues about the site came from nearby sounds. One was of a telephone. It didn't ring a lot, but calls did come in. The victim couldn't really hear the few muffled conversations that occurred, but he did occasionally hear the sound of an elevated train as it went past. Although Parrwalter was too terrified to realize it, his kidnappers' careful plan to avoid recognition was a sign that they didn't intend to kill him — unless necessary.

After what must have seemed an eternity, Parrwalter was again loaded into a car and driven back to Long Island. His kidnappers carefully placed him on the side of the road and sped away.

It was sunrise by the time I finished the debriefing. I wrote up my report and handed it in, thinking that the matter would be assigned to the kidnapping squad. Wrong. I got the case, the first kidnapping I'd worked.

Later, I interviewed the victim's father. During the ordeal he had received three telephone calls. This was in the days before caller ID or cell phones, so he had no idea who was calling.

When the phone rang the first morning after the kidnapping, a male voice said, "We have your son. If you want to see him alive again, it will cost you $200,000 in cash — all in twenties;

unmarked bills. And if you call the police or the FBI, he's a dead man. We're watching you, and have your phone tapped. Tonight you'll get another call." The caller then hung up.

The elder Parrwalter was beside himself with worry. Rather than call his banker, he got into his car and sped to the bank.

His banker was shocked at the request for such a large sum. "We don't keep that kind of cash on hand in the vault. I'll have to call the main bank; the money won't get here until the morning."

Refusing to answer questions about the matter, Parrwalter pressed for quicker action, but to no avail.

Late that evening, the phone rang again. "Do you have the money?" the caller asked. The father explained that it wouldn't arrive until the next morning, and asked to speak to his son before any money changed hands.

"Impossible," said the caller. "You'll receive a call before midnight tomorrow. In the meantime, go to the supermarket and buy a box of black Hefty brand garbage bags with the cinch top. Do this yourself; don't involve your housekeeper. Divide the bills into two even stacks and stuff them in the bags. We'll call you tomorrow night and tell you what to do next. Remember: one word to the cops, and your son will be dead."

The next thing James Parrwalter heard was a dial tone.

The Payoff

Throughout the next day and evening, Mr. Parrwalter worried. More than once he became physically ill, and thought he might be having a heart attack. But he had the money and plastic bags, just as ordered. As soon as his housekeeper left for the day, he brought inside the stacks of bills, which were in a bank bag in the trunk of his car. The elder Parrwalter was finally alone; he had been widowed several years earlier. As instructed, he carefully divided the money into two stacks and put it in the bags.

Two hundred thousand dollars in twenties is 10,000 bills, which weighs about 25 pounds. Mr. Parrwalter sat by the telephone the entire evening, afraid to move even to go to the bathroom.

Just before midnight the phone rang. "Immediately take a bag in each hand, and walk to your front gate," the voice said. "When you get outside your brick fence, drop one bag in the hedges to the left of your drive and the other bag to the right. Then go back inside your house. Remember, we're watching. If all the money is there, unmarked, and you don't call the cops, your son will be released before the night is out. Go now."

The caller hung up, and Parrwalter hurried outside to comply with their instructions. He then returned to his home, and waited in the dark. He didn't look outside, fearing that if he recognized anything or anyone, his son would be killed. The wait seemed like an eternity, but actually it was about two hours before the Nassau County Sheriff's Office called with the good news that Brian had been found alive and unharmed.

The older man was overjoyed when his son finally walked in the front door. Tears streamed down his face as they hugged. After Brian had taken a long, hot shower and changed his clothes, the deputy brought him to me.

Once I had interviewed both father and son, I began to realize what little we had to go on: no physical evidence at all, no recognition of the caller's voice, no idea of where the son had been kept during his ordeal; nothing.

Not being familiar with kidnappings, I hoped to get the case reassigned. My supervisor, Vinnie Daugherty, was empathetic but gave no ground.

"Vinnie, why was this case assigned to me?" I asked.

"Because you're an FBI agent and because you took the complaint," replied Daugherty, sober as a judge.

"But I have an accounting degree and I work corruption and financial cases," I protested.

Vinnie said, "Okie, the FBI investigates over 200 specific violations of federal laws. Agents without an accounting background can deal with only about 150 of them. You can work 'em all. Now quit your bitching and get to work." The look in my supervisor's eyes told me that the conversation was over.

I moseyed down to another floor where the kidnapping squad was located. The supervisor referred me to one of his most experienced agents for advice.

"What have you got?" he asked.

"Not much at all," was my answer. "The victim never saw his kidnappers. He thinks there were three of them — two men and a woman — but he isn't sure." I then repeated the impressions of his surroundings that young Parrwalter had given me.

The kidnapping expert thought it over. "Did he recognize any of the voices? It could have been a gardener or another worker with access to the property."

I shook my head, no.

He asked me to repeat the entire story, asked a few follow-up questions, and said, "You may not be aware of this, but most kidnappings are actually hoaxes. The so-called victim will get his buddies to kidnap him in order to extort money out of a wealthy relative. That's probably what you have here. If not, I have no idea how you can solve this; there simply isn't enough information. And you need to understand there isn't a resolution for every case. So first I'd determine whether this really was a kidnapping. If you can't confirm that it was, I'd close the case if I were you." He then stood up and shook my hand, signaling he'd given me all the advice he could.

Thinking Like an Accountant

Over the course of my career, there were many cases I couldn't solve. But at this time I had been in the Bureau for less than three years and, like many of my contemporaries, I had trouble admitting defeat. I spent a long time investigating the possibility that Brian had staged his own kidnapping. That led nowhere. He didn't have the motive. All the money he could spend was at his disposal. He was sole heir to his father's fortune, and his father was getting quite old; he was psychologically well adjusted; and then there was my interview of him. I'd spoken with young Parrwalter within two hours of his release by his captors. The degree to which the ordeal had shaken him would have been hard to fake.

I went over what I knew: half an hour from his home; bustling traffic; empty apartment; telephone; elevated train. That's all I had. But then I developed a theory, much as with the Klegmeir case. Suppose the apartment had been rented for the sole purpose of the kidnapping? And suppose a phone had been installed for exactly the same reason? Suddenly, I had an idea. It might take an accountant's mind to solve this one.

First, I got a map of Manhattan that also included Nassau County. Using the elder Parrwalter's home as a starting point, I drew a circle with a 25-mile radius. I assumed this distance would be more than sufficient. Then I marked off the location of every elevated train within the circle. Next, assuming the train couldn't be heard from more than a certain distance away I used that measurement on both sides of the tracks and marked it off. This gave me a corridor, inside of which I hoped the apartment was located.

Then, on a hunch, I requested from the telephone company a list of Manhattan phone numbers that had been connected and disconnected for a month before the kidnapping and a month after, within the streets in the corridor I had identified. In those days, the phone company was very helpful to law enforcement. These days, because of privacy laws, you can't get this information without a subpoena.

Within a couple of weeks I had the addresses for about 20 phone numbers. In the FBI, the cost of an investigation isn't the primary driver. Theoretically, almost any resource could be used to resolve a case. So, with the assistance of the kidnapping squad, I visited every one of them. Only one was for an apartment on the second floor, and it was in a seedy area of the city.

I interviewed the superintendent of the apartment building; he remembered renting the place on a six-month lease to a lone white male. Required up front was a month's rent plus a security deposit. He recalled it being unusual that the renter paid two months in advance plus his deposit. But the super never saw his tenant again. When he visited the apartment to collect the past-due rent, the place was vacant except for a telephone. He picked it up but the phone was dead. In an effort to enforce the lease, the super tried to call his renter's supposed employer, but it turned out that there was no such company. The super didn't pursue the matter further, and rented the apartment to someone else.

At my request, he handled the rental application form carefully, made himself a copy, and gave me the original. A routine check of indices in the NYO turned up nothing, which was no surprise. I then sent the rental agreement to FBI headquarters in Washington to be processed for fingerprints. At that time there was no computerized system for identifying prints; the process was a time-consuming chore done entirely by hand, using a complicated series of loops and whorls.

Perhaps two months later, I had my answer from headquarters: One of the latent prints belonged to a bank robber out on parole. He had a long rap sheet. It looked like I'd identified at least one of the bad guys. A quick phone call to his parole officer was revealing. The criminal had requested that his parole be transferred to California less than a month after the kidnapping.

Smart crooks, like this one, don't skip out on parole. If they're later fingerprinted for any reason — detained by the police, applying for certain jobs, etc. — they'll be nailed and their parole revoked. I sent a teletype to the Los Angeles division to locate and interview the felon. By some miracle the agent in the L.A. office found him and got a confession to the kidnapping. He was living the high life in Hollywood, and furnished the names of his cohorts. We even got back about $100,000 or so of the ill-gotten loot, which was turned over to the elder Parrwalter. All three of the kidnappers received long prison sentences. Score one for the accountants.

Enter the Okie

The infamous Watergate break-in occurred in June 1972 — about the time I entered the FBI Academy. For the uninitiated, Watergate was one of the most important political scandals in American history. It began with the arrest of five men for breaking into the offices of the Democratic National Committee at the Watergate complex in Washington, D.C. Their purpose was to obtain political intelligence that could be used in the upcoming presidential race that pitted Republican incumbent Richard M. Nixon against Democratic Senator George McGovern.

The five soon were charged with burglary and wiretapping, as were former White House staff member E. Howard Hunt and G. Gordon Liddy, the general counsel for a Nixon White House fundraising organization, the Committee for the Re-election of the President (CREEP). Only a few months before the break-in, John N. Mitchell, CREEP's director, had resigned as U.S. attorney general to head the re-election committee.

One of the burglars, James W. McCord, said during the ensuing trial that the White House had pressured him and his confederates to cover up the administration's role in planning the break-in. As the probe continued, Jeb Stuart Magruder, assistant director at CREEP, told a grand jury that Mitchell and John W. Dean III, the president's legal counsel, had coerced him to deny any CREEP or White House involvement in the conspiracy.

At this point, in July 1972, Mitchell left CREEP and returned to private practice in New York. However, the government hardly forgot his role, and field offices throughout the Bureau were involved in the case. By mid-1974, the investigation had clearly implicated Nixon, Mitchell and many other highly-placed officials. Nixon resigned in disgrace in August 1974 — the only U.S. president ever to have done so.

Late one spring day in 1974 I was in the office, pushing paper during lunchtime. Save Neville Jones and me, no one else from the squad was there.

"Okie!" Neville shouted out from his cubbyhole. "Come here!"

On my way, I thought about the advice I was given in El Paso: If you don't have anything to do, don't do it in the office. Well, I had plenty to do, but from Jones's perspective I was the only live body around when he needed someone.

Once I was in front of Neville's desk, he shoved at me a tele-type from FBI headquarters. "Here's a new case for you," he said without emotion.

I scanned the top of the document, which bore the heading *United States of America v. John N. Mitchell.*

When the enormity of it had sunk in, I said quietly, "Jesus, this is the former attorney general."

Neville simply nodded.

"For Christ's sake, why are you assigning this to me?" I asked. "I've got less than three years in the Bureau."

With a sly smile, Jones said, "Because you're the only one in the office right now."

Drat, I thought. Big cases mean big paperwork.

"What do you want me to do with this?" I asked earnestly.

Jones drummed his fingers on his desktop impatiently. "Joe, what do you do with a crooked lawyer?" he questioned.

I shrugged my shoulders with an unknowing look.

"Okie," he said testily, "you put the lying bastard in prison."

End of discussion.

When I returned to my desk, I carefully read the four-page teletype. It requested that the NYO contact Mitchell's lawyer and set up an appointment to interview the attorney general under oath. There were perhaps a dozen questions, the meaning of most of which was unclear to me. However, the communication briefly described answers to perhaps half of them. A common investigative technique is to mix questions to which you already knew the answers with ones that you didn't. If a suspect lied on the control questions, one could fairly conclude that he was lying on the rest.

It was unusual indeed that an investigation was directed by headquarters; at that time, I had no experience with it. But this was Watergate. At one time or another, at least several hundred agents conducted some part of the investigation.

Locating Mitchell's attorney was easy enough; his phone number was in the teletype. Arranging the interview was also easy. The lawyer had been expecting my call, and we scheduled a meeting for the following morning at Mitchell's apartment on Central Park South, one of the priciest sections of Manhattan.

I didn't know what to expect when I knocked. The door was opened at once by the maid. After I introduced myself and Nick Esposito, the colleague who accompanied me, we stepped inside. It's difficult to describe how stunning the place was. It was tastefully furnished, and the walls were filled with original art — expensive, I presumed, though I didn't recognize the names of any of the artists.

The very same Martha Mitchell, still in a robe, was sitting on a lounge chair. Although she wasn't fully dressed in her daywear, her hair was carefully coiffed and her makeup was already applied. She eyed us suspiciously as we were led into Mr. Mitchell's library.

Crooked Lawyer

Inside, Mitchell sat at one end of a rectangular conference table surrounded by a phalanx of lawyers sitting stiffly in their chairs.

I introduced myself first to Mr. Mitchell and shook his hand firmly while looking him in the eye, per FBI training.

He repeated my name and motioned for me to sit at the other end of the conference table.

Mitchell's principal attorney in turn had each of the lawyers introduce themselves, but they didn't get up, and we didn't shake hands.

I took my seat as Nick sat beside me, but slightly to the rear.

The table was now getting crowded, and I got the impression they had expected me to show up by myself. Fat chance; headquarters had specifically instructed that the conversation not be recorded, which meant that I wanted a witness to my questions and Mitchell's responses.

While I was taking the documents out of my briefcase, I discreetly let my eyes wander about the room. It was wood-paneled and stacked nearly floor to ceiling with books. I wondered if our esteemed former attorney general had actually read them or whether they were strictly for show. Later, because of his answers, I'd have bet on the latter. There were also several comfortable overstuffed chairs around the room near the bookcases. But it appeared that the most elegant chair at the conference table was at the head, reserved for Mr. Mitchell. I have no idea where it came from, but it looked like one a Supreme Court justice would occupy — a high back with beautiful scrollwork on the wooden part of the arms. The heavily padded chair rocked to and fro at Mitchell's command; very comfy.

"Mr. Mitchell," I began, "I've identified myself and my associate as Special Agents of the Federal Bureau of Investigation." With that, I passed my credentials and Nick's around the room.

Each one of the attorneys carefully examined them, and copied down our credential numbers. Both Nick and I made sure our credentials never left our sight. Normally an agent would not hand them to anyone. But this was the former attorney general, and it seemed like the thing to do.

Once the IDs were safely back in our hands, I said, "Mr. Mitchell, as the former attorney general, you are aware that FBI agents are empowered to place respondents under oath in certain cases, this being one of them. Please stand and raise your right hand."

Mitchell struggled to his feet and feebly raised a paw. His attorneys — in a knee-jerk reaction — stood too.

While administering the oath, I was struck by the fact that Mitchell appeared to be a tired old man, not one of the most powerful men in the former Nixon administration. The strain of possibly facing prison had obviously taken its toll.

Lies, Lies, and Damned Lies

With the formalities out of the way, we all sat down. I prefaced my questions by saying, "This interview is being conducted at the specific request of the Justice Department via FBI head-quarters. The questions that I will be asking were prepared by Justice. We are not recording this interview but my associate, Mr. Esposito, will be taking detailed notes. Are there any recording devices turned on in this room?"

Mitchell and all of his lawyers simultaneously shook their heads. The questions prepared for me were follow-ups to Mr. Mitchell's testimony before the federal grand jury. The Justice Department's lawyers could have easily called the former attorney general back to the grand jury, but the questions were worded in a way that called for yes-or-no responses, and inter-viewing him in the comfort of his home was an accommodation made for his previous high position in government. The passage of time has dimmed my memory of the exact questions I asked.

I do recall that when I asked a question, Mitchell's lawyers — I believe there were seven — scribbled down, word for word, what I said. I was amused at the overkill. Even though the attorneys were charging 1970s rates, Mitchell was doubtlessly paying a few thousand dollars an hour for what amounted to overpriced scribes; the attorneys did not utter a word during the interview. Mitchell thought carefully before answering each yes-or-no question. He evidently wasn't sharp enough to use the fail-safe response: "I don't recall."

A pattern emerged early in the interview. When he told the truth, he answered fairly promptly. But when he was getting ready to lie, Mitchell took a long puff on his pipe and looked up, as if the answer would be revealed to him on the ceiling. He then would lie though his teeth. The former attorney general had been coached well enough by his lawyers: Answer the question, and stop. Don't explain; that could lead to more questions.

The whole interview lasted maybe an hour. When we got ready to depart, Nick and I shook hands with each lawyer, and each gave us his card. I saved my last handshake for Mitchell, and thanked him for his time.

When we were clear of the building and out of earshot of the parties, Nick gleefully exclaimed, "We got him by the nuts!"

Although I agreed, I wasn't happy inside; in fact, I was sick to my stomach. Here was the chief law enforcement officer of the United States, whose position I'd been taught to respect. But in reality he was just another slimeball lawyer, one of several I eventually would help send to prison.

The results of the interview were sent by teletype to FBI headquarters, and I thought my role was over. But with lightning speed, I received a response asking for follow-ups to a few more questions. So Nick and I repeated the process in Mitchell's apartment once again and with the same results.

John N. Mitchell was convicted at trial in February 1975. Evidence would show that he controlled a secret slush fund used to pay for the Watergate break-in. I was happy not to have been called to testify. Mitchell was convicted with the overwhelming evidence gathered by the Justice Department and the grand jury. He served 19 months in a minimum security federal prison, and died in obscurity in 1988. The irony of the whole Watergate affair is that it was so unnecessary. A paranoid Richard Nixon somehow felt it necessary to gather political intelligence on his Democratic rival. But Nixon won handily anyhow, pulling in 61 percent of the popular vote and enough in the Electoral College to ensure his reelection.

Chapter 4

Jackson, Here
I Come!

T he NYO Bribery and Political Corruption Squad had
20 agents and two telephones. On a hazy morning in the
summer of 1976, one phone rang.

Someone answered it, and called out: "Wells, it's for you!"

I got up from my desk.

It was Don Selman, my old SAC in El Paso. "Joe, good to
talk to you," he started. "How do you like New York?"

The work was great, I answered, but the job was very tough
on an agent and his family.

"I might be able to arrange a transfer out of there for you,"
Selman said. "I'm now SAC in Jackson, Mississippi. We need

someone here with your background, and there isn't an accounting type on the office of preference list."

If Selman could get me out, I mused, I'd escape the grind of a three-hour commute and the oppressive cost of living in the New York metropolitan area.

"Joe," he continued, "Jackson is a small town and the division, which covers the whole state, has only 60 men. I've heard about your fine work against corruption; this part of the country is crawling with it."

Selman wasn't kidding. Everyone in the Deep South knew it had been plagued by political deception for generations. But few realized that hominy-flavored graft was nearly as old as the United States itself. In 1794, unscrupulous land speculators bribed Georgia state legislators to sell them at artificially low prices title to enormous parcels — the Yazoo Lands — just west of the state. These 18th-century fraudsters planned to then flip the land in profitable sales to the general public. The problem was that the Yazoo Lands — which were named after a nearby river, and later would become Alabama and Mississippi — weren't yet American possessions; in fact, they were claimed by Native Americans and the Spanish. So Georgia couldn't legally sell what it didn't own. It wasn't until 1815, after a landmark U.S. Supreme Court case, *Fletcher v. Peck*, that Congress could settle the resulting legal disputes.

Massive Southern corruption continued unabated in the 19th century. President Rutherford (aka "Rutherfraud") B. Hayes secured his 1876 election victory by means of what came to be known as "The Corrupt Bargain." That scheme delivered to him the electoral votes of Florida, Louisiana, and South Carolina in return for the removal of federal troops that had been enforcing post-Civil War political reforms.

And in 1935, Huey "The Kingfish" Long, former governor of, and then U.S. senator from, Louisiana, was assassinated.

Long had consolidated his power in state politics by aggressive tactics, including, some assert, extorting campaign contributions from state employees and from companies bidding for state contracts.

In my day, one of the more well-known Southern corruption scandals involved Texas farmer and financier Billie Sol Estes, who in 1964 was convicted on federal charges related to mail fraud and conspiracy. Opinion still is divided on whether Billie Sol had violated the law. But it seemed likely that someone among his business and political connections had done so. In other words, Deep Southern corruption was centuries old, with no end in sight.

So here on a silver platter was my opportunity to make a dent in this wall of fraud. I jumped at the chance, not even checking with my wife first. That same day I changed my office of preference to Jackson from Dallas, and less than a month later, the transfer letter arrived. My NYO colleagues, most of whom hated being in Manhattan, were happy for me but envious too. It took me little time to wrap up or reassign my cases. The Bribery and Political Corruption Squad usually had a fairly low caseload because, by its nature, the work tended to be long and drawn out. The other squad across the way from us worked primarily bank embezzlements. This was in the days before the savings and loan scandal of the '80s, so the typical bank embezzlement was rather small and fairly easy to resolve: one teller or one loan officer helping him- or herself to the financial institution's money.

The reaction to the transfer by Dawn and Beth, my wife and stepdaughter, surprised me. I was thrilled to leave but they weren't. Dawn would now have to quit her high-paid office job at Johnson & Johnson, and Beth had settled into her new school system. Prior to moving to Jackson, the FBI permitted us one three-day house-hunting trip to Mississippi. We decided to try to find a home to buy instead of renting and then moving again. There were only about 25 agents assigned to Jackson proper; the remainder was in resident agencies scattered throughout the state. The personnel in the headquarters office welcomed us warmly. I immediately gravitated toward W.K. "Bill" Peterson, and he helped us find a home in his neighborhood. It was a great place and compared to New York prices, a veritable bargain. Bill would become one of my closest lifetime friends; we still talk to this day.

The area we selected to buy in was northwest Jackson, a 15-minute drive from the office. We bought a four-bedroom brick single-story house on a corner lot. Like so many other homes in the neighborhood, it was surrounded by tall, beautiful pine trees. And it had a fenced-in backyard for our new dog, Simon. Bill lived about four blocks away. He and I would jog in the early morning before work. But the neighborhood was not ideal by the Mississippi standards of the mid-1970s: Slowly but surely, blacks were moving into the area to the south — the next subdivision over. When that happened, every "white" home would be on the market, often at fire-sale prices.

Not having grown up in the Deep South, I couldn't understand the fuss. But my home came at a bargain rate because of fears that blacks would move into the neighborhood. By my thinking, this racial attitude was insane. At the time, the populations of Mississippi, Alabama and Georgia were mostly black, and Louisiana wasn't far behind. I thought whites should accept this, but many of them felt otherwise.

The school systems were almost completely segregated. Blacks attended well-funded public institutions. Whites attended "private" schools where the parents paid tuition, but these weren't the fancy, schmancy private schools one would imagine. To keep the tuition as low as possible for whites, they most frequently were located in prefab metal buildings, often without air conditioning adequate for the South. Because extracurricular activities or sports would cost more money, there were none.

After the move, we were critically short of dough. The government supposedly reimbursed your costs, but that was a cruel joke. I'd not known an agent who was transferred and didn't end up flat broke. We simply couldn't afford to enroll Beth in a private school. Although I don't remember the exact numbers now, the tuition would have been about a third of my net pay. So my stepdaughter attended public school. One time she came home with her class photo, in which hers was the only white face in a sea of black ones. Beth put on a brave front, but being a minority was difficult for her. Many whites don't think much about what it's like to be a lone black person in a group, but I'm certain that person feels very much isolated. So it was with Beth.

Dawn was furious at the situation — then again, she was furious about a lot of things, most of them out of my control. Our life in Jackson together was a miserable one, but it wasn't much different from that of many agents whose families had to sacrifice for an FBI career. Within a few months, Dawn announced that I had to make a choice: the Bureau or her. Truth be known, I loved Beth more than Dawn, and the notion of being without my stepdaughter was almost more than I could bear. However, I also knew that it was simply a matter of time before Dawn and I would split up, and so we did.

While in Jackson, Dawn landed a job with the Social Security Administration. Later, after I was transferred to Austin, Dawn — who hated Mississippi anyhow — got a job transfer there too, under the pretense of making it possible for me to see Beth. But it seemed to me that Dawn later tried everything she could do to turn my stepdaughter against me, and it finally worked. I've not seen or talked to Beth in at least 35 years, and I have no idea where she and her mother ended up. Both of them, I hope, are happy.

Three-Dollar Bill

During his heyday in Mississippi politics, few could match State Senator William G. Burgin, Jr., for good old Deep South corruption. Or at least that was the unspoken message of the television show I was watching. Now that I'd been transferred from the Manhattan office of the FBI to Jackson, Mississippi and my wife had left me, there was plenty of time to watch the tube after work.

"The citizens of this state," said the TV reporter, "have a right to know if the controversial Senator Burgin has stepped over the line this time." She was referring to her station's investigative report, which concluded that Burgin had been using the power of his office to collect money owed to his private-practice law clients. The reporter had obtained secret copies of letters Burgin had written.

Waving them in front of the camera, she said, "These letters were written on state stationery. They were signed by Senator Burgin personally. But the letters have nothing to do with state business. They're on behalf of his personal clients. Can you imagine owing money to a private party, and receiving a letter about it from one of the most powerful people in state government?"

Burgin's power came from his position and seniority. As chairman of the senate Appropriations Committee, he had a virtual stranglehold on every dime the state spent. If Burgin didn't like a project, it didn't get funded with state — and matching federal — money, period. In reality, as the reporter pointed out, "Bill Burgin has more power in this state than the governor does. But," she asked in conclusion, "is he using that power for citizens, or for himself?"

Since I was new to town, I asked around the FBI squad room the next day, "Who is this Bill Burgin guy?"

"Oh, just one of the state political crooks," said one agent.

118

"A pretty smart one, I hear," said my newfound friend, Bill Peterson.

"Yeah, he's been around for years — always a lot of smoke, but no real fires," said still another agent.

"Why haven't we looked at him before?" I asked. "Surely in his position as chairman of the Appropriations Committee, there must be some federal money he handles, which would give the FBI jurisdiction."

Bill said, "Joe, the reason we haven't investigated him is that we've been waiting for you. Welcome to Mississippi."

So began my investigation of William G. Burgin, Jr. It seemed like a piece of cake after working on — or, perhaps more accurately, surviving — the Watergate investigation. But suspecting someone of being a crook and proving he is one are two different things.

One of the more interesting aspects of conducting investigations is the creativity you can employ. In the instance of Bill Burgin, all I had to go on were television reports that he was using state resources to collect debts for his private clients. That certainly seemed untoward, but hardly enough to make a federal case out of it. To investigate a powerful politician like Burgin, one must have the imagination to develop a theory.

It was my theory that Burgin, if he were a crook, would be involved in some sort of fraud related to his power to disburse money on behalf of the State of Mississippi. As chairman of the senate Appropriations Committee, he ultimately decided where the state spent billions of dollars. So it would be logical to theorize that Burgin would take bribes and kickbacks for the awarding of state contracts. But what contracts? The State of Mississippi — like many other government bodies — had tens of thousands of them. Where could I start? It certainly wouldn't be practical to review tons of paperwork, looking for mysterious clues.

Then I thought of sneaking a look at Burgin's personal bank balances to see if I could pick up some clues. But this idea had a flaw: Without probable cause, the United States Attorney would not issue a subpoena for Burgin's bank records. And although I had the contacts to secretly check his bank accounts, doing so would be illegal. I had committed fraud in the past, ostensibly for a good cause. But maturity and experience as an agent kept driving home the point I'd ignored before: If you can't win playing by the rules, you don't deserve to win.

After I'd wrestled with the temptation to look at Burgin's bank records anyway, the banking angle gave me another idea. There was a bank within spitting distance of the state capitol building. I felt sure that because of its proximity to the capitol some politicians and state employees would bank there. So I reasoned it might be worthwhile to get to know the bank's staff. Perhaps they could tell me something useful.

Two New Relationships

On a dark and dreary Mississippi winter morning, I walked into Fidelity Bank, and introduced myself to the president's assistant. "Hello; I'm Joe Wells from the local FBI office. I've just been transferred to Jackson, and want the presidents of the local banks to know they can contact me if they ever need our help."

The assistant, Sally Mulcasey, looked me up and down. With a dazzling smile, she said, "Really, Mr. Wells? Suppose *I* need your help?" She looked to be in her late twenties, was blonde and very attractive. I was single, sort of. She wasn't, according to her wedding ring.

I smiled back. "Then all you have to do is whistle."

Ms. Mulcasey offered me a seat outside the president's office, and with little delay, I was led in to meet George S. Sewell, Jr., the president, majority shareholder, and CEO of Fidelity Bank.

The bank was on the small side, located catty-corner from the state capitol building. Mr. Sewell's office was elegantly furnished in leather and oak paneling — a striking contrast to its occupant's silver hair. Sewell appeared to be in his early sixties, and was of medium height and somewhat portly. He welcomed me and ushered me to a seat across from his highly polished desk. On the wall were framed photographs of him many years ago, next to a variety of World War II airplanes.

"Do you still fly?" I opened. Experience taught me to *not* get right to the subject. FBI agents, whether they mean to or not, often create a natural paranoia in people who have done nothing wrong. It comes with the image.

Sewell responded with a light laugh. "Not in 40 years. But I still keep those pictures around to remember what's really important. When people are shooting at you in an airplane, your only thought is to stay alive. So when I'm having a bad day now, all I do is look at those photos, and they always make me smile."

I had just met this guy, and already I liked him. "Mr. Sewell, as you may know, the FBI investigates over 200 violations of federal law," I said. "Many of them affect banks. I've just been transferred to the Jackson division, so I'm trying to meet with the local bankers and explain how we can help each other. My specialty is white-collar crime. So if you suspect an employee has embezzled money, or an officer has made a phony loan to himself, the case would be assigned to me. And if you're unlucky enough to have a bank robbery, you can call me or anyone else at the office right away."

Sewell smiled, thanked me for my visit, and asked, "You said I might be able to help you. How's that?"

"Well, because my specialty is white-collar crime, I also handle political corruption cases," I said. "So if you ever hear of something I might be interested in at the state or local level, call me. We can discuss it confidentially, without you getting involved."

With that, our first meeting ended. I didn't realize it was only the first of many meetings with Sewell. But the look he gave me on the way out implied he expected to see me again.

Sally Mulcasey gave me a look too, but I couldn't figure out what hers meant.

Free Money

I didn't have to wait long for the second meeting with George Sewell. Within weeks, he called and invited me to lunch. Sewell, in addition to being a decorated World War II hero, knew food like no one I'd met before. He was a master at locating out-of-the-way small restaurants with meals to die for. At our first luncheon, he did all the ordering. I had a delicious local fish — the pompano — the memory of which still makes my mouth water. As I had been taught, I waited until Sewell was ready to talk business. After we had stuffed ourselves, the waiter poured two cups of steaming coffee with chicory and discreetly departed.

"Supposing I could help you in state politics," Sewell said. "How can I be sure you'll handle my part confidentially?"

"You can't," I said. "You'd just have to trust me."

Apparently that did the trick. I guess if I had promised him the moon, he wouldn't have carried the conversation further. But since I didn't, he found comfort in that somehow.

"Okay," Sewell finally said, "I'm going to trust you. I know there's a lot going on in government, but I can't prove it."

I told Sewell he didn't have to prove it; that was the FBI's job.

After a long silence, he then told me that some — but not many — banks received most of the state's deposits. "Those deposits amount to free money for the banks that get the business, because they don't have to pay interest on the state's checking accounts," Sewell explained. "For years, it's been rumored that you had to pay off the state politicians if you wanted those deposits. I don't know if that's the case, but I know my bank doesn't get much state money at all."

"Who makes the decisions on who gets state money?" I asked.

"It depends on which state agency is involved," Sewell replied. "In Mississippi, the agency with the most money is the public welfare department, headed by Fred St. John."

I didn't know St. John. He turned out to be a political appointee of Governor Cliff Finch. I knew only enough about the governor to wonder about him. When I first moved to Mississippi, Finch's election campaign was under way, and his commercials were all over television. (Remember, I had a lot of time to watch the tube.) The commercials were surreal. Many of them displayed Finch — a lawyer — loading trash, sweeping streets and performing other menial tasks to prove he was "for the working man."

So the fact that Fred St. John had been appointed welfare commissioner by Governor Finch didn't exactly impress me. But his control over such a large block of the state's money piqued my interest.

"Does that mean the governor ultimately determines where the welfare department and other state agencies deposit those funds?" I asked Sewell.

As I sipped the last of the coffee and chicory, Sewell looked at me with a bemused smile, as if he were answering a completely obvious question. "No," he said. "In Mississippi, the governor doesn't have very much power. That belongs to the senate Appropriations Committee."

Although I already knew the answer, I asked the question anyhow. "Who controls the senate Appropriations Committee?"

"Bill Burgin," Sewell said, eyeing me evenly.

Undercover Job

As soon as we finished lunch, I returned to the office. Under the theory that two heads are better than one, I sought some advice on what to do. Special Agent Ross Laben just happened to be handy, so I sat him down in the squad room, and told him a five-minute version of the information I had gleaned from George Sewell.

Ross listened carefully. Although he wasn't as experienced as I was in corruption cases, Ross had at least ten years' seniority on me and I greatly respected him. He had seen it all — from the early violence of the civil rights movement to kidnappings — and most everything in between. Laben looked something like your grandfather. Graying, with more than a little bald showing on top, Ross could have lost 20 pounds. "Joe," he said, "we've all known there's been corruption in state politics around here for a long time. But with what you've told me, I think we could get the Justice Department to authorize an investigation."

But investigate what? I thought to myself. All we knew is that Sewell said Burgin controlled where money was deposited for the state. That wasn't a secret. The question was whether Burgin was getting kickbacks. That was something we didn't know.

After my conversation with Laben, I called Assistant United States Attorney James Beauregard Turner on the phone, and asked to meet with him. He invited me right over — it was only a two-block walk from the FBI office. If there was ever a classic Type A personality, it belonged to James Beauregard Turner. Slender with a full head of brown hair, Turner lit the end of one cigarette with another, and his eyes were constantly bloodshot, reputedly from drinking himself to sleep every night. But he was one hell of an aggressive prosecutor. He preferred to be called James. Knowing that, we universally referred to him as Beauregard.

When I walked into Beauregard's office, he was in his classic pose: sitting behind his desk, barely visible amid huge stacks of files. A constant stream of smoke emanated from his nostrils.

After listening to the details of my lunchtime conversation with Sewell, he pointed out the obvious with his usual directness. "Joe, you don't have shit. But as long as I've lived here, I've heard Burgin is dirty. If you can develop some specifics, then we'll have probable cause to investigate. Have you considered an undercover operation?"

I had already flirted with the idea briefly. But as glamorous as undercover operations sound, most FBI agents know they're a paperwork nightmare. I thanked Beauregard for his input and returned to the office to come up with The Plan.

Laben suggested I approach Sewell about working undercover for us. Perhaps Sewell could invite some politicians to his office at the bank, Laben said. The idea would be for Sewell to pretend he was interested in getting state deposits for the bank and to hint that he'd be willing to pay for them. And we'd secretly tape all those conversations.

From my own experience, I knew two fundamental problems would have to be overcome.

First, when law enforcement works with an inexperienced operative such as Sewell, he must become highly educated in the fine points of the law. And under the law, entrapment is illegal, and occurs when an individual or individuals are induced to commit a crime they would not otherwise commit. To avoid entrapment charges, the operative must walk a very fine line. On one hand, Sewell could hint that he was interested in getting state deposits for his bank, but he couldn't suggest an illegality; that had to come from the other side.

The second problem with such an operation involves the logistics of taping, transcribing, marking, and handling records of the conversations, which could be used later as evidence.

That's where the paper war in undercover operations begins. The agent in charge of the case is responsible for adding volumes of paper to the investigative file, often without sufficient time or resources to do it, just as I'd done in the Klegmeir case in New York.

Despite these logistical challenges, I finally acknowledged that using George S. Sewell, Jr., president of Fidelity Bank, as an undercover operative was probably the only way we were going to penetrate the murky world of Mississippi political payoffs.

Complete Trust

Sally Mulcasey, Mr. Sewell's assistant, spotted me at the front door of the bank. Her eyes followed me all the way up to her desk, where she greeted me with her trademark smile. "Great to see you again, Mr. Wells. Mr. Sewell is expecting you," she said. "Go right in." As I turned to go into his office, Sally said, "By the way, I am taking whistling lessons."

It took me a second to recall what I'd said to her when we first met. When I did, for some reason I looked down at her hand. The wedding ring was still there.

Once in Sewell's office, I closed the door and got right to the point. I explained the proposed plan — for Sewell to work as an FBI undercover operative. This would be an unglamorous, unpaid and possibly dangerous assignment, if he accepted it, I told Sewell, and he wouldn't ever be able to talk about it.

When I'd finished, Sewell looked behind his desk at the pictures of the much younger man standing beside a Navy fighter. "Joe, 'danger' is having three Japanese Zeros on your tail," he said. "Compared to that, this assignment will be a walk in the park. Count me in."

People like Sewell volunteer for a variety of reasons. In his case, it was my impression that he was first and foremost a patriot. The notion of the government of the people being corrupted by dishonesty offended Sewell's sense of right and wrong. The second reason was more practical — Fidelity Bank, at least in the opinion of its president, was being slighted in regard to state deposits. And third, being an undercover operative for the FBI *sounded* exciting.

It was several weeks before a real plan began to take shape. In the meantime, we worked on the logistical issues: How would we actually record the conversations? Could the recording device we selected be turned on and off? How often would we have to replace its tapes and batteries?

In one of our planning sessions, we decided that Sewell should have a confidant at the bank to help him.

"But who can we trust?" I asked.

George, with the corners of his mouth crinkling upward, immediately said, "Sally Mulcasey, your number-one fan."

I didn't immediately say anything, but the look on my face must have been one for the books: Sewell burst out in one of his laughs.

I wondered how he could trust such a beautiful and flirtatious woman? But all I said was, "What makes you think you can trust her?"

"Joe, don't let those gorgeous eyes fool you," George said. "Sally is 27, and has been with me five years — ever since she graduated from college. She's smart as hell, and I trust her completely. Besides, since Sally took an instant shine to you, I'm sure she'd do just about anything you want."

Later, I'd learn why Sewell trusted Sally. And again, I thought and said two different things. I thought he probably didn't mean the double entendre; I said nothing.

Laying a Trap

The recording equipment we installed in Sewell's office was assembled by the FBI lab. They hollowed out a book, and fitted a Nagra recorder inside it. The Nagras were considered the best recorders made — so sensitive they could capture the sound of a pin dropping. We concealed the microphone in the spine of the book. To turn it on, all Sewell had to do was pull up on the bookmark. The book was strategically located in a small bookstand next to his desk. Since the Nagra was so sophisticated, we had to give George detailed instructions on how to operate it and change the tapes and batteries.

After that, we turned to the most difficult assignment of all — deciding whom to invite to Sewell's office and what to tell them once they were there. We figured it would seem suspicious if Sewell invited Bill Burgin right away. After all, Burgin didn't know George, and vice versa. So instead Sewell suggested to us that he invite State Senator Ellis Bodron from the senate Finance Committee. Even though the two were not close, Sewell had known Bodron for quite some time. But inviting Bodron to George's office had one big disadvantage — Bodron was totally blind. The likelihood of the senator coming to Sewell's office was remote. We therefore decided to have George invite Bodron to lunch. Bodron accepted, but that introduced a whole new set of operational difficulties: We would have to place a body recorder on Sewell to pick up the conversation.

FBI agents don't like body recorders. They're easily detected with a pat-down, and more than a few operatives have met their demise when it was discovered they were wired. But agents like the alternative — body transmitters — even less. Body transmitters have the advantage of being easily concealed. But transmitters are notoriously unreliable. Interference from buildings, garage door openers, and other electronic devices can cause them to transmit nothing more than unintelligible noise.

We rightfully reasoned that a blind state senator going to lunch with a bank president is unlikely to pat him down. In this instance, it was advantageous that Bodron was blind. So this would be a great opportunity to test this risky equipment. We decided to go for it. Sewell got taped up under his shirt. The recorder was under his armpit, and the microphone was attached to a shirt button, covered by his necktie. Theoretically, all Sewell had to do was turn it on and off at the right time. The right time to turn on the recorder would be when Sewell picked up Bodron from his office. And the right time to turn it off was immediately after Bodron was returned to his office. That gave us 90 minutes — no more, no less. We wanted to pick up the entire conversation — if the tape ran out, Bodron could claim there was more that had not been recorded.

Because we were very careful about the timing, the Sewell lunch with Ellis Bodron took about 80 minutes — 10 minutes to spare. Luckily, Jackson, Mississippi, was not a large town. When Sewell returned from lunch with Bodron, I was waiting for him at the bank. Sally Mulcasey helped pass the time by flirting with me.

What is with this woman? I kept asking myself.

Sewell returned to the bank with his tape. In his office, we removed the recorder from under Sewell's arm and played it. George was brilliant in his performance on the recording. In essence, Bodron told Sewell that he would have to "play ball" with Bill Burgin in order to get state deposits for Fidelity Bank. Bodron did not in any way indicate that he himself was interested in any shenanigans. But he certainly didn't seem to mind telling George — in a very matter-of-fact voice — that politics was an expensive game.

Bodron also mentioned that Burgin was tight with Fred St. John, the welfare commissioner. Bodron repeated that the state welfare system held the largest bank accounts and that to get some of that money for Fidelity Bank, Sewell would probably have to work a deal with Burgin or St. John. We were pleased with the way the conversation went, but the tape didn't contain any solid violations — no "smoking gun."

Nonetheless, the tape had to be transcribed and added to the evidence file. The steno pool was not crazy about transcribing tapes; after all, they had to hear conversations over the noise created by lunch — glasses tinkling, mouths full, patrons talking. Because of my own experiences in the Klegmeir case in New York, I fully appreciated this problem. But little did I know when I gave the Sewell-Bodron tape to the steno pool that future events would greatly strain their resources. Many more tapes would be recorded over the next few months. Sewell secretly recorded conversations with a host of state officials: the banking commissioner, the welfare commissioner, and even Governor Finch's brother. Every time I walked up to the steno pool with a tape in my hand, heads would duck. Still, after all the effort, there was no smoking gun.

Running Out of Time

Overwhelmed by my transcription requests, the head stenographer had complained to the special agent in charge of the office, Homer Hauer. A chisel-faced Dutchman, he had succeeded Don Selman soon after I arrived in Jackson. Homer was a no-nonsense guy from the old school. He and I had an odd liking for each other. But because my hair was roughly an inch longer than regulation, he seemed to regard me as somewhat of a closet hippie.

Hauer summoned me upstairs to his office, and told me to close the door. Bad sign. He got right to the point. "Betty in the steno pool tells me your case is clogging up the works, Joe, and we're not authorized to pay overtime. What am I going to do with you?" he said. His serious expression was undermined by the upturned corners of his mouth.

Betty must have laid it on, I surmised. "Well, boss, as you know, this case hasn't exactly gone as planned."

He looked at me carefully.

"We have an operative who is recording conversations with a variety of politicians," I continued. "But it's going slower than we thought. What we have on tape is a great deal of political intelligence, but we haven't seen a violation yet. We've found smoke, but no fire yet."

The amused part of Hauer's expression disappeared instantly. "Joe, the FBI isn't the goddamned fire department. Do you understand?"

I understood. Hauer told me I had 30 days to turn up something good. The only thing left to be understood was exactly how I was supposed to pull that off. Dejected, I left Homer's office.

Ross Laben, who was in the squad room when I returned, put an understanding hand on my shoulder when he heard the news. But Ross didn't have any flashes of genius as to how we could get the case kick-started within the next month.

The next few days I reserved for head-scratching. If Burgin was a crook, how could I get some leverage? Where could I get started? Could I offer a bribe to Burgin through Sewell without entrapping the senator? It would be tricky, I surmised. So I walked the two blocks to the United States Attorney's office, hoping Beauregard could help me think it through.

As usual, when I walked into the prosecutor's office, Beauregard's eyes were blood red. I couldn't tell if it was because of what he had to drink last night or because of that constant stream of cigarette smoke curling from his nose and mouth, directly into his eyes. While I waited for him to get off the telephone, I looked around at the cramped office, which was on the second floor of the two-story federal building. The décor was decidedly early battleship, with walls of varying gray tones. A huge nicotine stain spread across the ceiling above his desk. I had to move some files to sit on one of the few chairs in his office.

Beauregard finished his conversation, and I brought him up to date: lots of good intelligence but no violations yet. And I told him of Homer's ultimatum.

"Wells, when you came in here before, I told you that you didn't have shit. Now, after all this time, you still don't have shit," Beauregard opined. Leave it to Beauregard to cut to the chase.

"I know that, James." It wasn't the time to call him Beauregard.

"Then why are you wasting your effort?" he asked.

I wondered about that too. Christ, I thought to myself, I have better things to do. Other cases were piling up, and I wasn't working them. And Homer and the whole steno pool were on my ass. As an experienced agent, I knew that Homer, the boss of the Mississippi division, would probably be transferred within 18 months. In that way, the FBI promoted people through the ranks. But I also knew that the steno pool would be there forever, and until Betty retired — in another 10 or 15 years — I'd have to work with her. Pissing off Betty was therefore much worse than getting Homer mad at me. When the steno pool didn't like an agent, his dictation would be mysteriously "lost" so he would have to repeat the entire process.

Yet Another Woman

Because of my difficulty with the steno pool, I decided to close the case; it just wasn't worth Betty's wrath. As I was thinking about that, I left Beauregard's office. But in the hallway, those thoughts disappeared when I saw another fine example of Mississippi's beautiful southern lasses.

"Hello," I said, as we crossed in the hall.

"Hi," she said, holding out her carefully manicured hand. "I'm Roxanne Hurley." She was the local legislative liaison to U.S. Senator John Stennis, and her office was just down the hall. She said she'd seen me come in and out of the U.S. Attorney's office several times.

My eyes ran slowly from her bright red fingernails, up her arm to her sensuous, curving neck, then on to her soft, parted lips, colored to match her nails. And then I saw her eyes, iridescent green, seeming to look deep inside me.

I was impressed. Before returning her greeting, I glanced at her left hand. Damn, I thought. Not only is she married, but the size of that stone indicated Roxanne Hurley had bucks.

Roxanne immediately caught me looking at the ring.

"I'm Joe Wells," I said, slightly embarrassed that I had even looked at her ring finger.

"Are you one of the federal agents?"

"Yes," I replied.

"Which agency?" she asked.

"FBI," I said. "Is it that obvious?"

"Not really," Roxanne said in her lovely southern drawl. "All the federal investigators deal with the United States Attorney's office." Then her eyes dropped from my face to below my belt. "And under that coat, either you have a gun, or you're very glad to meet me." She broke out in a hearty laugh, no doubt because of the stunned look on my face.

And I was glad to meet her. Even if she was married, she was still beautiful. Not tall, but not petite, Roxanne Hurley was blonde like Sally Mulcasey. But that's where the similarity ended. Roxanne's curly blond hair was long and spilled over her face and shoulders. Speaking of her face, it looked like it could have been cast from alabaster; her complexion was flawless. But past that, it took only a few minutes with Roxanne Hurley for me to figure out she was a genuine firecracker. And she loved to laugh.

Almost every sentence that spilled from that lovely mouth was a one-liner. Before I left, Roxanne said, "Tell Bill Peterson I said hello. And come back to see me sometime." Bill had obviously been holding out on me. He had never even mentioned that this beautiful creature existed.

I put Roxanne Hurley out of my mind while I drove over to Fidelity Bank to tell George Sewell that I had decided to close the case. Sally, as usual, was smiling at me the moment I started through the lobby. She'd been very helpful to Sewell, maintaining the recorder, replacing the batteries, and rewinding the tapes. She knew he was our operative, but she didn't really know exactly what he was doing. This fundamental element of information security was drummed repeatedly into every FBI agent's head: You can't tell what you don't know. Therefore, information is shared on a need-to-know basis.

"Special Agent Wells," she said mockingly as I approached her desk. "The big man is waiting to see you. Go right in," Sally said.

Sewell took the news without surprise. Within a half hour, I had retrieved the book and recorder from George and was on my way.

Sally wasn't at her desk.

I guess I'll see her later, I thought.

When I got back to the office, Bill Peterson was standing next to the sign-in register. He was just returning from a day in the field. Bill saw the book/recorder in my hand. "What happened?" he asked.

I told him the news too.

"By the way," I said, "I met a real fox over at the federal building. Her name is Roxanne, and she said to tell you hello."

Bill's face lit up. "She sure is a fox," he chimed in. "If I were single like you, Joe, I'd go after that."

"Bill, she's married. That's trouble for an FBI agent," I observed.

He looked at me quizzically. "Oh, you mean the wedding rings," he finally said. "She has been divorced from this rich guy for a year or two but still wears the rings."

"Oh, that sounds just great, Bill," I joked, "sending me after someone who holds a torch for her ex-husband." I was neurotic enough already.

"Joe, she doesn't hold a torch for her ex-husband," Bill said. "She's richer than he was. Roxanne designed and bought those rings herself. The reason she wears them is to keep guys from hitting on her."

I could immediately appreciate the problem, having seen Roxanne. "Why didn't you introduce me to her before, Bill?" I asked.

"She may be out of your league, Joe," Bill said.

Aha, I thought: a challenge at last.

The other challenge was the deadline. A month after I talked to Hauer, I had come up empty. I wrote a memo to the file stating that the investigation had been closed for lack of specific evidence of a violation against Burgin or any of the others in state politics. I have no doubt the news was bearable because I was now completely distracted by Roxanne Hurley.

About a week after she and I met, Bill saw Roxanne at the courthouse. She suggested that he and I accompany her and one of her friends, Leah, to a political bash at the Old Capitol Inn in downtown Jackson. Bill and I were unsure if we could attend; I was driving the surveillance van on another case, and Bill had to respond to a bank robbery earlier in the day.

But we finally made it downtown. I parked the van on Capitol Street and joined Bill. We then met Roxanne and Leah for drinks before the party at the bar in the penthouse level of the hotel. Bill and I sat on one side of the table, across from Roxanne and Leah. Frankly, neither Bill nor I considered this a date. Neither did the two ladies — we were just all going to the party together.

That changed when Roxanne and I got on the elevator alone to go down from the bar; Bill and Leah followed in another elevator. Before the doors closed, Roxanne and I were locked in a passionate embrace. I was totally surprised. By the time we arrived at the political party downstairs in the hotel, Roxanne and I were holding on tightly to one other. Although there were hundreds of people at the party, we didn't see them. Bill and Leah were there too. But we didn't see them either. Less than a half hour after arriving at the party, Roxanne and I left and walked up Capitol Street to the van and climbed in the back.

Two hours later, when we left, we were inseparable. It would be a while before Bill Burgin, George Sewell, Sally Mulcasey, or corruption in Mississippi politics would dominate my thoughts again.

Sally vs. Roxanne

Six months later, in the early spring, a surprising message was waiting for me when I arrived at work. The note was in the scrawl of Steve Gavin, the morning clerk. It said simply, "Call Sally Mulcasey. She said you know her number by heart." I smiled after reading the note. Like most of my conversations with Sally, it could be taken several ways. For example, "knowing her number by heart" could mean that I was so taken with Sally that I still remembered her business telephone number. Or perhaps she was referring to my strange inability to forget digits of any kind, like my telephone number when I was in high school (255-8272).

At any rate, she was right — I did know Fidelity Bank's number by heart, and I called her right away.

As soon as Sally came on the line, she began teasing. "Hey, G-man."

I could hear the smile in her voice.

"Don't you love me anymore? I haven't seen you in months."

"Yeah," I replied, "I've been doing some undercover work."

Sally could no doubt appreciate the double entendre, since she seemed to be the master of it.

What I didn't tell her is that "undercover work" in the FBI was the classic line agents like me would use on unsuspecting women. That excuse was one of the fringe benefits that came with the lowly salary of an investigator.

Sally immediately retorted, "Yes, I'm sure you've been doing 'undercover' work. Now you could legally do some on me — I've gotten divorced!"

Well, I thought, she sure came right out with that. I could have told her at that point about Roxanne, but I didn't. Perhaps I was flattered by the notion of having two beautiful women interested in me.

So I simply said, "We'll have to see about that, won't we?"

Then Sally Mulcasey got serious. "I do want to see you privately. There's something I think you should know, and I don't want to talk about it over the telephone," she said. "One lesson you taught me is to realize that your conversations may be recorded. I guess I'll never trust the phone again." It was easy to see how she got that way, working with the FBI.

Sally and I met after work at one of the bars in Jackson. The months and her divorce had been kind to her. When she joined me at the table, she was wearing a simple burgundy suit, cut high, revealing her beautiful thighs. Sally noticed that I was looking at her, and she drank it in. Before she sat down, she grazed her lips against my cheek. "Good to see you again, Joe," she said simply.

As she scooted into the booth on the opposite side, I was cursing myself for being attracted to her. After all, Roxanne was incredible. And Roxanne surely wouldn't want to see me here with Sally. But, I told myself foolishly, it is business.

It took Sally and me two drinks to get around to talking business. By that time, my tongue was slightly numb. And the more we drank, the less I thought about Roxanne. I was having a great time with Sally. Even though Roxanne and Sally were both blondes, the similarities ended there. While Roxanne was certainly no one's fool, she had an innocence about her that was missing in Sally. Indeed, Sally seemed very worldly for her age and despite the fact that she had been working for George Sewell since she got out of college.

Finally, a Break

Sally got to the point. "I didn't want to tell George Sewell," she said. I didn't ask why. "Anyhow, I saw something last week that I think would be of interest to you. Have you ever heard of Flavous Lambert?"

I said I hadn't.

"Flavous is a good friend of Bill Burgin's. They went to college together," she said. "Flavous was in the bank last week."

As I listened, I drained the rest of my vodka martini. As if by magic, the waiter appeared, eager to refill my glass. Since I was already having a little trouble focusing on Sally, I switched to a vodka and tonic — the perfect drink for the deep, steamy South.

Sally waited until the waiter left before she continued. "Flavous has this really flaky reputation. No one knows exactly what he does, except that he's a lawyer and does some lobbying. He and Burgin are like that," she said, crossing her fingers.

Sure enough, even in my slightly drunken state, I could see the wedding rings were gone. There wasn't even one of those indentations on her finger where the rings used to be. That meant it had been a while since Sally had worn them. Wait a minute, I thought. Why do I care? After all, Roxanne is my girl.

Sally snapped her fingers. "Hey," she said. "Listen up."

I looked up at her about the time the waiter arrived with my third drink. After he departed, Sally leaned closer to me. "Flavous opened a safe deposit box at the bank today, and I saw what he put in it." The look on her face told me that she was proud of her efforts.

"Well?" I said impatiently. It was about the only word I could pronounce without a slight slurring of my words. Damn, I thought. I hate this. Drinking excessively, paying attention to the details of what Sally was saying, having to drive home in my FBI car, telling Roxanne where I'd been — suddenly it all seemed too much.

Sally looked at me closely. Even through the fog, I could see how serious she was. "Before I tell you anything, you must promise me that Mr. Sewell will not know. And you have to promise me you won't ask why I'm making that request. It's a take-it-or-leave-it deal." Sally leaned back and drained the last of her third drink. I wondered why she remained so sober.

Immediately, I became paranoid. What's going on? I wondered. Why is Sally asking me to cut George out of this? Had he done something wrong? Is he not to be trusted? Is the relationship between George and Sally more than business? Has she done something wrong?

I'd had too much to drink, but at least I realized it. So I wasn't going to agree with Sally to do anything on this particular evening. "Sally," I finally said, "Let me mull it over and I'll get back to you."

Sally didn't seem a bit surprised. "Want me to drive you home?" she asked with an amused expression. Her hand closed over mine.

Naturally, I did what the public service spots tell you not to do: drink and drive. I got in my FBI car and headed out. I was thinking, I'll be damned if I'll let some woman outdrink me. If she's sober enough to drive, so am I. And of course, I also thought about Roxanne, who was probably waiting for me at my apartment. It certainly wouldn't do for Roxanne to see Sally and me together. No, that wouldn't do at all, I thought as I pulled into my driveway.

Mata Hari

The next time I saw Sally, we went to lunch. No drinks to fog my judgment. She went over the same information about seeing Flavous Lambert put something into a safe deposit box. And she repeated that Sewell was not to know.

"Sally, why are you putting me in a bind like this?" I asked. As I looked into her eyes, something told me that Sally could cut your heart out without flinching. I shivered involuntarily.

"Cold?" she asked.

"No, I just had a chill."

"What I could tell you about Lambert would warm you up nicely."

"So tell me."

"Not until you agree to my conditions."

"What were those again?"

Sally's eyes narrowed. "Joe, you really were drunk the last time we met, weren't you?"

"I had one too many. I was not drunk," I said a little too emphatically.

"Let's go over it again," she said. Her patience obviously was wearing thin. "If I tell you what I know, you can never involve me in it, and you can't tell Mr. Sewell. And you can't ask me why you can't tell Mr. Sewell. Remember now?" I'd had about enough of Sally's attitude.

"Sally, I really can't make you any absolute promises," I said quietly through clenched teeth. "You're already involved just from what you've told me. If you've witnessed something important, that makes you involved. I can't pretend you don't exist."

What I didn't tell Sally is that I had the power to get her subpoenaed before the federal grand jury. There she wouldn't have much of a choice other than to repeat what she'd already told me. Then she'd have to provide all the details. After all, I had made no deals with her so far. But I hoped it wouldn't get to that. If Sally really knew anything, she could be helpful behind the scenes.

She broke my thought process when her eyes fell to the table. "So in other words, sooner or later I'm going to have to tell you what I know," Sally said.

I simply nodded.

She stared at me a long time. I thought she was getting ready to slap me. But then she gradually broke into her trademark smile. "Does that mean I'd get to play Mata Hari?"

I hadn't thought about that legendary spy in years. Mata Hari's standard information-gathering technique was to seduce men. I suspected Sally Mulcasey would be very capable of that. Despite her outward innocence, I speculated to myself that Sally had already seduced more than her share of men.

"Sally, for all I know, you *are* Mata Hari," I said, returning her smile.

She looked at me thoughtfully for a while. Then her smile gradually disappeared, and she said, "Flavous Lambert put a contract in a safe deposit box at Fidelity Bank. I saw the top of the contract, which said 'Learning Development Corporation and the State of Mississippi, Department of Public Welfare.'" She said she'd seen the contract when it was in Flavous's hand, and that he had put it down momentarily on her desk while signing the paperwork for the safe deposit box.

Since I didn't have anything to write on, I committed the contract's name to memory. If the state had signed a contract, it would be public record. I could probably get a copy.

"Did you see the date of the contract?" I asked hopefully.

Sally shook her head. No, she had seen only the top of the first page of the document.

This information meant nothing right now. But with a stretch, you could theorize that somehow Flavous scored the contract through his connection to Burgin. The contract itself must be important to Flavous; otherwise, why would he rent a safe deposit box to put it in?

Looking across the table at Sally, I could tell she had already figured that out before Flavous had left the bank. But I couldn't tell if she was thinking what I was: Could this be the break I needed?

Complicated Relationships

After six months, things between Roxanne and me had started to get complicated. We thought we were passionately in love, but fought constantly. And we both were at fault. For my part, there were two major issues — Roxanne's looks and her money. They were both threatening to my male psyche. And from Roxanne's side, there was only one thing that really bothered her — my career. In all her prior male relationships, there was no doubt who was in charge: that blonde with the infectious laugh. But in my relationship with her, she had extreme difficulty adjusting to me going off on the spur of the moment, unable to tell her where I was going or when I would return. And I specifically had kept her in the dark about the Burgin investigation, Sally Mulcasey, George Sewell, and Flavous Lambert. Roxanne was from a prominent, well-connected family, and was very close to her mother — one of the last of an older generation of genteel southern belles. Both Roxanne and her mother would instantly recognize all the names involved, except maybe Sally's.

So, during the Burgin investigation, I felt very isolated, almost as if I were leading two completely separate, secret lives.

That certainly added to the tension between Roxanne and me. And if she had any idea that Sally Mulcasey was the Mata Hari, Roxanne would absolutely flip.

Sally had given me one slim lead — the name of a contract, "The State of Mississippi and Learning Development Corporation." A quick check with the secretary of state's office in Jackson failed to turn up the name of such a company in Mississippi. And I really didn't know how to locate a contract in the bowels of the state government. If I could find it, however, the contract should be public record, I reasoned.

For the next few days, I spun my wheels looking for the location of all the public contracts. Finally, I discovered the contracts were maintained by the respective state agencies. Unfortunately, I didn't know which agency might be involved in a contract locked in a safe deposit box at Fidelity Bank. Briefly I considered getting into the safe deposit box for an unauthorized look at the paper. But that presented its own problems — getting Sally involved in what we used to euphemistically refer to as a bag job — an illegal break-in. No, I finally decided, it's too risky. There had to be a better way. That turned out to be taking an educated guess at which agency would have issued a contract. The Department of Public Welfare, with its head, Fred St. John, would be a logical start.

Once I had made that decision, locating the contract was a piece of cake. I simply walked into the contract office at the welfare department and asked to see a list of them. Because it was a public record, I didn't have to identify myself or my mission. Sure enough, I found a two-page document involving the State Welfare Department and Learning Development Corporation, Nashville, Tennessee. St. John had signed the contract himself on behalf of the State of Mississippi.

The records custodian at the Department of Public Welfare made me a copy of the contract. I studied it carefully. The contract was for a one-year period, and called for Learning Development (LDC) to provide "educational services and counseling to disadvantaged youths" living in Mississippi. LDC was to be paid at the rate of $65,000 a month, or $780,000 over 12 months. At once, I wondered why the State of Mississippi was farming out work to a Tennessee company. After all, any state politician worth his salt would prefer to sign such a contract with a Mississippi enterprise. That would give him bragging rights for bringing jobs to the state. Then I looked at the date on the contract. It had been in force about 10 months and was getting ready to expire.

I wondered why Flavous Lambert, if he were concerned, would wait that long to put the contract in a safe deposit box. I went through several scenarios in my mind, none of which made real sense. I recalled the words of nameless experienced agents over the years: "Joe, only a rookie overcomplicates a case. Most often, the explanations are simple." With that thought, I left the State Welfare Department to contemplate my next move.

Protecting My Source

Ross Laben was munching on a doughnut.

Staring at his expanding waistline, I teased him. "Ross, all you need is a blue uniform, and you'd look exactly like the cop in the Dunkin' Donuts commercial," I said.

Ross looked at me for a few seconds, then retorted with a grunt.

He and I liked each other. But either of us would have stood in front of a bullet before admitting it. That was simply something a macho agent would have never said. So we showed our affection for each other by teasing a lot.

I showed Ross my copy of the LDC contract and explained that a source told me of its existence. Agents respected the confidential nature of a source's relationship with an investigator. So I didn't have to explain that Sally Mulcasey had turned me on to the document.

"Does your source suspect this contract is flaky?" Ross asked.

"My source doesn't know," I answered. "But my source suspects a guy by the name of Flavous Lambert may be involved."

Ross's eyes lit up immediately. "*The* Flavous Lambert?"

"Who is he?" I asked.

"He used to be a state senator years ago. Since he left politics, Flavous has been hanging around the back rooms of the capitol as a lobbyist," Laben said. "Flavous and Bill Burgin go back to law school at Ole Miss."

"That's great," I exclaimed enthusiastically, recalling that Sally had told me essentially the same thing. But I didn't tell Ross what I knew — that Sally Mulcasey had seen Lambert put a copy of the contact in a safe deposit box.

When I thought about it for a second, I realized I couldn't tell anyone what I knew without compromising Sally. Even though I'd promised her nothing, I was going to do everything I could do to protect her. Would I have gone that far, I wondered, for someone who was not flirting so outrageously with me?

Ross snapped me out of my trance. "So if you have Flavous Lambert involved in a state contract, I'd say that Burgin can't be far behind," he observed. "But proving a connection between them may be difficult."

Hello, I'm a Reporter . . .

I decided to start the process by running some checks on LDC, the Nashville company. Through public records, we were able to establish that LDC was a small outfit owned by someone from Tennessee. The owner had no black marks on his record, and as near as we could tell, he had been in business for about five years. An agent in Nashville drove by LDC's address and determined that it was a small space in a retail strip mall. The agent thought maybe fewer than ten people worked for LDC.

After gathering the preliminary information, I had to decide if I was ready to talk to LDC. The prospect seemed premature; I really didn't know anything other than that LDC had the contract and that Flavous Lambert was somehow involved. I didn't even have a direct connection to Burgin. So I decided to try to establish some sort of paper trail between LDC and Burgin. I reasoned that there would be some documentation of the procedure leading to the contract award. But locating the paper turned out to be more difficult than I had thought.

So far, it hadn't been necessary to identify myself to get a copy of the LDC contract. But I wasn't sure I could get the right documentation from the state — if it even existed — without revealing that I was an FBI agent. The answer was to conceal myself behind the telephone. So I called various state agencies, posing as a reporter for the Jackson *Clarion-Ledger*, the largest newspaper in Mississippi. I said I was writing an article on doing business with the state, and that I wanted to find out exactly how people and companies were awarded contracts. After getting the normal bureaucratic runaround, I finally landed a nice lady who had nothing better to do than talk to me in her slow, southern drawl.

"A reporter," the lady repeated. "Now, that must be a real interesting job."

I assured her that it was.

"My daughter is in college, and she said she'd like to be a reporter," the lady said. "But I heard that a reporter's job doesn't pay very much."

I told her it didn't — having no real idea if that were the truth.

Lynchburg, Virginia, 1971: Escorting Miss U.S.A. Deborah Shelton

San Antonio, Texas, circa 1950: Vola, Cotton, Sue and Joe Wells

Duncan, Oklahoma, circa 1990: My mother Vola, her husband V.K. McMasters, Judy and me

New York, New York, 1991: John Stossel and me during filming of ABC News' *20/20*

Rural west Texas, circa 1987: My friend Rob Parnell and me having a laugh on the ranch of client Max Vance

Duncan, Oklahoma, circa 1949: Joseph Thomas Wells

Brenham, Texas, 2006: Me with my Pulsar airplane

Washington, D.C., 2004: Delivering the opening remarks at the ACFE Annual Fraud Conference

MACHINE SHOP

MACHINE SHOP MORNING CLASS

Duncan, Oklahoma, 1961: My Machine Shop class with Mr. Brown

Austin, Texas, 2002: Official ACFE photograph

Quantico, Virginia, 1972: With classmates at the FBI Academy

Londonderry, Northern Ireland, 1963: The memorial service for slain U.S. President John F. Kennedy

San Diego, California, 1962: Leading Company 306 at U.S. Navy recruit training graduation

Vola and Coyle Wells, circa 1940

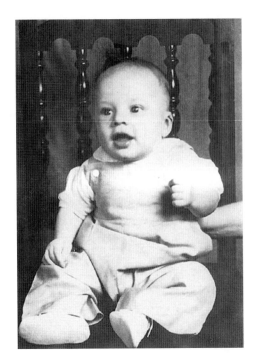

Joseph Thomas Wells,
circa 1944

Duncan,
Oklahoma, 1973:
Margaret and
Tina Dean and me

California desert, 1951: My cousins and me (on right)

Duncan, Oklahoma, 1954: My first-grade class

Quantico, Virginia, 1972: My FBI Academy graduating class

Duncan, Oklahoma, 1962: The prettiest girl in high school

Austin, Texas, 2000: ACFE Headquarters Staff in front of the Gregor Building

Bellville, Texas, July 4, 2005: I'm proud to be an American!

Berlin, Germany, September 2003: East Berlin is on the other side of the fence

Chicago, Illinois, July 2006: Academy Award winner Cliff Robertson and me

Austin, Texas, circa 1978: FBI agents and me clowning around

Jackson, Mississippi, 1976: Saying "No comment" to a television reporter on the investigation of State Senator William G. Burgin, Jr.

Austin, Texas, 1983: My wedding to the former Judy Gregor

Londonderry, Northern Ireland, 1964: Answering questions about
transmitters from the undersecretary of the U.S. Navy

Quantico, Virginia, 1972: On the FBI Academy firing range

Gruene, Texas, 1984: Playing guitar with the Lee Roy Parnell Band

San Diego, California, August 1962: Receiving the American Spirit Honor Medal

Austin, Texas, 1988: Filming a training video with Academy Award winner Robert Stack

Santa Barbara, California, 1985: Meeting Dr. Donald R. Cressey for the first time

Austin, Texas, 1990: The cover photo for the album *Standing in the Middle of the Stream* by Joe and the Debits

Austin, Texas, 1981: In the recording studio owned by Christopher Cross and me

Londonderry, Northern Ireland, 1964: In the Navy barracks with Marty Lowman

Austin, Texas, 1983: Attendees at the wedding of Judy and me

Duncan, Oklahoma, 1962: Graduating from high school

San Diego, California, 1962: The last time I saw my dad

Bellville, Texas, circa 1985: Judy with her parents, Jenny and Jerry Gregor, and me

Shannon, Ireland, 1963: Me kissing the Blarney Stone

Bellville, Texas, 1993: Judy with her brother, Rusty, his wife, Carrie, and me at the Blue Bonnet Ball

Austin, Texas, circa 1994: Playing with friends in a local club

Austin, Texas, 1998: Jim Ratley, Kathie Lawrence and me

Finally, after several minutes of chitchat, the nice lady finally asked, "Now, what was that you wanted again?"

"I'm trying to find out what a person — say me — would need to do to get business from the State of Mississippi," I repeated.

"Oh, yes." she recalled. "It's kind of complicated. But the first thing is for the state to request a product or service. Most of the time, these are developed by the agency that needs it. You would look at the public postings for all the contracts. They're either published in the state register or are advertised through the largest newspapers in the state, including yours," she said. "So after you got notice of the request, you'd submit a sealed bid to the proper agency, which would review it and decide who would be awarded the business."

Recalling that Burgin's responsibility with the senate Appropriations Committee was to allot state funds, I asked, "How are the funds allotted to the agency itself?"

"The agency prepares an annual budget which includes their request for a particular product or service. That budget is then submitted to the senate Appropriations Committee, which can adjust the final numbers up or down," she explained.

The nice lady seemed to be telling me that — in the case of LDC — Fred St. John, the head of the welfare department, would request $780,000 from the senate Appropriations Committee, headed by Bill Burgin. She also pointed me to the source of the documents: the state welfare department. In other words, in order to delve further into the LDC contract, St. John's people would have to pull the paperwork. I thought for a minute and decided I didn't want my interest getting back to St. John just yet.

I thanked the lady for her time and assistance, and then called the state treasury. I found out that all of the checks issued by each agency were maintained in the treasury's archives. I could therefore get copies of the checks from the state to LDC; I might even be able to get the originals without revealing my hand.

Digging for Dollars

Next, I spent three days in the basement of the treasury building, thumbing through thousands of canceled checks maintained in the archives. On the first day, I located one LDC payment. The second day, I didn't find any. But the third day, I found four checks paid by the state to LDC. By wearing surgical gloves, I managed to keep my prints off the checks. Eventually, the state treasurer allowed the FBI to have the actual checks, and copies were substituted in place of the originals.

Now I had five checks payable to LDC from the state treasury. This gave me information on where the LDC bank account was kept. But that didn't tell me much I didn't know already. Perhaps, I mused, one of the high-ranking officials — Burgin or St. John or Lambert — may have touched the check. The idea was worth wasting a couple of weeks to find out. I submitted all five checks to the FBI Identification Section in Washington to have them dusted for prints.

I killed the interim time working on a variety of other cases. The television image of a detective doesn't capture the real story: You never see one of those heroes working on one of the many piddling cases that must be processed through the system. But in real life, my bread-and-butter white-collar crime offenses normally involved bank employees — including a lot of tellers — who couldn't keep their fingers out of the till.

One day, when conducting just such an investigation of a single female employee, I thought about Sally Mulcasey. In a way, she was the ideal bank embezzler: someone you wouldn't suspect. I wondered to myself what Sally was really like. Obviously, something was behind those beautiful, calculating eyes. I remembered back several months ago, when we first talked about her helping in the case, Sally demanded that I not ask too many questions. I've learned over the years that people who don't want to answer questions usually have a self-protective reason for not doing so. Her secretiveness puzzled me.

In the middle of one of my many thoughts about Sally, the fingerprint technician called me from the Identification Section in Washington. It had the effect of throwing ice water in my face.

"We ran the five checks," the technician reported. "The only useful prints are on the check dated December 15. We have two different sets of prints on that one. The first set of prints belongs to Fred W. St. John. The second set belongs to William G. Burgin, Jr."

The technician — who had no idea of the details of the case — heard me suck in hard. "Evidently, you're shocked at that information," he said.

That was an understatement. I couldn't imagine why both the chairman of the Mississippi state senate Appropriations Committee and the state welfare commissioner would have their fingerprints on a check made payable to Learning Development Corporation of Nashville, Tennessee.

I thanked the technician for the oral briefing. He told me he'd confirm the results in writing. Like clockwork, I received his written report two weeks later. When it arrived, I was still debating with myself what the fingerprints of two state officials on a vendor's check meant. The most logical explanation was that Burgin, St. John, and the head of LDC were in some sort of meeting together where the threesome handled the check. When the report from Washington reached Jackson, I walked over to the United States Attorney's office with the document. James Beauregard Turner, hunching over the report with a cigarette, let the smoke drift into one eye while he read with the other. Ashes from the cigarette fell onto the report, prompting me to say "Damn, Beauregard, don't set my case on fire."

He looked up long enough to catch my eye, and then returned to reading the report. "It sure as hell is curious why

Burgin's and St. John's prints are on this vendor's check," Turner mused aloud. "Perhaps this is enough predication to commence an active investigation."

Mixed Feelings

The term *predication* was almost holy in the criminal investigative field. It was the legal basis upon which an investigation was commenced. Investigations could not be started on mere suspicion, which is what I had until the prints turned up on the check. If Beauregard believed I had sufficient predication to start investigating Burgin, then one major hurdle had been overcome. From there, it would become a matter of figuring out the best way to accomplish the investigation of William G. Burgin, Jr., et al.

I left Beauregard's office much happier than when I arrived. Since Roxanne's office was just down the hall, I stopped in to say hello. We had been a couple for nearly a year now, and it continued to be a volatile relationship. I don't know what we liked better — fighting or making up. When I stepped into Roxanne's office, she greeted me with a delightful squeal and a hug.

"Hey, G-Man," she said, "what a great surprise."

I told her, without being specific, that I had received some good news on an investigation.

"Well," Roxanne said, her eyes sparkling, "does that mean we should celebrate?"

"I guess so," I said. "Perhaps I can afford to take you to dinner tonight."

"I don't want dinner, and I don't want to wait. No one's in the office today but you and me," Roxanne said as she closed and locked the door.

A bit later, after leaving Roxanne's office, I dropped by Fidelity Bank to see George Sewell, who hadn't heard from me in a while. As usual, Sally was sitting at her desk, outside Sewell's office. But not as usual, Sally didn't seem either surprised or happy to see me. Rather than her usual flirtation, she simply said, "I guess you're here to see Mr. Sewell." She didn't even look me in the eye.

I had no official reason to see George Sewell, but I wanted to keep in contact with him in case he could help in some way later in the investigation. Or was it just an excuse to see Sally Mulcasey again? After spending a few minutes with Sewell, I went back to the lobby and sat down at Sally's desk. She looked up at me this time, staring for an instant too long.

"Sally, is something wrong?"

"Well, I was going to ask you the same thing. I haven't heard from you lately, and I thought maybe you didn't like me anymore." Sally's eyes searched mine for a reaction.

"Of course I like you, Sally."

"Then what do I have to do in order for you to ask me out?" she asked. "I've done just about everything I can think of except throwing myself in front of a train."

"I'm already seeing someone," I said simply.

Sally looked at me silently for a while. Then she asked, "Are you engaged or married?"

"No," I replied, shaking my head.

She smiled. "Then I still have a chance?"

I returned her smile. "Sally, any man would be lucky to have you, including me."

"Well, I've been wondering," Sally said earnestly. "Since I got divorced, no one has asked me out. It's starting to bother me."

All of a sudden, it bothered me too, but for the wrong reason. For an instant, I felt a wave of jealousy at the thought of Sally going out with other men. I had no claim on her, though, and I was involved with Roxanne. My feelings made no sense whatsoever, but there they were. I got up from Sally's desk before she could see the look on my face. "Sally, it's only a matter of time until you find the right guy," I said optimistically.

The Third Man

After deciding to approach Fred St. John, I dropped by his office. I didn't have an appointment, but had called to be sure he was in. I had learned long ago that important interviews are best conducted by surprise. Had I called ahead and made an appointment, St. John could have been unavailable. Or he could request that his lawyer be present. Or he could have had time to make up a story. It wouldn't do to try to see someone like St. John without an appointment if I were a constituent or an ordinary citizen. But when an agent identifies himself as being with the FBI, it is surprising how many important people can make the time to see him. It was no exception with St. John — when I walked into his office, I could see the look of curiosity on his face.

"Good morning," I said, introducing myself.

St. John's office was what you could expect from a high-level state politician — large and cheaply furnished. Behind his desk were the requisite photos of him standing with other notables. I guess the purpose of those pictures is to impress visitors with your high political station. I couldn't help but notice that there was a photo of St. John standing with Burgin, their arms entwined.

"Mr. Wells," St. John acknowledged. "Is the FBI making a courtesy call?" he asked, with no attempt to conceal his curiosity. After showing me to a chair in front of his desk, he pulled one up for himself. St. John's aristocratic name fit his demeanor and appearance. He was obviously from good stock, and was impeccably dressed. Tall, slim, with thick salt-and-pepper hair, he could have passed for an aging athlete.

"No, Mr. St. John, I'm afraid this isn't a courtesy call, although I'm certainly happy to meet you," I said, trying to disarm him with a smile. It didn't work.

St. John was looking carefully at me for a clue as to why I was there.

I wore my best poker face. It was risky talking to St. John at this point. One way or another, he was likely to tell Burgin of my visit. That may not be bad, I thought to myself. But I had to be careful what I disclosed. "As you know," I continued, "the FBI's responsibility partly involves situations where federal funds are parceled out to the states. More specifically, we're interested in any contract irregularities in that regard. I know the Mississippi Department of Public Welfare is largely funded with federal money. So, I wonder if you have any information that some of the contracts you have signed on behalf of the state were forced on your agency by politicians."

St. John took his time answering. He had on his poker face too. "I'm afraid I don't understand, Mr. Wells," he finally said.

"Has any state official forced you to sign a contract against your better judgment?" I asked pointedly.

"No," St. John claimed with a questioning look.

"Okay. That's all I need for now," I said, getting up from the chair.

If St. John was worried about my question, he would probably try to get additional information out of me.

"Wait a minute," he said. "Surely you wouldn't come all this way to ask a question like that. There must be more to it. What's going on?"

"That's what I'm trying to figure out, Mr. St. John. I thought, since you have the largest budget in state government, you might know. I guess I was wrong."

St. John followed me out into the hall and all the way to the elevator. I suspected the average constituent wasn't afforded that courtesy. I shook hands with him as I stepped on the elevator, and told him I might be in touch. When the doors closed, something told me St. John would be the one calling; he looked worried.

Good, I thought.

Lay Down, Sally

This time I called her. Sally had been on my mind since yesterday, when Roxanne and I had a big argument. Roxanne had grabbed a suitcase and headed off to her mom's. That was all too common for Roxanne — to say she was a spoiled brat would be an understatement. When Sally answered the phone, I said, "This is one of your many admirers. I wonder if you could crowd me into your date book for dinner sometime."

"Now, you have to define 'dinner' before I can answer that question," Sally retorted. "Here in the South, 'dinner' is lunch. So are you asking me for dinner or supper?"

"Take your pick," I said.

"Then I'll take supper. How about my place at eight tonight? You can bring a bottle of Stoly and I'll make you one of my killer martinis. We can grill steaks."

I was relieved that she was having me over. If we went out to dinner, there was always a chance I'd be spotted by a friend of Roxanne's. But I didn't say that. Instead, I said, "Don't you want me to take you to a fancy restaurant and spend some real money on you? After all, this is an official date."

"No," Sally said, "I want you all to myself. See you at eight." The phone clicked in my ear; end of discussion.

On my lunch hour, I went to one of Mississippi's state-controlled liquor stores. A bottle of Stolichnay was almost $20. I wondered why, when the government was involved, things almost always cost more. In Texas, where the free market ruled, the same bottle was half that price. My cynical self decided it was because of the corruption in state government. I took the bottle home on my lunch hour, and put it in the freezer. It would be ice-cold by "supper."

At 8:00, I rang the door to Sally's apartment. It took her a while to answer. When she finally opened the door, it appeared at first that she had grown by several inches. Then I looked down. She was wearing a very short, tight black skirt and spiked high heels. "Hope you don't mind the outfit," she said, grinning. "Since I've been out of circulation, I haven't had a chance to really dress up for a guy. I enjoy it."

So did I. Sally looked incredibly sexy standing there.

I was speechless, so I simply handed her the bottle of Stoly.

"Great," she exclaimed. "It's been in the freezer. I didn't realize you were so urbane."

Neither did I. But in the more-than-a-few martinis I'd had over my short life, I discovered that the vodka tasted better when it was icy cold. When it came out of the freezer, it was thick, like syrup. But with all the alcohol in 100-proof Stoly, it would never freeze.

Sally quickly and expertly made a shaker of martinis. We toasted, and downed our first drink. Like most martinis, this first one tasted harsh; much better to sip carefully. I guess we were both nervous. In a mere few minutes, the warmth of the martini came over me, and I was ready for a second. Sally poured for both of us. Then she sat down in an overstuffed chair and motioned me to sit on the sofa beside her. We drank silently, savoring the feeling of the ice-cold liquor.

She looked at me seductively and broke the silence. "You know, it's very nice of you to take pity on a lonely divorcée." Sally then sat down on the couch beside me, pulled me to her, and closed her mouth over mine. Even though I'd been drinking myself, I could taste the Stoly on her.

"Sally, are you trying to seduce me?" I slurred slightly.

"Of course I am," she said. "But you knew that when I invited you over, didn't you?" She took my hand and slid it up the inside of her thigh.

"I guess I did," I admitted to her. And to myself.

Follow the Money

The phone rang. It was Assistant United States Attorney James Beauregard Turner. I could hear him sucking on his cigarette even before he said anything. He told me my request for a subpoena for the records of Learning Development Corporation in Nashville had been approved. I could pick it up at my convenience at his office.

I went over right away. After punching the elevator button, I got off on the second floor of the federal building. Roxanne's office was to the left; Beauregard's was straight ahead. I turned left. It had been a week since our last argument — the night I saw Sally. Although Roxanne and I were pretty much living together, I still kept my apartment, thank God. It came in very handy when we were fighting.

Roxanne wasn't glad to see me. I was glad she wasn't glad. Right now, I felt guilty about Sally, and I didn't want to make up with Roxanne. For one thing, I was getting sick of the arguments. Even though Roxanne may have been the most beautiful woman on earth to me at the time, nothing could convince her of that. She was one insecure, rich, spoiled, southern princess. And the highest-maintenance woman I'd known.

So after exchanging a few frosty sentences with Roxanne, I went to Beauregard's office, and picked up the subpoena. I had the option of sending the subpoena to Nashville to get it served by a local agent there, or of serving it myself. I decided to make the trip.

A few days later, I was standing in the office of LDC in Nashville. The owner was surprised to see a subpoena for his records, to say the least. I explained to him that he had two choices at this point. First, he could appear at the federal grand jury in Jackson with all of his business records. Or second, if he preferred, he could turn certain records over to me. In that case, he wouldn't have to make a personal appearance at the grand jury. Like most people, he chose the latter.

I immediately began the examination of his records, which lasted two hours. It didn't take very long to find the smoking gun; the evidence I was after was in the checkbook. I was able to trace each monthly payment from the State of Mississippi to LDC's deposit slips. As far as I could tell, the state was LDC's only source of income.

Then I reviewed the canceled checks. It stuck out like a sore thumb — large payments to a Georgia bank for deposit to the account of DFL Enterprises. Indeed, every deposit from the State of Mississippi was $65,000 per month, and the checks to DFL from LDC, also paid every month, were for the sum of $32,500. So it was obvious that fully one-half of the monthly deposits were going back out somewhere. I smiled to myself at the possibility that DFL Enterprises could be D. Flavous Lambert. I obtained the necessary records from LDC and returned to Jackson. LDC's owner was extremely nervous during my visit, I told myself on the return flight. Good. We'll see if anything happens. It did.

My next day in the office, there was already a message to call State Welfare Commissioner Fred St. John. I was immediately put through to him.

"Mr. Wells," he explained, "I've been giving our previous conversation some thought, and wonder if you and I could get together and talk some more."

"Sure," I said.

We made an appointment for him to come to the FBI office the next morning. Mr. St. John had originally wanted to meet me in a restaurant for coffee. But from an investigative standpoint, it would be better to have him on my turf. Not only would that give me control over the situation, it would also provide me with a psychological advantage; St. John would be much less comfortable at the FBI office.

He arrived 15 minutes before the appointed time. Since agents had their desks in the squad room, it was not an appropriate place to conduct a sensitive interview. It was early in the morning, so the interview room was empty. It was small and windowless — on purpose — not a place to be used for idle chitchat. There were no distractions. No pictures. No windows. No place to escape. St. John didn't mince words once we were in the interview room with the door closed.

"I think you believe I'm engaged in some sort of impropriety," he began.

Leaning on my FBI training, I answered his question with another: "Why would you think that?" I asked.

"Mr. Wells, let's don't play cat and mouse," he said immediately at my attempt to be coy. "You didn't come to me just to ask if I knew of any improprieties in our contracts. You think I know something, and you're not telling me what I'm supposed to know."

Under Oath

Aha, I thought: a fishing expedition. He obviously knows I visited LDC and got those records. I wondered if he knew I had his prints — along with Senator Burgin's — on a $65,000 check to LDC.

I didn't answer St. John's question directly. Instead, I said, "Mr. St. John, in view of your visit, I think it's best to handle this matter formally. You may know that, as an FBI agent, I'm empowered to take sworn statements from public officials. Before we continue this interview, please raise your right hand and take the oath."

St. John looked at me quizzically; nonetheless, his right hand automatically shot into the air. He had fallen for a basic trick of the investigator: If you want someone's cooperation, don't ask for it.

Instead, act like it is a routine procedure and assume they'll go along. Once I had St. John sworn in, I knew it would be difficult for him to answer some very pointed questions.

I agreed with St. John — no playing cat and mouse. So I used the direct approach. "Mr. St. John," I began, "I'm curious as to why you called me when you did. Who told you that I had visited the offices of LDC?"

On purpose, I didn't ask if anyone had contacted him to convey the news; that would have called for an automatic denial by St. John.

The welfare commissioner was visibly shaken when I mentioned LDC. He quickly recovered, though. "I don't know what you're talking about," St. John said, sounding not very convincing.

I had expected no less from him. But over the next two hours, I managed to get the basics of St. John's story. The key was telling St. John I had his fingerprints on a check made payable to LDC. When I finally shot that rifle, St. John looked as though he had been wounded. As a result, he told me an interesting story.

St. John said he never heard of LDC before Burgin called him. Burgin told St. John LDC was a great company that could help the state welfare department provide educational services to disadvantaged youths. Although St. John did not press the issue, he quickly got the message that doing business with LDC would please Burgin, the source of most of St. John's funding. It was easy to understand why St. John did not ask many questions of Burgin — something about biting the hand that feeds you.

So St. John knew what was going on, in an indirect sort of way. But like many natural politicians, he was interested ultimately in deniability. That deniability was severely compromised by St. John's fingerprints being on a state check for $65,000. So after mentally assessing his options, the welfare commissioner finally opted for the truth.

"In early December of last year," St. John began, "I got a call from Bill Burgin." The welfare commissioner exhaled audibly. "Burgin said that LDC had not received its December check from the state, and he asked me to look into it. Burgin told me that LDC was a small company and that its employees would be depending on the state's money to pay them for the holidays."

Burgin asked St. John to follow up and see if he could get LDC's check for $65,000 cut right away. Within a day, St. John had the money in his hand. He called Burgin, who insisted on picking up the check personally. So a couple of days before Christmas, Burgin visited St. John's office, and St. John handed him the LDC check. That, St. John said, was why the fingerprints of both Burgin and St. John were on the December check. Boom. Just like that, I had the makings of a case. St. John left the office, and my brain was reeling.

Flavous in the Flesh

Since our last argument two weeks earlier, I hadn't seen much of Roxanne. And even if I had, it wouldn't have been appropriate to tell her I was developing a pretty damn good case against Bill Burgin. Such a disclosure would not only have been a violation of FBI protocol; there was the issue with her parents. I'd begun to realize a permanent relationship between Roxanne and me wasn't possible, but I wasn't ready to inform her of that — yet.

My next stop in the investigation was the bank in Atlanta to examine the records of DFL Enterprises. It came as no surprise to me that this wasn't a business; it was simply a bank account, and only one person had signature authority — D. Flavous Lambert.

I traced the deposits to DFL Enterprises' bank account from LDC, and it was all there; not a penny was unaccounted for. The DFL checks, in their entirety, were made payable to Bill Burgin's law firm account, and were personally endorsed by him.

I thought to myself: How stupid or arrogant can a man be to accept bribes by check? But that is what he did. He wasn't stupid at all; he'd just been corrupt for so long that he had built an illusion of invincibility around himself.

I shared the news with Beauregard, who was elated. "Damn!" he exclaimed. "Why would Burgin be so stupid to leave a paper trail so clearly marked?"

I repeated my theory about arrogance; Beauregard held his chin and nodded.

Although we could have taken our case directly to the grand jury, it was FBI policy to interview suspects before that happened. In this situation, it would be Lambert and Burgin. The standard Bureau technique was to start interviews at the outer edges with people least likely to be deeply involved, and to work your way inward, ending up with your main suspect. You just had to make sure you secured all the physical evidence you could before conducting interviews. Otherwise, documents and the like had a way of disappearing.

Lambert was where I began. I located him in a dingy, one-room office not far from the capitol. I knocked on the door and Lambert, I presumed, shouted, "Come on in!" He was talking on the telephone and motioned for me to sit in a chair across from his desk. While he was on the phone, I took the liberty of looking around his office. The paint was peeling from the walls, there were stacks of files scattered haphazardly on every level surface and many ashtrays, filled to the brim with stale cigars. This was not a place to which I'd have brought a potential client, so I surmised this was Lambert's hideout.

I'd never seen Lambert, but had developed a mental picture of what I expected him to look like. I thought he'd be short and overweight, and he was. As a matter of fact, cigar ashes had fallen on his ample gut while he was on the phone. I had imagined that he'd have a blustery demeanor, and he did. I had surmised that since he was in his mid-fifties, he would either be balding and/or have salt-and-pepper hair, but Lambert had neither. His locks were coal black, with not a trace of gray. He wasn't wearing a toupee (who among us couldn't spot one of those things from 50 yards away?), so I concluded that the blackness of his hair came from a bottle. Although I'm no fashion maven, I thought the look was totally bizarre.

Lambert got up from his desk, smiled, and shook my hand. I said "I'm Joe Wells from . . ." and that's as far as I got.

The smile quickly disappeared from his face and he finished my sentence. ". . . from the FBI," he said. "I have nothing to say to you. Get out of my office."

"Mr. Lambert, of course you don't have to speak to me. But your other choice is to be called before a federal grand jury," I advised.

Lambert said, "I thought you FBI guys had to take a hearing test. You obviously flunked yours." Then he cupped his two hands around his mouth, megaphone style, and said in a louder voice, "I told you to get out of my office. And I mean now!" The veins in his forehead and neck looked as though they would burst at any second.

I got up from the chair, left the room without saying a word, and softly closed his office door behind me. I knew it'd be only be a matter of minutes before Lambert would call Burgin about my surprise visit. Good.

Time to Say Goodbye

Roxanne called me at the office, something she rarely did. There was no place in the squad room for private conversations. "I need to see you after work," she said solemnly.

I had an idea of what was on her mind, but agreed to meet her about 6:00 at one of our favorite watering holes.

As I sat at the table opposite her, Roxanne's beautiful eyes were glistening. She was on the verge of tears. "As you know," she continued, "we spend almost as much time fighting as we do making love. I can't take it anymore."

I simply nodded.

"When we first met and fell in love," she said, "I was certain we'd marry someday, and raise a family in a nice home with a white picket fence around it. But you've never asked me to marry you, and I don't think you ever will. I'm over 30, and still want children. After we started dating, it gradually sunk in that you're eventually going to get transferred somewhere else. I love Jackson. I was born and raised here, and all my friends and family are here. I won't live anywhere else. And one of my friends spotted you with a gorgeous blonde recently. You needn't deny it; I know it's true. Her name is Sally, and she works for a bank. Why would you do that to me?"

I stared down at my glass for what seemed like an eternity, rubbing the top of the rim with my finger, saying nothing.

Roxanne finally asked, "Were you intimate with her?"

I looked up at Roxanne, who by this time had tears streaming down both checks.

I was silent.

Then she burst out crying and said, "Well, I've never been unfaithful to you, but during our many troubles, I went to dinner with another man a couple of times. He's someone I think I could have a relationship with."

After she gathered what she could of her dignity, Roxanne said, "Joe, we both knew this would end sometime, somewhere. This is the time, and this is the place. I wish you the best." Then she stood, turned on her heel, and left.

I never saw her again. Within three months, she was engaged to the guy she described to me, and married shortly thereafter. He was a banker. Ironically, within a year he was indicted for bank fraud, and spent a year or two in lockup. It wasn't my investigative case. Roxanne divorced him while he was in prison.

Confronting Burgin

The day had finally come to try to interview Burgin. We knew he was in the capitol building. My mentor on the case, Ross Laben, was out somewhere so I asked John Max, another agent, to accompany me.

You could tell that Burgin was about to explode in a fit of rage. "Wells," he almost screamed, "get out of my office!"

"Senator," I replied, "this is not your office. It belongs to the citizens of Mississippi, and I have as much right to be standing here as anyone else. This is Special Agent John Max, who is familiar with the case. We'd like to ask you some questions about your role in awarding the LDC contract."

With a distorted smirk on his face, Burgin said, "I'll bet you would. But it's clear you're trying to frame me, an innocent man, for your own reasons, and I'm not going to fall for that."

"Senator," I said, "you have two choices: Tell your story to me or tell it to the grand jury. That's not a threat; it's a promise."

John Max and I quietly left the room. Burgin, through clinched teeth, said, "Wells, you don't know who you're messing with. You are toast."

We closed the door behind us, walked directly to Beauregard's office about three blocks away, and reiterated the conversation with Burgin. An hour later, we left with four grand jury subpoenas: one each for Burgin, Lambert, St. John, and the guy who owned LDC.

Lambert's office door was open and, as usual, he was on the telephone. I just dropped the subpoena on his desk without saying a word. He looked at it while he was on the phone. To add an element of drama, Lambert wadded up the subpoena and threw it in the trash.

We had the U.S. Marshals serve the subpoenas on Burgin and St. John, and we forwarded the one for the LDC owner to the Memphis FBI field office so they could deliver the not-so-good news.

Speaking of news, I got home to my tiny apartment that evening and switched on the TV just in time to hear Burgin ranting about me. "Agent Wells has cooked up this witch hunt to try and destroy my reputation. Why? I don't know, but it wouldn't surprise me if Wells is getting under-the-table money for this from one of my political enemies. All I ever did was recommend a contract that would bring educational services to disadvantaged children in Mississippi. My attorney will attempt to get this subpoena quashed but, failing that, I won't get indicted because I've done nothing illegal."

I had a good, hearty laugh and switched off the television. Before I fell into a deep slumber from a successful day, my last waking thought was being thankful that I had an unlisted phone number.

Not too surprisingly, the FBI office the next morning was ringed with television cameras, and newspaper reporters were standing on the steps.

"There he is!" one reporter was yelling and pointing in my direction. With that, the throng descended on me, shouting questions simultaneously. All that was seen on the evening news was me saying "No comment." This case easily drew more press than any in Mississippi since the brutal murder of three civil rights workers in the 1960s.

Burgin was wrong on both counts of his press conference predictions. The judge refused the motion to quash the subpoena, and Burgin was indicted for official corruption, along with his pal Lambert.

That led to more press conferences where Burgin could claim that I was "after him" and that I was "probably on the take."

Laughable as that was, I stuck to my "No comment" line. When the crowd finally dispersed, I went inside the FBI office and started working on other cases. I was sick of hearing Burgin's name, and besides, the investigative work was about 90 percent complete. With a trial at least several months away, I'd have plenty of time to wrap up any of the loose ends.

Sally's Secret

"Hello," I said to her on the phone, "would you like to go to dinner with me to celebrate our small but significant victory in the Burgin case? I couldn't have done it without you."

"Sure," she immediately responded. "My place?"

"No, I want you to dress in your finest, so I can take you out to the best restaurant in Jackson and show you off," I replied.

She came to her door in a breathtaking woman's winter off-white tuxedo, replete with satin lapels and stripes down the side of the pants. She was easily the most beautiful woman in the whole place, and I was proud to be with her. Sally ordered scallops, and I requested lobster with drawn butter. Although it's my favorite meal, because of the cholesterol I limit myself to having it only three or four times a year. Our dishes were prepared to perfection, and we enjoyed every bite. The meal cost me almost two weeks' salary, but was worth it.

The waiter brought around the dessert menu, but Sally told him it would be at least ten minutes before we ordered. She got right to the point. "What happened with you and your other girl?" she asked.

"Sally, we fought nearly all of the time. I'm not going to live like that."

She nodded knowingly, and then changed the subject. "Do you think I'll be called as a witness in the Burgin trial?"

"I seriously doubt it," I replied. "All you did was direct me to a public document, which anyone has the right to see. I've never written your name in an FBI report; no one knows of your involvement but me, and if somehow I were asked about it on the stand, I'd claim the law enforcement informant privilege. Ultimately, it'll be the judge's decision, though."

Miss Mulcasey looked at me for a time, not saying a word. She finally said, "You and I have a chance for a serious relationship. To me, truthfulness is at the top of the pyramid, and it's one of the things I respect about you the most. So I've decided to tell you why I wouldn't allow questions about Mr. Sewell.

"By the time I moved to Jackson after getting out of college, my marriage was in tatters. My husband probably didn't stay here two months. I came home one day after work, and all of his stuff was gone. I was alone. About six months later, Mr. Sewell asked me whether I'd like to make an extra $500 a week. That would have effectively doubled my salary. My head was reeling. What would I need to do to earn this extra money? I thought I knew the answer, but he'd be the one to ask the question."

"Sally," she said Sewell told her, "my wife hates oral sex, giving or receiving. I think in 30 years of marriage, she has maybe given me oral sex two times, and both times she was drunk. So to cut to the chase, you'd have to do that once a week."

Sally said she thought about it for quite a while. She was completely broke, had no groceries in the house, and wondered if she even had enough gasoline to get home.

"Do you have $500 on you?" Sally asked.

"Yes, I do," said George.

"Then go over and sit in that chair," she said she'd told him. And George did so.

Now it was time for my head to reel, but not about her peccadilloes. Who knew about this arrangement?

No one, Sally insisted.

How was she paid? Always in cash.

Where did the cash come from? She didn't know but doubted it came from bank funds.

Where did these trysts occur? Always in his office with the blinds closed.

Did they ever travel together and spend the night in a hotel? No.

Were they seen in public together for dinner, drinks, or social events? No.

Had Sally told any of her close friends or family about seeing Mr. Sewell on the sly? No, she said emphatically.

Is your "business relationship" still active? No.

How long did it go on? About two years.

Why did you stop? Sally sighed and said, "Because I met you, Special Agent Wells. Mr. Sewell completely understood when I told him; he likes you very much."

The Grand Jury

The newfound knowledge of the Sally-George relationship couldn't destroy a case against Burgin or Lambert, but it is exactly the kind of information that crafty defense attorneys would have a field day with if they found out — a smokescreen to make witnesses seem untrustworthy or immoral. It's one of the oldest tricks that lawyers use: If you can't attack the evidence, then attack the witness. I decided that a visit to Beauregard was not only prudent but necessary.

Without revealing Sally's identity, I told Beauregard most of the story. "Damn!" he said. "I sure hope none of this comes out at trial. It's irrelevant anyhow. Let's take this case to the grand jury."

Under the American system of justice, grand juries are somewhat of an anomaly. They are some of the few court procedures where a defendant or his attorney has no right to be present and listen to the allegations and discussions; the prosecutor is completely in charge of the show. Grand juries typically comprise 18 citizens who vote on one of two recommendations: dismiss the case or hand up indictments. In some instances, the grand jury can delay a decision, pending further investigation. But that rarely happens. There's an old saying in legal circles, "A good prosecutor can get a ham sandwich indicted."

A few weeks later, the grand jury convened to hear the Burgin-Lambert case. A mob of reporters milled around outside the courthouse, waiting for a decision. But inside, the situation was much more serene, thanks in part to the small army of federal marshals assigned to keep the peace. The grand jury session couldn't have been simpler. Beauregard provided a concise summary of our investigation to date, and made sure the jurors saw the checks from the state to LDC, from LDC to DFL Enterprises, and then directly to Senator Burgin. Beauregard called only two witnesses — St. John and me.

The whole process took less than an hour. By the time I arrived at my apartment late that evening, all of the local channels were covering the event live. As I pulled the bed covers over my head, I was once again thankful that the media didn't have my home number. The following morning, I padded out on the patio to get the paper.

The front-page headline screamed in gigantic type, "BURGIN, LAMBERT INDICTED."

Meeting Judy for the First Time

The FBI office was housed in the top two floors of the Unifirst Savings and Loan Building, at the corners of Capitol and State streets in Jackson. I'd worked a couple of fraud cases involving tellers at Unifirst, and knew some people in management. The others I sort of recognized from riding up and down with them in the elevators.

One of them was Judy Gregor, a beautiful, slender, auburn-haired girl. She looked to be in her mid-twenties, and I found out that she ran the S&L's steno pool and was recently divorced. Even though I was attracted to her, there was the not-so-small matter involving Sally Mulcasey.

Over a period of months, Judy and I got into the habit of meeting at an ice-cream place around the corner once a week or so in the afternoons to share a dish. To complicate my life, I asked Judy out, fully knowing that I was sort of involved with someone else and had just ended another relationship.

Luckily, Judy was already dating someone, and unlike me, she was prepared to be faithful to him. Oh well, I thought, there are more fish in the sea. Little did I know then that she would be my third and final wife.

Day of Reckoning

The trial of Burgin and Lambert took place at the Federal Courthouse in Gulfport, Mississippi. Because of all of the publicity in Jackson, the defense requested and was granted a change of venue. The legal proceedings lasted about two weeks. Beauregard Turner called numerous witnesses, but his key ones were the LDC guy and St. John.

On the witness stand, the LDC guy said that he had heard that Flavous Lambert was the person to see if he wanted to get a contract from the State of Mississippi. He had contacted Lambert, who said that such a contract could be arranged for a large finder's fee — in this case, half of the contract amount. The LDC guy had never met Burgin, but Lambert had told him that he had the connections with "the right people."

The contract was approved in a short time, he said, and Lambert told him where and how much to pay. The LDC fellow admitted that minimal services were provided under the contract, but he did defend what he had done for his money.

St. John testified that Burgin had contacted him by telephone, and told him that he wanted a contract awarded to LDC, but didn't explain. St. John knew better than to argue with Burgin, who held his agency's purse strings. St. John testified that Burgin had called him about the so-called Christmas check that LDC had not gotten. Burgin picked up the check himself from St. John's office.

Lambert declined to testify in his own behalf.

The last witness was Burgin. He spun a yarn that he had no idea that Lambert was collecting money from LDC. The "Christmas check," Burgin claimed, was a favor he did for Lambert without knowing the significance. The senator said that the money paid to him by Lambert was for attorney fees that Lambert had owed for years.

I was sitting at the prosecution table near the front of the courtroom, and could tell by their faces that the jury didn't believe Burgin.

Toward the end of his testimony, Burgin managed to get tears welled in his eyes and said, "There is no way that I would deprive the citizens of the great State of Mississippi of their hard-earned tax money." He then pulled out a red bandana handkerchief, and loudly blew his nose.

The scene was just too much for me; I burst out laughing. Then the jury started snickering.

The defense lawyer was on his feet immediately, shouting "Mistrial!"

Beauregard stared at me. The judge called for a recess and took me into his chambers alone. I don't remember exactly what he said, but he chewed my ass up and down.

Then the trial resumed, and both sides made their closing arguments. The jury got the case, and in less than four hours convicted both Lambert and Burgin on all counts.

After their appeals were exhausted, Lambert spent two years, and Burgin three, in federal prison. The LDC guy and St. John were not charged. Both Lambert and Burgin are now dead.

Part Three

MY OWN MASTER

Chapter 5

A New Start

Word got around of my success as a corruption fighter in Jackson. So in late 1977 when suspicions arose of corruption in the administration of then–Texas governor Dolph Briscoe, the Bureau sent me to Austin to investigate.

Ultimately, I concluded that the allegations were nothing but hot air. But it took longer than the 90 days I had been allotted for the case, and the easiest way for the FBI to handle that was to let me remain in Austin, which it did. That spelled the end of Sally and me. I didn't want to marry her, and although she didn't say so, the feeling was probably mutual.

When I got to Austin, I felt I'd arrived in heaven. The resident agency consisted of about a dozen agents. On my first day, the only other single guy in the office took me to Barton Springs, a beautiful park near downtown. Lying in the sun were at least 20 topless women, most of them probably coeds from the University of Texas. I decided right then and there that Austin was my home.

Moreover, the city, whose population at the time was about 200,000, had an outstanding music scene. Any night of the week, you could walk along Sixth Street and hear bands from all over the world play original songs. Austin now hosts a yearly music event, *South by Southwest*, which attracts hundreds of musicians and tens of thousands of fans. I lost count of the number of nights I spent in the club scene. It was a true paradox: FBI agent by day; rocker by night. My Bureau colleagues looked askance at my bohemian lifestyle, but I didn't care.

Because I played guitar — mostly rhythm — it was easy to find guys to jam with. Several later became famous. At a joint called the Austin Outhouse, I played the blues standard, "Crossfire," with the legendary Stevie Ray Vaughn, and I also jammed on rhythm for Christopher Cross — his real name is Chris Geppart — around Austin. Eventually, Chris scored big and recorded a hit album in L.A. I asked him why he didn't call me to play on it.

"Joe," he replied, "you know the answer to that — you ain't worth a damn."

At one point, Chris and I owned a recording studio together. It was a financial disaster, but we managed to get out of it by the skin of our teeth. As they were literally tearing down the walls to the studio, I managed to get in and record four original tunes.

I spent my first three months in Austin in a motel at the government's expense. When I was officially transferred in early 1978, I got a small furnished apartment. Because I'd not yet met a circle of friends in Austin, I spent weekends driving around aimlessly, familiarizing myself with the territory. Once I ended up on Lake Travis, one of the five Highland Lakes constructed during the 1930s for flood control on the lower Colorado River. Lake Travis was the largest — about 65 miles long — and the deepest, nearly 300 feet at the dam.

I happened on Briarwood Marina, which was managed by a retired Air Force pilot, Joe Potts. We became friends, and I returned to the marina nearly every weekend. A month or two later, I spied a 40-foot yacht for sale and carefully checked it out. By doing a bit of math, I discovered I could finance it at the bank for less than I was paying in rent, so I bought it and converted the vessel to a live-aboard. The drive from the marina to the FBI office was nearly 30 miles, but since I had a government car and gas allowance, living on a boat made perfect sense. I had two generators, a television, and air conditioning. The fuel was expensive, but worth it.

I had the boat for nearly three years, and discovered some facts previously unknown to me: In the winter, a marina is the loneliest place you can find; in the summer, it was almost impossible to get rest, especially on the weekends. A party atmosphere prevailed from Friday to Sunday night. Often I was pitched out of my bed after midnight by drunken boaters speeding into the marina. That soon caused me to find a quiet cove each weekend and anchor off.

The Love of My Life

The first three years I was in Austin, living on the boat, I didn't date seriously. My FBI colleagues thought I was getting laid constantly by a legion of women. And indeed, I tried to live a bachelor's dream, and bedded as many women as I could. Perhaps there were five or so at one time.

It helped that I could make up stories about my FBI work. That way I kept the bevy at bay, and saw each girl once a week. Rather than being a bachelor's dream, it was a nightmare. If I was exhausted from the night before and didn't want to have sex, the next woman would think I didn't want her any more. Constant lying and nonstop sex were wearing me out. Moreover, it was a very shallow existence — not my style. One by one, I quit seeing each of those women.

The life of an unmarried FBI agent was an odd one. Although I'd joined the Bureau after my LRB&M fellow auditor, Dan Imhoff, had told me that women would dig an FBI agent, the reality of using your macho-sounding occupation to attract females was a bit different.

Most of us learned the hard way how foolish it was to try impressing women by telling them what we did for a living. Many people were paranoid around FBI agents. Every human being has committed wrongs, some against the law and some not. So when people learned what my occupation was, they'd often be concerned I was listening carefully for evidence of offenses and might arrest them on the spot. Of course, the public at large didn't really understand what we agents did and that drumming up insignificant cases didn't interest us.

Then there was the type that would pester you with ridiculous questions, wanting to know, for example, how many people you had killed. Finally, there were law enforcement groupies, male and female, who were attracted to the power associated with being an agent. I avoided these kinds of people in social situations. When asked what I did for a living, I normally replied that I was an accountant for the federal government. It usually stopped talk of my career dead in its tracks.

One time my friend Bill Peterson and I stopped by a bar in Mississippi for a beer after work. At an adjacent table, two attractive women were chatting. Suddenly, a shrimp of a guy appeared at their table and sat down. Bill and I weren't trying to eavesdrop, but the tables were close together.

One woman asked the young man — who was trying to impress them — what he did for a living.

"I'm an undercover agent for the FBI," was his reply.

Bill's and my ears perked up. We knew this was bullshit. First, if he really was an undercover agent, he had just blown his cover. Second, at the time an agent had to be at least five foot seven, and he was a couple of inches short of that.

The ladies, however, didn't know they had an impostor on their hands, and he regaled them with tales of his phony exploits.

It was all Bill and I could do to keep straight faces. Just for fun, I leaned over and said to the guy, "Excuse me. We weren't trying to listen in, but that sounds like a really fascinating job. Can you tell us more?"

The shrimp happily complied, and his stories got wilder. When he'd complete one unbelievable tale, we'd ask for another.

Finally, one of the ladies asked what Bill and I did for a living.

Bill said, "I manage a shoe store at the mall."

"Oh, I'm just an auditor for Sears," I said.

The little guy was, of course, merely trying to get laid. But impersonating an FBI agent is a felony, and we could have dragged him out of the bar in cuffs. We said nothing, though, and paid our bill. But outside in the parking lot, we erupted into laughter. We never found out if the guy was successful with either woman.

In Austin, I had accompanied a date to a party at the home of one of her coworkers. I didn't know anyone there. We walked into the kitchen, where several people were standing around, sharing a joint. This was obviously not a comfortable situation for me. I was about to turn around and leave the room, when one person offered me a toke. I declined, and headed to the den.

But before I could make my getaway, my date exclaimed without thinking, "Oh, no, he can't smoke marijuana; he's an FBI agent."

Everyone fled that kitchen pronto — as if Scotty from *Star Trek* had beamed them up. That was our first and only date.

Months later, a wonderful, fateful thing happened — Judy Gregor walked back into my life. I hadn't seen her since two years earlier, in Jackson.

Dan Morelock, the security director at a local bank, called me. "Do you remember Judy Gregor?" he asked.

Of course I did, I replied.

"Well, she's working here in Austin for our bank, and she asked about you, wanted to know if you were married. I told her you weren't, but that I didn't know anything else. Judy said she'd love to hear from you."

Completely floored, I immediately called her, and was sitting before her desk within an hour.

Judy had grown up in the small Texas town of Bellville, married her high school sweetheart, and brought home a paycheck while he attended college. He took a job in Jackson and she followed him there, only to get divorced a couple of years later. When I had first met her in Jackson, she was dating someone else. But that later ended, and she longed to move back to Texas. In Austin, she was less than two hours from her family, with whom she had a very close relationship.

When Judy said she'd always been attracted to me, my heart soared. I told her that I too was divorced, and we immediately made a date. I took her to one of Austin's finest restaurants, Jeffrey's, where we had a romantic meal by candlelight. When it came time to pay the bill, I whipped out my American Express card, the only one I had. The waiter smugly told me they didn't accept American Express. Unfortunately, I didn't have much cash on me, so Judy got stuck with the tab on our first date. Terribly embarrassed, I promised to pay her back the next day, but she made light of the situation. We left the restaurant hand in hand, and I was smitten. I tenderly kissed her goodnight at her apartment door, and skipped all the way back to my car.

There is some controversy about our second date. At the end of the evening, we stood inside her apartment for several lingering kisses. Then she touched me in a sensitive place. Judy doesn't deny touching me, but claims that I put her hand there. Naturally, I've blamed it all on her for many years. She won't admit it, though.

I could write a book about how wonderful Judy is. She is the kindest, most giving and supportive person I've ever met. On top of that, she's beautiful, and takes great care of herself. I can't even imagine how my life would have turned out sans her support and love. After two failed marriages, I wasn't thrilled about the possibility of getting divorced again. So we dated for more than two years before I made a commitment. As I write this, we've been together for going on three decades. We tried for years to have children, but it simply wasn't in the cards.

I quit the FBI while Judy and I were dating. When we actually married, I had no real means of support; she didn't marry me for my money — I had none. But I'm getting ahead of the story.

My time with the FBI in Austin was largely a waste for two reasons. First, by the time I landed in Texas I had a bad attitude about the Bureau, even though I shouldn't have. Second, I had 13 years to go before I would even be eligible to retire, and I knew my chances of spending it all in Austin were small. However, there was no way I was going to leave my new adopted home so the thought was in my mind to find something else to do eventually.

Part of my bad attitude was because my second wife, Dawn, had followed me to Austin by getting a job transfer with the Social Security Administration. Supposedly it was to bring my stepdaughter, Beth, nearer to where I was. But by this time Beth was in high school, and I saw little of her. I didn't see much of Dawn either, and when I did, an argument almost always erupted.

Closing One Door; Opening Another

After I'd been in Austin for nearly three years, I walked into the office one day and a transfer letter awaited me. I was being sent to the division headquarters in San Antonio. Although the Alamo City is a nice place, I didn't like it; the division was located downtown in an ancient federal building, and there was little political corruption work, my specialty.

I made up my mind then and there to resign and gave 90 days' notice. I had no idea what I would do to earn a living, but at least I wouldn't have to worry about getting transferred. The life of an agent seemed to be living in a place you hated and scheming to get out. Or being in a place you loved and scheming to stay there.

My supervisor, Greg, told me that I was getting assigned to San Antonio because I was "overqualified" to be in Austin. But I suspected that the powers that be at the division headquarters worried about my lifestyle. The FBI wasn't a great place for a single agent. Believe it or not, premarital sex — even among singles who were consenting adults — was frowned upon even then. If a former girlfriend complained to the FBI about you for some reason, trouble was sure to follow. It hadn't happened to me, but it did to other unmarried agents.

In my final year as an agent, I interviewed a young college student who'd lost perhaps $10,000 in an investment swindle. That was not a life-changing amount of money for most employed professionals, but it was a small fortune to a college guy. Or so I thought. We spoke in a private apartment complex near the University of Texas campus.

The victim, David Scofield, was a young business student. After I got the details of his loss through the investment swindle, we chatted a bit. I found out I had no reason to feel sorry for him: He owned the apartment building where I was interviewing him, and had two small businesses on top of that — an amazing feat for someone so young who hadn't inherited money.

One of these small businesses was called University Refrigerators. Its sole purpose was to rent dorm refrigerators on the University of Texas campus to students. David was graduating soon, and said he was going to sell his apartment complex and both businesses. Under him, University Refrigerators was extremely profitable.

He'd deliver the refrigerators on the first day of the fall semester, pick them up on the last day of the spring semester, and store them over the summer. His sole advertising was notices posted in the dorms, with a phone number for students to call. On the rare occasion when a refrigerator broke down, he'd replace it with a spare from among several hundred in his inventory.

After speaking with David two or three times, I finally decided to buy the business from him — plunging myself headlong into debt. I hired a student to take orders, collect money and replace any malfunctioning refrigerators. I had the business for about three years — one year before I left the Bureau, and two years afterward.

The second year I embarked on a serious expansion effort that nearly broke me the third year. I'd managed to grow the operation to six campuses, both within and outside Texas. I borrowed the money for that too. At the time I bought the business, the dorm refrigerator rental market was only about five years old. I didn't know — and had no way of knowing — that a national refrigerator rental chain had been formed, and was expanding quickly.

Suddenly, it showed up on the University of Texas campus and immediately undercut my price. Until then I had a near monopoly. My powerful new competitor, headquartered in Tulsa, soon would expand into all of my markets. So I sold the entire business at a loss to them, and spent the next three years digging myself out of the hole. It was a painful but valuable lesson: Don't get into a business you know nothing about.

Around that time, Dawn and I got into a screaming match in the upstairs of her condo — probably over Beth, who wasn't home. It wound up ending my FBI career about a month earlier than I had planned. During the argument, Dawn went downstairs, saying she'd be right back. The next thing I heard was the downstairs door close.

Dawn had been scheduled to leave in a couple of hours for an out-of-town business trip, and I then realized she'd gone to the airport early. I was furious that she'd walked out on our argument, so I jumped in my car and followed hers, honking for her to pull over. She ignored me, which made me even madder.

At the airport, instead of parking, she pulled up, and motioned for a security guard. I stopped directly behind her. When she started talking to the guard and pointing back at me, it was clear I needed to leave, so I went home.

An hour later my FBI supervisor, Greg, phoned.

"Joe, did you just follow your ex-wife to the airport?" he asked.

"Yes, I did, Greg," I replied.

"Well, she complained to the airport police, and told them you were armed and following her," he continued.

Both of those statements were true; I always kept my extra pistol in the locked glove compartment of my car. But I never threatened to use it on her. The thought never entered my mind.

Rather embarrassed, Greg said, "Well, the San Antonio office has already been advised. They've instructed me to come out to your place and disarm you. And they want to see you first thing in the morning."

That bitch, I thought. Being a former FBI wife, she knew exactly which buttons to push. The following morning, Greg and I drove together to San Antonio. He didn't know what was going to happen but I did. When I went into the SAC's office, I pitched my credentials and FBI-issue revolver on his desk.

"I quit," I said quietly.

Then Greg and I returned to Austin. He was in shock. In total, my FBI career lasted nine years, three months, and two days. Greg couldn't understand why I was so gleeful. After all, I had no other job to go to. But I felt as though I'd been let out of a straitjacket. And quitting is something I've never regretted. The previous evening was the last time I saw or talked to Dawn. Someone said later that she'd moved out of Austin with Beth.

When I left the FBI, I had about $20,000 in retirement savings that was returned to me. I figured that with careful planning, it might last a year or so, but I was broke within six months. So much for careful planning. I applied halfheartedly for several jobs but prospective employers couldn't figure out what to do with me — a nonpracticing CPA who was an expert marksman.

Judy was very much in favor of me leaving the government, but there was no way, on her modest salary, that she could support the both of us, and I wouldn't have let her anyhow. Job or no, our relationship flourished. We continued to hit the music scene. We'd gone to the Austin Opry House, closed long ago, to see Delbert McClinton, a Texas legend. Delbert had a repertoire of blues that we both liked a lot.

Opening for Delbert that evening was the Lee Roy Parnell Band, a group I'd never heard of; they were great. I noted his name, and next day went to buy his CDs, but found he hadn't made any. By asking around, I found that Lee Roy was playing in a local restaurant at Barton Creek Mall, and Judy and I went to check him out.

I loved his music; he was an excellent singer and one of the best slide guitar players I'd ever heard. We introduced ourselves during a break, began following Lee Roy to his various gigs around central Texas, and became friends. Eventually Lee Roy asked me to be his business manager; he'd not had one before. Even though I didn't know anything about the music business, I consented because I had a lot of time on my hands.

Soon I learned that although I loved music, I hated the music business. I kept his books, which was easy enough. But I also had to land him gigs, and collect the money for them. That's what I disliked; I've not dealt with a flakier bunch than club owners. For example, they'd frequently double-book artists, and Lee Roy would show up only to find another band playing.

And collecting money from these guys was like pulling teeth. It was customary at that time for the artist to be paid immediately after performing. Conveniently, some club owners would disappear right before the end of the show. Others would make various excuses why they couldn't pay at exactly that moment. But being Lee Roy's business manager wasn't a full-time job, so I still had time on my hands.

Chapter 6

Self-Directed: Wells & Associates

S oon I was one payment overdue on my condo. Then two. But my luck turned; the phone rang. "Is this the Joe Wells who used to be with the Austin FBI?" the voice on the other end asked.

When I answered yes, he continued.

"You may not remember me. I'm Frank Mahoney, an attorney here in Austin. A year or so ago, I was representing a loan officer who was about to be charged with bank embezzlement. I made him available at your office for an interview, and I was impressed with how you handled the matter."

I recalled Mahoney not so much because of his client but because of the lawyer's physical appearance. A land mine had blown up in Mahoney's face during the Korean War, and had left him horribly disfigured. But Mahoney had great credentials. He'd graduated with a law degree from an Ivy League school, was a former prosecutor, and taught as an adjunct professor at the University of Texas.

During my interview of his client, Mahoney never objected to the questions I had asked, and didn't direct his client to be quiet. The FBI didn't like interviews conducted with lawyers present because it was typically a fishing expedition; they wanted to know what the government had on their client without actually letting the client answer questions. As it turned out, the guy Mahoney was representing was innocent. But if he had stonewalled my questions, the client would surely have been indicted.

Mahoney continued our call. "Mr. Wells, I tried to reach you at the FBI office to discuss another bank client with you, but I was told you're no longer with the government. So I took a chance and looked you up in the phone book. Would you be available to consult with me on this client?"

I had no idea what he was talking about. "What do you mean by consulting?" I asked suspiciously.

"This is kind of a complicated fraud case," Mahoney said. "It's a bit out of my expertise, and I frankly don't know if my client is telling me the truth. I'd like you to investigate him just like you would have as an FBI agent, and tell me what kind of case you think the government could develop. I'll give you a list of witnesses that you can expand on. I'll make available all of the client's records. You'll have carte blanche to do whatever makes sense. And I'll pay you $75 an hour with a $2,500 retainer."

Seventy-five dollars an hour! I nearly jumped through the telephone. The retainer would more than cover the $1,600 I owed in past-due condo payments, as well as some other bills. But I tried not to appear overly eager.

"We can get together and talk about it," I replied.

This was my first case in the private sector, but it certainly wouldn't be the last. Mahoney was prominent in the legal community. Within a month, he'd referred enough cases to me that I was making more from my kitchen-table office two days a week than I ever made with the FBI. And thus my firm was born. With this first client, I'd done the work needed. Not too little; not too much — just enough.

"Frank," I reported, "your client is screwed. The government is going to cream him."

That's what Mahoney needed to know. Later on, he negotiated a plea for the banker/defendant. Although the guy drew some jail time, it was much less than what it would have been had he gone to trial.

Something's Wrong at the CIA

On one occasion, I was contacted by a young woman with a case that had an interesting twist. She had dated a man who subsequently went to work for the CIA. Although they'd theoretically broken off their relationship, they talked on the telephone nearly every day and she'd made the mistake of confessing to him that she had dated and had been intimate with another man after her boyfriend left for the government. The CIA guy went off the deep end and started threatening her, she said.

"What do you want to do?" I asked.

"I just want him to stop," she pleaded.

"Then why don't you just hang up on him?" I questioned.

"I'm afraid to do that. He has a gun and he has threatened to kill me."

That piqued my interest. I gave her a telephone recorder with instructions on how to use it. A few days later the woman brought in tapes of several conversations with the CIA agent. As I listened, I wondered who was sicker — him or her. There was a definite pattern of role playing. She would play the helpless woman, and he would play the aggressor. But on one part of the tape, he did indeed threaten to kill her. If the CIA knew of this conversation, the former boyfriend could probably kiss his new career good-bye.

I called the young man on the phone and told him I was a private investigator hired to look into his relationship with his former girlfriend. The agent asked to call me right back. I knew why; he was connecting his own recording device to his phone.

In a few minutes, my line rang and it was him. I was candid with what she told me but didn't mention that she had recorded his conversations at my request.

"Did you ever threaten her?" I asked.

"That's absurd," he replied, "I think she's lost her mind."

Then I said, "Listen to this." I had spooled the tape to start where he had threatened to kill her. Then I played that part of the recording. There was silence on the other end of the line.

"Sir, I am not trying to make trouble for you," I said. "But I used to be an FBI agent. If I had talked to a woman like this, it would have cost me my job," I advised. "If you ever call her again, I am turning this tape over to the CIA."

End of conversation; end of calls to her; end of case.

Big Publicity in a Big Town

Within a year I had bitten off some overhead by moving into an office suite. It provided the basics for an up-and-coming business person: a small office, telephone and secretarial services, and a real address. Since my space had no windows, Judy was kind enough to hang some Austin skyline photos in window frames. If you didn't notice that nothing was moving in the pictures, you almost could believe that they were actually windows and that was my view of the outside world.

I didn't initially have a desk, but Judy found an antique in her hometown that I could lease-purchase. It was quarter-sawn oak, and nearly 100 years old. Eventually I paid it off, and it is the only desk I've used in my business; it graces my office to this day. A few months after moving into my new quarters, I received a phone call that would rocket my small operation into the stratosphere.

Hal Monk, a former federal employee I knew, phoned to ask if I'd seen the newspapers about the fire that had occurred the previous evening in the State Capitol Building; I had. In Texas, both the governor and lieutenant governor maintained apartments in the capitol for occasional use. The lieutenant governor's daughter was staying overnight with a young male guest when the fire started. The young man died of smoke inhalation, and the papers were full of speculation about how it happened.

Was he freebasing cocaine? Did the television or some other electrical appliance catch fire? Were the young man and the lieutenant governor's daughter involved romantically?

Hal asked, "Joe, do you know anything about arson investigations?"

"Not a thing," was my reply.

"That's fine," he said. "I'm now an assistant attorney general for the state, and we'd like to hire you to be in charge of the investigation. I've already cleared it with the attorney general. The state fire marshal and employees of the attorney general's office will assist and be at your disposal. Please come on down, and we'll discuss it further."

The investigation took the better part of four months. During that time, I was in the newspapers and on television a lot. The fire marshal's investigation into the cause was inconclusive. The attorney general believed the television was the cause, and he hired experts to try and re-create a fire started by the TV, using the same model and employing different scenarios.

This group, well respected in their field, could not get the television to catch fire. My own conclusion seemed obvious: The young man was a smoker, and had fallen asleep on the sofa with a lit cigarette. But the AG didn't even bother to ask me what I thought; he sued Zenith, the manufacturer of the television. So when reporters called me about the AG's lawsuit, I had to answer with a terse "No comment," reminiscent of my Burgin days.

During the course of the investigation, Judy and I got married on Valentine's Day, 1983. It was a small ceremony attended by fewer than a dozen of our relatives. Lee Roy Parnell sang, and was my best man. The wedding was beautiful, held in the capitol's chapel. It was tiny but had a stained glass window that ran from floor to ceiling.

On our wedding night, we splurged and stayed at the Hyatt in the honeymoon suite. There wasn't time go anywhere because I had to work on the fire case the next day. I left Judy asleep in bed. A steak breakfast for two with champagne was included with the suite; Judy had to enjoy it by herself.

One of the reporters who'd stayed on the case was Rick Fish with the *Dallas Morning News*. He and I had become friendly, and he had a fascination with the kind of work I normally did. So he asked about doing a profile on me for the paper and I readily consented. One Sunday morning the article ran, complete with a picture of me.

The piece had two significant outcomes. First, it was read by Ross Perot. Second, Jim Ratley saw it.

I was sort of familiar with Perot but didn't know much about him; he had yet to make a national name for himself. Shortly after the article, which was quite flattering, I got a call from one of Perot's aides who wanted to make an appointment to talk to me in person. He turned out to be a lawyer on the staff of Electronic Data Systems (EDS), headquartered in Dallas.

EDS had made Perot a billionaire. His staffer wanted to know if I was interested in moving to Dallas to work full time doing "special investigations" for Perot; I wasn't. Since I had quit my FBI job to stay in Austin, I wasn't going anywhere. Besides, I didn't much care for Dallas.

I received a phone call later from the same staffer wanting to know if I would work for EDS on a consulting basis. That would turn out to be much more lucrative in the long run. But first I had to fly to Dallas to meet with Perot. From the outset I didn't like the guy. His office was gigantic and filled with mementos to himself. Perot was quite short, and I judged him to have a Napoleon complex. Later events would prove that to be true.

I asked what I'd be "consulting" on.

Perot was vague, spending an inordinate amount of time on whether I could keep a secret.

"Mr. Perot," I replied, "I had a top-secret clearance in the FBI. So the answer to your question is yes."

He then asked me a whole bunch of hypothetical questions. One stands out. "Let's say that one of my employees is committing a crime and I asked you to bug his phone. How would you do it?" he queried.

"Mr. Perot, that's called 'interception of communication,' and it's against the law. I wouldn't do it at all."

He pressed on. "But I own this company and all of the telephones. Don't tell me you wouldn't do it. You're getting paid to do what I say."

I rose, signaling the end of our meeting.

"Sorry, Mr. Perot, you've got the wrong guy." I left him with a smirk on his face as I shook his hand.

The next day I got a call from the guy on his staff. "Ross was very impressed with you. That wiretapping question was a ringer; you said just the right thing. Had you said you would do that, he wouldn't want so badly for me to hire you. Name your price."

I quoted him twice my usual rate, which at that time was $100 an hour. Over the next two years, I handled some very sensitive assignments and got well compensated for them. But I didn't do anything illegal; my days of overly aggressive and questionable investigative techniques were over. It had finally sunk in: If you can't win by the rules, you don't deserve to win.

Meeting Jim Ratley

The second significant outcome of that newspaper article was a call from Jim Ratley, who identified himself as a Dallas police officer. Jim said he traveled to Austin frequently and would like to stop by and meet me sometime. He had an accounting degree, which was unusual for a cop. I met with Ratley a few weeks later in my tiny office. He explained that he was ready for a change, and wanted to know if I was interested in hiring him.

Not possible right now, I replied; the only person in my company was me.

But we agreed to stay in touch. Within a year of opening my business, I was getting quite busy. I leased a new office in a beautiful Victorian building near downtown. My first hire was not Jim but Kathie Green, an administrator in the Austin office of the FBI. Kathie was a real workhorse, keeping track of a dozen agents and all of their paperwork. She was eager to quit the Bureau and was the right employee at the right time; I kept her very busy.

Not long after that, I decided to talk to Jim about working for Wells & Associates. Until then there were no "associates" except for Kathie. I was candid with Ratley. This was a start-up business. There were no guarantees; he had to agree to go anywhere at any time for the company. I offered him only a modest increase over his police salary but without the perks that come from a government job. He took the offer.

Jim was divorced with custody of his two young daughters, Leslie and Sarah. He moved to Austin to start his new life. When he came to work on Monday, I asked, "Jim, do you have a passport?"

"Yes," he replied.

"Well, dust it off. We're going to London on Wednesday."

I didn't know Jim very well when he started with me, but we sat next to each other on the long flight, and I began to understand this amazing man. He was born and raised in Marshall, Texas, to divorced parents. His mother, Patsy, whom I have come to know quite well, is an elegant woman. I didn't meet Jim's father, Harry, who died at 62.

Jim's daughter, Leslie, first came to work for us at the age of nine — stuffing envelopes on Saturdays. She bragged then that she had even been entrusted taking out the confidential trash. But after Leslie grew up, finished college and worked elsewhere for a couple of years, she came back to the ACFE, where she has been a key cog in the wheel ever since.

Immediately after high school, Jim joined the Dallas Police Department as a patrolman. He married his high school sweetheart, but they later divorced. Ratley worked his way up to the rank of detective. Then he went to night school and got his accounting degree; like me, he hated the stuff. Eventually he became the department's "one-man fraud squad." But Jim soon got restless and realized that his options for advancement were limited.

Jim's a wonderful storyteller. I enjoy listening to him so much that I won't interrupt when he tells the same tale again. And I laugh at the punch line like I'm hearing it for the first time. At this writing we've been together 25 years and counting.

The London trip was for a New York lawyer who wanted some intelligence gathered on an adversary. Jim and I spent four nights in England. Since Jim had never been there, he figured he could sleep when he got back to the United States. I, however, had been to Europe countless times, and didn't attempt to keep up with him.

Our client had a lot of money, so we stayed in the famed Dorchester Hotel, frequented by royalty. Late one evening Jim and I were in the hotel bar, which was nearly empty. But Jim spotted an attractive young lady, and invited her to our table for drinks. I got tired and went up to bed. The next morning Jim told me that he'd plied her with drinks and invited her to his room, only to find out she was a prostitute. Jim wasn't buying but when he told her this, she said she'd missed the last train back to her home in Nottingham, and didn't have a place to stay. So she offered Jim sex in exchange for sleeping in his room. Jim said he threw her out into the cold London night.

Making Lemonade and My First Film

Business was booming at Wells & Associates, thanks to H. Ross Perot and EDS. I worked principally with Claude Chappelear, general counsel for the company. The assignments ran the gamut. One big case involved a competitor that EDS sued as a result of losing a contract to provide data processing services to the State of Massachusetts. Thus began our long weekly commute from Austin to Boston and everywhere in between. A lot of money was involved. It wasn't unusual for Jim and me to jump on a plane in an attempt to conduct a surprise interview at the other end of the country.

Once we found ourselves on the western coast of Florida and decided to travel to Fort Lauderdale for another interview. We rented a convertible, stocked the car with a six-pack of beer, and drove across Alligator Alley heading east. The road was almost completely straight from one side of the state to the other and we encountered little traffic en route. We kept seeing road signs that read, "Only 37 Panthers Still Alive." That almost became 36 as one darted out in front of the convertible. When we arrived at our destination, we stayed at a hotel on the Intracoastal Waterway. Both of us marveled at the 100-foot yachts parked alongside the hotel. The prices started at $1 million and went up. We were wistful, wondering how much money it must take to live like that, and sadly concluded we'd never know.

At one point, EDS's security director retired. His replacement, John Handley, would be the first to tell you he knew nothing about investigations and security. So, he relied heavily on Wells & Associates, which had now grown to three or four people.

The president of EDS had received a series of threatening letters from an employee. From the way that the communications were worded, Jim and I were able to narrow a list of several hundred possible suspects down to a dozen or so. We then had their employment applications pulled, and I submitted handwriting samples to an expert.

The exemplars were less than ideal; in a number of instances, we had only the signatures of the employees. Nevertheless, our expert was able to further trim the list down to about four suspects. For no particular reason, we picked one employee, whom I'll call Marvin. He sat at a table across from John and me, and vehemently denied any involvement. I held a copy of the original document in my hand.

Then I said, "Marvin, please write down the following," reading to him what was on the paper.

He started writing but stopped after the first sentence, wadded up his cursive, and dropped it on the table.

"Damn, you got me," he muttered. Then he looked at Handley and me and asked, "How in the hell did you do that?"

Before John could tell him it was just luck, I said, "Marvin, we don't discuss our methods. But we knew it was you all the time."

I could barely conceal the smile on my face. When Handley and I left the room, he burst into laughter.

"Joe, if this is all there is to investigating, I'm not going to have any trouble at all."

I just shook my head; if John only knew. Marvin was fired but not prosecuted.

Another case we worked on for EDS involved a computer programmer named Nelson. The company acted as the data processing center for a number of banks. Nelson lived in Dallas but wanted to be transferred to New Orleans, his original home. The company arranged that, and advanced him $15,000 for the move — a "bridge loan." It was supposed to be repaid after Nelson sold his house in Dallas, but that didn't happen; he was in hock up to his eyeballs and used the profit from his home sale to pay his most persistent creditors.

Nelson's manager in New Orleans, at the behest of the company, kept pressuring him for the money. The manager finally said, "Nelson, if you want to keep your job, you're going to have to pay this loan back. Do you understand?"

Nelson understood, alright. He managed a bit of computerized sleight of hand to defraud the bank of $150,000 — enough to pay all of his bills. Since customers of the institution received their checking statements on different days of the month (e.g., Adams on the first and Zwick on the thirtieth), Nelson wrote his own program to "borrow" money from the ending balance field of the checking account. He figured that he could keep the money for 29 days, after which he would return the funds by debiting the account of someone else who just received their statement.

Numerous accounts were involved so he wrote his own little program to keep track of when to move money. But Nelson's program had a fatal flaw: There were only 28 days in February; this wasn't a leap year. Customers started calling and streaming into the bank with two consecutive statements in their hands that showed one amount for the ending balance of one month and a different amount for the beginning of the next.

Nelson's manager figured out something was wrong and phoned Dallas. They called me. I showed up at Nelson's office in New Orleans unannounced and had a confession within an hour, complete with a signed statement. Nelson pled guilty and was a guest of a state prison for a couple of years.

Wanting to make lemonade out of the lemons, I approached the company about the possibility of doing a training program for it on fraud by employees. Although the idea was a bit ahead of its time, EDS consented and made its audio-visual department available so I could create a video for company-wide distribution. Thinking that Nelson would make the perfect illustration for the program, I wrote him in prison and asked to videotape his story; he consented, much to the disbelief of his former employer.

It was quite the emotional ordeal. Nelson broke down and cried at how he had ruined his life and his family's. I helped the A-V people put together a script, and they edited the video down to about 20 minutes. It was a cautionary tale: Steal from the company and you'll be prosecuted and ruin your job and perhaps your life. EDS had about 20,000 employees at that time and at least half of them saw the video. Several months later a manager sent me evaluations. It received rave reviews.

Getting Into Crime Prevention Education

That got me thinking: If this training aid worked for EDS, why wouldn't it work for banks? Financial institutions had a particular problem with fraud; after all, their stock-in-trade was money. Tellers were especially vulnerable because of low pay and constant exposure to drawers full of cash. I spoke with my colleague Dan Morelock (who had reintroduced me to Judy) about my idea.

"Joe," he said, "you may be on to something. We have training tapes on what to do if an employee is robbed but nothing on embezzlement, and that's a much more common problem, as you know. I'd certainly buy a tape like that for our bank if it were done right."

I checked around carefully. There were 33,000 financial institutions in the United States at the time, and I couldn't find a single embezzlement prevention video in the market. According to my calculations, I'd need to sell to only 1 percent of them to recover my costs; the rest would be profit.

I approached my own bank, which agreed to lend me $50,000 toward the project. But I had to pledge all of my available collateral. That would later become my hallmark as a businessman — if I believed in an idea strongly enough, I was willing to bet the farm. Armed with my loan, I realized it was time to come up with a plan.

My colleague Jeff Mirkin was a Hollywood associate producer. I'd met him a couple of years earlier when Judy and I were in California and, on a whim, went to a taping of the original *People's Court* with Judge Joseph Wapner. Jeff worked on that show, and we chatted and exchanged phone numbers. He was glad to hear from me, and said that he and a friend could easily produce my video idea and deliver me a turnkey product. In the meantime, I rounded up three embezzlers who were willing to tell their stories.

At my request, Jeff hired Efrem Zimbalist Jr., to do the narration. Zimbalist was popular from being on the original television series *The F.B.I.* when it was rated number one. The bank thieves were taped, and then we went back to Hollywood to edit the tape, write a script, and videotape Efrem.

This was in the days before computerized editing so Jeff, his friend, and I sat in Jeff's apartment playing VHS tapes over and over until we had selected exactly the snippets we needed. Then Zimbalist read his lines into a camera, and we went into the studio to put the final product together. Editing was an expensive proposition: of the $75,000 I had budgeted for the project, probably $30,000 was spent in editing. Now it can be done inexpensively on a computer.

Finally I had something in my hand: a 22-minute video entitled *Embezzlement: The Thieves Within*. We marketed it strictly by mail. I'd bought a list of banks, but since I couldn't afford to send an advertisement to all of them, I took a random sample. Within 90 days, the video broke even; by the time it was all over, I had grossed well over $1 million. The cost of production and marketing was less than $200,000.

Over the next three years I wrote, produced, and edited about two dozen video training programs for diverse markets and on a variety of crime-related topics. I'll always be thankful to Jeff Mirkin for showing me how to do it.

Good Advice From Death Row

One of the videos I conceived and produced was a bit out of the norm. For it, I videotaped an inmate on death row at the Mississippi State Penitentiary in Parchman. Richard Gerald Jordan had been sentenced to death for the murder of a banker's wife in Gulfport about ten years previously.

I knew of the case because I had been involved in the investigation. Jordan, who was from Louisiana, was driving through Gulfport when an idea struck him: He'd kidnap a banker's wife and hold her for ransom. But it's not easy to get away with a kidnapping; the perpetrator, at some point, must expose himself to pick up the payoff.

That's what happened here. On Jordan's drive through Gulfport, he noticed a large bank on Highway 90, along the Gulf Coast. He stopped at a pay phone and made a pretext call to the bank in order to find the president's name. Then he looked up the banker's home address in the phone book, and found his way there.

Jordan gained entrance to the home by posing as an electrical repairman. He then kidnapped the wife, leaving a two-year-old child at home alone. He took the wife in his car to the piney woods outside town, and knelt her down. From behind, he put a .357 Magnum at the base of her skull and pulled the trigger. The victim fell over, face first, dead.

Only then did Jordan call the banker and say, "We have your wife. If you want to see her alive again, get $50,000 together and I'll call you back. Don't call the cops."

Jordan hung up and the banker called the FBI. We immediately swung into action, placing recording devices on his home and office phones, and waited. The following day the banker received a call telling him where to drop the money.

"You'll take the main road north toward Hattiesburg. When a car comes up behind you and flashes its lights, pull over on the tarmac and drop the package of money. Then drive away. Your wife will be released shortly after that."

The FBI covered the drop from both the ground and the air. I was assigned to ride in a helicopter with a state trooper — a most unpleasant experience. The trooper was somewhat of a cowboy, and took great delight in putting the helicopter at odd angles for the sole purpose of making me sick to my stomach. It worked.

But from high in the air, we saw the package drop, and we followed the car that picked it up. At a shopping mall, Jordan stopped and went inside a store. He returned with a complete change of clothing, and we almost didn't recognize him. However, the car was a dead giveaway. When he tried to make good his escape from Gulfport, the police and the FBI stopped him, and recovered the money. He then confessed to the kidnapping.

But where was the banker's wife? With great reluctance, Jordan took us to the scene. She was lying face down on the top of a knoll in a stand of trees. Without the kidnapper's assistance, it would have been weeks or months before she was discovered.

As we were approaching the body, Jordan said, "She might be hurt. The woman tried to run away from me and I got off one lucky shot." But she wasn't hurt; she was dead.

When we lifted her lifeless body, her forehead had been completely destroyed and her brains spilled out on the soft, damp ground. It was too much for a couple of us; we threw up.

Forensic evidence would later show that Jordan didn't shoot her from a distance; she had powder burns on the back of her head, indicating that she had been shot at close range, execution-style, before he made the first call to the banker. What a waste of a life.

Jordan went to trial in an attempt to be convicted of something other than first-degree murder. It didn't work, and he was given the death sentence. In America, it takes a long time to execute someone — sometimes decades. Every conceivable legal appeal can be filed to delay or stop the execution. Most killers hope that public opinion will soften as time goes by, and that their death sentences will be converted to life terms. That was Jordan's strategy.

He had been on death row for over a decade when I wrote asking to interview him for a video we were doing. Jordan readily agreed, thinking that his assistance in saving the lives of others would cut some soap with the appeals courts; it didn't. He is the longest-serving inmate on Mississippi's death row and, at this writing, still has not been executed.

The gist of the letter I wrote Jordan was "Remember me? I helped put you where you are. We're producing a video for bankers on how to avoid becoming a kidnap victim. Would you be interested in us taping you?"

He answered right away, giving his consent. Getting through the legal mumbo-jumbo and dealing with the prison was no easy matter, but finally I taped him on death row. He was behind bars and was shackled to a chair. Prison guards stood on both sides of him for good measure.

Jordan told his story, and gave good advice on how to avoid being a victim like the banker's wife he had killed. It was a chilling video, and sold extremely well in the financial services industry.

Money for Nothing

When I was making and selling training videos, I was also doing work for EDS and other clients. But when Perot decided to sell EDS to General Motors, he established Perot Systems, which consisted largely of Perot and his son, Ross, Jr., whose constant eyelid-flickering led me to call him "Blinky" behind his back. For this new entity, Perot again retained my firm. Thus I found myself working both for Perot Systems and EDS.

Perot wanted me to check out his potential competitors; how I got results was up to me. On one occasion, Jim and I traveled to Dallas, where one such company had offices in a high-rise. We figured our best initial course of action would be to raid the building's dumpster to see what it held. So at about 3:00 A.M. we did a drive-by, and saw that the dumpster was huge. This meant that one of us would stand watch while the other climbed inside it.

Jim laughs when he tells the story, "There was no doubt who was going in the dumpster, and it wasn't Joe." He was inside, tearing open trash bags when we were surprised by a security guard who must've been 70 years old.

"What're you doing here?" he demanded of me, the only person he saw.

"I'm just waiting for my girlfriend," I stammered, and stepped away.

My pulse shot up, though, when, Jim made a noise, and the old geezer thrust his flashlight inside the dumpster. But Jim quickly flattened himself against the wall, and escaped detection.

Satisfied nothing was amiss, the guard continued on his rounds and we got away with several bags of garbage. Back at our hotel with the booty, we sifted through it one document at a time, and discovered we'd hit the mother lode: balance sheets, income statements, future plans, minutes of board of directors meetings — you name it.

As was our custom, we didn't tell clients we got our information from the trash. Instead, we repackaged the relevant details in a formal memo and attributed this intelligence to a "source in a position to furnish reliable information."

Shortly after turning our report over to Perot Systems, I got a call from Blinky, who wanted to see me at once. When I entered his office, Blinky had my report on top of his desk. "Are you sure you can rely on this source of information?" he demanded.

"Yes," I said, "you can take it to the bank."

Blinky looked off into the distance and said, "It's scary that you can get this sort of thing. Did you have someone inside the company as a mole?"

"Ross," I replied, "we never discuss our methods. You can assume whatever you want, but I can assure you that the information is reliable."

He then said, "Well, if you can find out this kind of stuff on a potential competitor, what can you find out about me? I'd like to hire you to do an investigation of me and my family."

I swallowed hard. With considerable effort, I talked him out of the idea.

When I told Jim he laughed, and said to me, "Blinky, what we can find out about you depends on what you throw in the trash!"

I did work for both Perot Systems and for EDS for about a year.

But then John Handley, EDS's security director, approached me. "Joe, we don't like you working for Perot. I realize that he used to own this place, but he doesn't now and we can't trust him. We'd like you to quit doing assignments for Perot Systems."

This was not what I wanted to hear; both Perot and EDS were good clients, and I was making money hand over fist. After some discussion, Handley sweetened the pot by offering me a guarantee of $150,000 annually for five years. I could bill time against this retainer at my usual rates, but any leftover was mine. Eventually I negotiated $180,000 a year for six years.

Do the math: The total was $1,080,000, and all I had to do was *not* work for Perot. I inked a deal with EDS before anyone could change their minds. Within a year, Handley had retired from EDS and a new guy took over as security director. He was well experienced and didn't need me much. Later the company approached me about buying out my contract for a lump sum. On December 31 of one year, it cut me a check for $375,000. And on January 1, it signed another check for $325,000 — a total of $700,000, and I didn't have to do anything for the money. Jim, Kathie, and the other members of my small staff were incredulous.

After cutting the deal, it appeared that I was completely through with Ross Perot, but in 1992, he decided to run for President of the United States. Knowing the guy, I thought other people would figure him out too. But by the summer, he was actually leading in the polls, beating both George H. W. Bush and Bill Clinton.

However, in response to a reporter's questions, Perot denied that he had ever hired a private investigator. That was flatly untrue, and it took enterprising media types only a short time to find my name connected to Perot in one of the many lawsuits that he had filed against competitors.

I was inundated with telephone calls from reporters wanting me to comment. I had a difficult decision to make. Perot, in my view, would have made a great dictator but a terrible president. And he didn't tell the truth. My decision was whether to violate my sense of client confidentiality for what I believed to be the greater good: stopping this man from maybe ascending to the highest office in the land.

For better or worse, I decided on the latter and gave an interview to the *New York Times* refuting Perot's false claims. The next day, it was on page one. That led to a flurry of more media calls from all of the major television channels wanting me to go on camera. I declined any further comment; I'd said what I wanted to say — the truth. But Perot was heavily damaged.

Several days later, he was on *The Today Show* being interviewed by Bryant Gumbel, who was waving the *Times* story in Perot's face. Rather than admit that he had hired me, Perot didn't deny it;

he said, "If this guy Wells calls himself a 'private investigator' and he is talking to the media, what does that tell you about him?"

I wanted to climb through the television and strangle him.

Perot was extremely sensitive to criticism, and sometimes would believe the worst of people. Later, he hired another private investigator, who evidently told Perot what he wanted to hear. In this case, it was that the Republicans had taken compromising pictures of his daughter in order to disrupt her wedding. On the basis of that, Perot withdrew from the presidential campaign, only to later claim that he was back in the race. Both investigators had done mortal damage to Perot, and he got only 19 percent of the popular vote in the election, which Bill Clinton won.

Several years later, the other private investigator disclosed that the story about Perot's daughter was a complete fabrication. In the end, one investigator had told the truth and the other had lied.

Meeting Mike Lawrence

One day not too long after I had gone into business as Wells & Associates, I received a call from G. Michael Lawrence, an attorney and partner with Graves, Dougherty, Hearon and Moody, one of Austin's premier law firms. We hadn't met previously, and he invited me to his expansive high-rise office, which had a perfect view of downtown. When I arrived, Lawrence explained that he needed help locating a key witness for a case of his that was coming to trial. One way and another I was able to track the guy down, which made a good impression, I thought, and earned me a nice fee.

But I didn't hear from Lawrence again until nearly two years later, when he called regarding a high-dollar family dispute over land in south Texas. Lawrence wanted me, as a potential expert witness, to accompany him to the client's ranch to examine some records. Because it would've been an eight-hour drive, he chartered a private plane.

When our work was done, bad weather ruled out a return flight, so we rented a car. And on the long drive home, we discovered our mutual love of music. By coincidence, Lawrence played guitar and wrote tunes, and I did too. So when we parted ways after the trip we vowed to stay in touch. Over the years, Mike became my dear friend.

Meanwhile, Judy and I continued to enjoy life in Austin. Take, for example, our home on Townes Lane. We had bought it for four reasons: It was in the best part of old Austin — it was an easy ten-minute drive to the office; the property was owner-financed; and it had a separate garage apartment that I could convert into a music studio.

I had inherited a great eight-track recorder from Christopher Cross in lieu of some money he owed me, and it was ensconced in the garage apartment. But I was clueless on how to operate it. Still, that didn't prevent Mike and me from regularly meeting to play guitar in the garage/apartment studio — just him and me. Some of his original tunes were terrific, and others were just incomplete bits and pieces.

Now I was acquainted with a great musician, Robert McEntee, from my days of studio ownership with Christopher Cross. And Robert could play almost any musical instrument very well, especially guitar. So Mike and I invited him to join us for some of our half-baked sessions.

Thankfully, Robert quickly figured out the eight-track recorder and mixers I had in my home studio, and he became our engineer and backup all-around musician.

Although Robert had played with some very famous musicians, he chose to live in Austin. After working with Mike and me, he went on to be the lead guitar player for the late Dan Fogelberg.

For several years, Mike, Robert, and I would get together weekly — not to jam, but to write and record original music under the name of Joe and the Debits. We even played some gigs. In total, we laid down about 60 tunes. We were very proud of most of them. A bit like Lennon/McCartney, Mike and I were better together than either of us was individually.

We didn't write standard love tunes; far from it. Here's a sample:

The Dawn of Inertia, horizons far away
This song is beginning on a most peculiar day
Objects in motion, rhythms in a trance
The laws of physics are beginning a slow dance
Do you feel the gravity? It's all around
And what about the elements coming up from the ground?
Scorched by the sun, frozen by the heat
Trapped in a place where space and time meet
The weight of the future, the waste of the past
At the Dawn of Inertia the motions rest.

Chorus
Does your experience confirm the theory too late?
Do your experiments validate
The Dawn of Inertia in its natural state?

Mike and I may have written these lyrics, but don't ask us to interpret them. We have no idea what they "mean." Having penned many songs, I'm convinced that the writer is merely a conduit for expressing concepts and feelings.

Indeed, one time I wrote a song with these lyrics:

I don't write the tunes, I just pick them from the air
And I don't write the words, 'cause they've always been there

Mike and I had wonderful times in our studio, getting together like clockwork every Thursday night. After a miserable first marriage and a very messy divorce, Mike eventually wedded Kathie Green, who had been with me for nearly 20 years when they married.

The Litigation Pie

I'd started Wells & Associates in late 1982. In 1984, I hired Kathie; Jim came aboard in 1986. We had other people working for us from time to time, but mostly we used independent contractors. I was fortunate enough to have former law enforcement contacts all over the country. When we had work and needed help, we easily found qualified people, and when business slowed, we didn't have the overhead.

But I was restless doing investigations, even though we'd been successful and made a wad of money. The problem was twofold.

First, nearly all of my cases were civil. Once you work criminal matters, and especially those for the FBI, you realize you've had the best cases of your career. Civil cases were all about money, not putting bad guys in jail.

Second, much of our work came from lawyers. I soon figured out what I called the "litigation pie." Clients have only so much money for lawsuits; many times that's millions of dollars, but there's a limit to it. That's the litigation pie.

Lawyers control how the pie is divided. The more money they spend on outsiders such as me, the less pie they have for themselves. Naturally, attorneys don't want to spend any more on experts than they have to. They want the best product at the cheapest possible price.

It was common for lawyers to "opinion-shop." They'd check with you about a case, and consider hiring you as an expert.

However, they frequently wanted to know what your opinion would be before you'd actually done any work.

I had one such case in the Silicon Valley. A law firm contacted me about representing an accounting firm in an audit failure. I wouldn't give my opinion until I'd seen exactly what the accounting firm had or hadn't done. I told their attorneys that I wouldn't look at the case for less than $50,000, and would bill against that amount at $400 per hour. After squealing a lot, the lawyers hired me.

It took me about two weeks to examine the depositions that had been taken so far, and to look at the workpapers the accounting firm had produced. I then called my client, the attorney in charge of the case.

"I know you want to take my deposition, and get me to give a favorable opinion that basically says the accounting firm had done a good job. That's a bad idea," I opined.

"Why?" the lawyer demanded.

"Because I can't testify truthfully without hurting the accounting firm," I replied. "I'd hate to damage your case after you've paid me this money."

But the attorney was insistent. "I just won't ask you about the problem areas."

"But the other side will," I answered, and that's what happened.

The opposing attorney knew just what to ask. As I had predicted, it was devastating to the accounting firm, which had failed to uncover a massive fraud committed by upper management. It was barely concealed, and any competent auditor would have found it.

Toward the end of this case, Vola Wells McMasters died of Alzheimer's at age 80. She had the fatal disease for about three years. At the end of her life she didn't recognize me or anyone else, including V.K. McMasters, the husband she'd married ten years previously. Two years into her illness, when she was lucid, I'd continually apologize for everything bad I'd done. But it didn't stick in her mind.

Dr. Donald R. Cressey

The accounting malpractice suit was among the last investigations I did for Wells & Associates. I found corporations' naiveté especially disheartening. Frequently, with major frauds right under their noses, corporate management would ignore all signs of it.

To me, it made much more sense to try preventing these problems than to deal with the mess afterward. Since I'd already made an embezzlement prevention video, I decided to learn as much as I could about the root causes of fraud, especially in the workplace.

My search began at the vast libraries at the University of Texas–Austin, which had exactly three books on fraud. I checked them out, and read each carefully. One made sense — a rather thin book, entitled *Other People's Money: Study in the Social Psychology of Embezzlement*, written in the early 1950s by Donald R. Cressey.

For his PhD dissertation at Indiana University, Cressey had interviewed 133 incarcerated embezzlers, and had developed a model that he believed most embezzlers conformed to; he called them "trust violators" rather than "embezzlers."

First, they had an unsharable need, such as excessive debt, gambling or addiction problems, or other difficulties that made their situation personally embarrassing. Second, they had a perceived opportunity to solve this unsharable need by violating their employers' trust in them. Third, they had the ability to rationalize their acts by diffusing the criminal nature of what they were doing — such as "borrowing" the money from the company — or by blaming their acts on, for example, inadequate pay.

Cressey's model immediately struck a chord with me. I'd seen this kind of behavior countless times, starting in El Paso with my very first fraud case. On a whim, I decided to see if Cressey was still alive, and, if he was, to establish contact with him. After making a couple of calls, I found he was chairman of the Department of Sociology at the University of California–Santa Barbara. He was in the phone book so I telephoned him, right out of the blue. Thus began our close friendship and collaboration, which lasted until his untimely death in 1987. During the years I knew Dr. Cressey, his unparalleled influence on me shaped my personal philosophy.

Shortly after we talked by phone, I visited California and met him in person. He invited me to his lovely home, which he'd occupied since the early 1960s, and I met his charming wife, Elaine. Later, he visited my home. Don and Elaine traveled to Austin frequently, and Judy and I delighted in their visits.

So in 1986, when Don asked Judy and me to join him and Elaine on a speaking junket in Australia, we agreed. His address was before the Sir John Berry Memorial Symposium on White-Collar Crime in Canberra. We had a great time, and decided to stop at Fiji for three nights on the way back. Unless things have changed, Fiji is not one of my favorite vacation destinations. Because of long-standing civil unrest, our plane was greeted by machine gun-toting soldiers — not a welcoming sight. We stayed at the Fijian Resort, a walled compound facing the ocean. For our own safety, we didn't leave its confines during our brief stay.

Although the weather was great and our rooms were right on the beach, the water was full of sea snakes — again, not a very welcoming sight. We spent most of our time simply sitting in comfortable lounge chairs on the sand. I could listen to Don talk for hours; after all, I was sitting at the feet of the master. I greedily drank in every word. He used to claim that he learned as much from me as I from him but that wasn't possible. Being a brilliant teacher, Don was able to put complex subjects in the simplest language.

One fateful evening while the sun was sinking low over the water, Don said, "Joe, it's time that America had a new corporate cop."

"What do you mean, Don?" I asked.

"Look at the situation," he continued. "You have accountants responsible for investigating fraud but who know nothing about how to do it. And then you have investigators who know nothing about accounting. The two disciplines need to be combined."

Or, as I have joked many times, we need to marry the accountant and the investigator, no matter how hideous the off-spring of such a marriage might be.

The significance of what Dr. Cressey said in that rather offhand remark didn't sink in until after his death, which occurred about a year later. He and Elaine were out for a Sunday drive; she was at the wheel. Don slumped over without warning, felled by a fatal heart attack. A reformed heavy smoker, Donald Ray Cressey was dead at age 67.

Before he left this world, though, Don's penetrating insight and generous spirit had planted a seed deep within my mind. Not long afterward, it grew into a practical concept that transformed fraud detection and prevention.

Part Four

FOUNDING A PROFESSION

Chapter 7

Vision of a New Breed of Fraud Fighter

The idea of the Association of Certified Fraud Examiners (ACFE) probably came to me in a dream spurred by Cressey's observation. I went into the office one early summer morning in 1988. Jim Ratley and I sat on the front porch, and I shared with him Don's offhand comment.

"Jim, there are tens of thousands of professional associations in the United States. As far as I know, not one of them is devoted solely to fraud. We've both done fraud work for many years, and yet there's no organization to represent us or recognize our expertise. What do you think about us starting one?"

"My God," Jim said. "What an idea! We've got to do it."

That's how it started. We pulled Kathie into the conversation later that day.

She asked the obvious question: "How much is this going to cost?"

We didn't know that, or how to start an association. I polled several colleagues, including John Handley of EDS; anti-fraud pioneer Jack Bologna, who taught at Siena Heights College in Michigan; David Battle, a bank and security director. All agreed it was a good idea but, like me, no one knew how to proceed.

A month later, I was teaching a weeklong fraud course at Bank of America's training facility near Oakland, California. My colleague Steve Albrecht — a PhD professor of accounting at Brigham Young University and also an anti-fraud pioneer — was teaching with me at my invitation.

Steve's been my friend for 25 years, but other than the anti-fraud field, we have little in common. He's a devout Mormon with six children, and has been involved in academia most of his professional life. Although Steve is brilliant, he's also one of the most modest people I've met.

One evening after dinner, he and I were sitting in one of the condos provided by the bank. Steve was having a sarsaparilla or whatever (Mormons are opposed to beverages containing caffeine) and I was drinking something, probably as strong as kerosene and water. I knew Steve had been on the board of directors for the Institute of Internal Auditors (IIA), the largest such organization for those in that field.

I shared with him my idea about a professional association for anti-fraud experts. He immediately recognized the value, and was very encouraging. Steve said that a profession was distinguished by its common body of knowledge (CBOK).

"Joe," he said, "I know quite a bit about fraud from the accounting side, but you're talking something different. What skills does a person need to investigate fraud?"

Almost offhandedly, I said, "It starts where accounting leaves off, Steve. People in this field are part accountant, part lawyer, part investigator, and part criminologist." I didn't know it then, but I'd just defined what would become the CBOK for our new endeavor.

I next asked Dr. Albrecht about the IIA's origin, structure, and revenue sources. Although volunteers had founded it as a nonprofit in the 1940s, its real growth, Steve said, began in the 1970s, when it introduced the Certified Internal Auditor (CIA) designation. At the time, the only eligibility requirements were to have been an internal auditor for five years and to pay a fee for the designation.

"By conferring the designation on many applicants through a grandfather clause in its charter, the IIA accumulated enough cash to buy a headquarters building for itself in Florida," he explained. "If you think about it, just about every profession — medicine, the law, engineering — started its association this way. It found people with expertise, persuaded them of the value of a professional designation, and charged a fee for the privilege of being exempted from a qualifying examination. Once these associations had attracted a sufficient pool of experts into becoming members, they were able to stop grandfathering, and have those same experts help determine what the admission requirements and exam contents should be."

For the next month or two, I mulled over what Steve had said, and I studied the bylaws, codes of conduct, and rules and regulations of similar organizations. Then in earnest I started drafting the same thing for what we originally called the National Association of Certified Fraud Examiners. I took a bit from one organization and a bit from another. (Within the first year, we changed to the Association of Certified Fraud Examiners [ACFE] because of a surprising number of international applicants.)

We chose the title "Certified Fraud Examiner" only after careful deliberation. Most states regulated who could describe himself as an accountant or investigator. But no one regulated use of the term *fraud examiner*, which seemed the most apt. After all, many potential members were accountants with few investigative skills, while others were investigators who knew little about accounting.

Only after I had all of my ducks in a row did I discuss the preliminary plans with anyone other than Jim and Kathie. I wrote the bylaws, the code of professional ethics, and decided on the organizational structure. Most professional associations were nonprofits, but philosophically that didn't work very well for me. I saw nonprofits as flaccid, do-nothing outfits that reminded me more of the government than private enterprise. To me, our organization should embody the entrepreneurial spirit. We wanted to establish an association that people could truly be proud to belong to, and not wanting to do things like the others was reason enough to choose a different path.

Moreover, most nonprofits that failed did so because of an obvious reason: They had no real incentive to raise and retain capital. So I decided that we'd be a regular corporation, but with a twist. There would be a board of regents, elected by the members, that would set standards for certification and admission to the organization.

But since we had no members yet, I appointed the first board, which consisted of eight people: Steve Albrecht; Jack C. Robertson from the University of Texas; David Battle; Jack Bologna; Kathie Green; Gil Geis, a PhD in criminology at the University of California–Irvine and friend and colleague of Don Cressey; John Handley; and me. I sent them letters describing their duties, but we didn't have an in-person meeting until the fledgling association got off the ground.

All of those I invited were enthusiastic, and applauded the new venture. Jim Ratley wasn't on the board because he became program director, in charge of reviewing and approving membership applications. Speaking of which, it took us quite some time to put together the application and get it approved by the board.

Since we hadn't yet designed an exam, the only way we could designate someone a CFE was to grandfather him or her in by granting a waiver of examination. We also had to establish qualification requirements. Obviously, successful applicants would need some actual experience uncovering, documenting, or investigating fraud, but how much?

Another question was whether we should apply numerical criteria. We decided to particularly closely review any applications that reported work on fewer than ten fraud cases. On the subject of educational requirements, we decided not to require college degrees; many qualified investigators attended college but didn't graduate. And when it came to other certifications, such as the CPA, we decided that applicants who had them should get extra credit, along with applicants who had advanced degrees.

Finally, we developed an application rating system that all regents supported. Under it, each full-time equivalent year of college was worth 10 points; each year of fraud-related experience was worth 5; a master's degree counted for 10 points and a PhD, 15 points. We decided that Jim would evaluate applicants who scored 80 points. Marginal applicants were rejected. Our theory was that if the CFE was too easy to get, it wouldn't be respected; too hard, and no one would apply.

Jim, Kathie, and I had calculated that we'd need at least 1,000 members paying $200 for a one-time application fee and $100 a year in dues for this to produce a positive cash flow. We had a small quantity of stationery printed up in the name of the National Association of Certified Fraud Examiners, along with some advanced standing applications. We then bought from a list broker the names of 20,000 or so internal auditors. Because we couldn't afford to send mail to the entire group, we selected a random sample of 200 names.

We figured that to continue our plan we'd need about four responses from among those 200 names. A month later, I went into the office on Saturday morning, as was my long custom, and found 19 applications, with the fees, lying on the floor by the mail slot. I was overjoyed and called Jim at home.

"I can hardly believe this!" I exclaimed happily.

"Believe it, Joe," he replied. "We're onto something."

What an understatement. I appointed myself chairman and Steve president, even though his role was largely advisory. Kathie became a vice-president and, in addition to being program director, Jim too became a vice-president.

The Certified Fraud Examiner

The first person we certified — CFE 00001 — was Nancy Smith Bradford, a CPA who headed the private insurance special investigations unit at Blue Cross Blue Shield of Florida in Jacksonville. Soon afterward, Jim and I got our certifications; we had been so busy taking care of members that we forgot to complete our own paperwork, and didn't do so until later.

Although Nancy's unit was initially staffed by auditors, it focused on detecting, investigating, and deterring fraud. She rightly felt that one of the best ways to do this was to prosecute offenders and publicize convictions.

But as the team's leader, she faced the persistent problem Cressey had emphasized to me: auditors are good at numerical analysis, but not at interviewing witnesses and suspects. It was clear Nancy needed to hire people with both investigative and interviewing skills. And she began to do so — retired Secret Service and FBI agents, postal inspectors and even a New York homicide detective. Yet though these new hires had the right kind of experience, Nancy still felt something was missing for them and the auditors she'd already had on her team.

"We wanted our investigators to have a professional designation," she told me, "and the Certified Fraud Examiner was the only one that matched the focus of our work: white collar crime. So when I received an invitation to join the ACFE, I looked into it."

Nancy of course checked us out thoroughly, and found that the ACFE was legitimate, well known, and respected. We had another characteristic she found appealing. At the time, women continued to encounter gender bias in the professions. Nancy was pleased to find, however, that the ACFE didn't discriminate against women — or anyone else, for that matter. Quite the opposite, she learned: We had open minds and focused on education, including training in interviewing, investigation, financial analysis, and many other fraud-fighting skills — just what she wanted in a professional association.

Nancy's close relationship with the ACFE deepened in 1994 when I asked her to join us as an employee in Austin. We were delighted when she accepted. It was a win–win situation: We benefitted from her considerable fraud-fighting expertise, and she expanded her skills, playing a dual role as CFO and deputy program director. Members voted Nancy onto our Board of Regents, where she served as its first chair.

Eventually, after 10 years with the ACFE, Nancy returned to her extended family and home state, where she is an associate at a firm that provides accounting, auditing and other services related to fraud and Sarbanes-Oxley Act compliance. It's always fun to see Nancy at ACFE events, where she networks with new professional contacts and spends time with me and her other longtime ACFE friends.

Other women — and members of minority groups — found the same welcome at the ACFE. For example, a young Baltimore fraud fighter of Puerto Rican descent, Isabel Mercedes Cumming, attended a conference I organized even before the ACFE existed in its present form. Prior to the NACFE, I'd done some fraud prevention education under the name of the Institute for Financial Crime Prevention. With KPMG we held the National Joint Conference on White Collar-Crime, in Washington, D.C. This was the first such gathering that focused on fraud. Isabel was a KPMG senior auditor and attended the conference, where we first met. In subsequent positions as a bank's director of internal audit and compliance, she worked on the savings and loan crisis and found the work fulfilling but didn't like what she saw. Not only were the white-collar crimes themselves disturbing to her, but so was the prosecuting attorneys' ignorance of accounting, which hampered their work against fraud.

Inspired by the presentations and networking at our sold-out conference, Isabel attended law school at night while working days at the bank. Her goal was to become a white-collar prosecutor, and she made it. In 1993 she left her $50,000-a-year job as director of internal audit and compliance, and accepted an unsalaried position in the Baltimore U.S. Attorney's office to gain experience and earn references for a job in law enforcement.

I liked that; as I had done, she bet the farm on a strongly held belief. And it paid off handsomely. A year later, Isabel became an assistant prosecutor in Maryland's Office of the State Prosecutor and then an assistant state attorney in the Baltimore City State Attorney's Office Economic Crimes Unit. Soon she earned her CFE credential as well. Today, she is chief of the Special Prosecutions/Economic Crimes Unit in Prince George's County, Maryland, adjacent to Washington.

What made Jim, Kathie, and me happy about stories like this is that we were meeting an important need that no one else was addressing. Isabel told me that when she was with KPMG — and I knew this well — there were no networking opportunities for fraud professionals who didn't work for the Secret Service or the FBI. And so, Isabel said, that first conference made fraud fighting her life's passion, and she joined us to gain access to our unique combination of accounting and detective skills, which are essential to effective fraud fighting, and previously hadn't existed.

Like Nancy Bradford, Isabel quickly made strong contributions as an ACFE member. She was the first woman to chair the Board of Review, which enforces the ACFE's Code of Ethics, a post she held from 1996 to 2006. And when the ACFE sought new regents in 1997, Isabel ran and was elected to the board by our members.

But I've gotten ahead of my story. In its first year of existence, the ACFE wrestled with the challenges that typically accompany rapid growth. The key management team was Kathie, Jim, and me. We had no computer system to speak of, so Jim kept most of our records on yellow legal pads. Kathie did our accounting, and when necessary we hired clerks to help us.

We began issuing certifications on my 44th birthday, June 27, 1988. The first 19 applications we had received turned out to be our best source of publicity, and our phone rang off the hook. At the same time, representatives from local law enforcement and several federal agencies stopped by our office to confirm we were legit. Jim answered countless questions. One fellow, whom we'd just certified, seriously proposed that we limit the number of CFEs to 500 worldwide. That way, he reasoned, he'd be in a more select group. I spoke with him myself and asked, "So in other words, you want to be a member of the most prestigious association that no one ever heard of?" By all signs, though, inquirers liked what they saw and heard. By the end of 1988, we'd certified more than 1,000 people, most of them referred by their peers.

As a part of the requirements for certification, applicants were obliged to provide copies of their college transcripts, three separate letters of recommendation and a detailed questionnaire about their anti-fraud experience. Jim paid more attention to the last category and, when there was any doubt, checked with me. We were pleased to be attracting senior anti-fraud professionals, which is what we were after. On average, the applicants we certified had a college degree, eight years' experience, and had worked on about 100 fraud cases.

A profession is judged by its CBOK, and it was no easy task to distill one for ours. We hired Jack Robertson of the University of Texas to write the ethics section. Mike Kramer wrote about the law, Steve Albrecht covered accounting, and I wrote the investigation section and coordinated the rest of the parts. Much of what I wrote was done on a small pseudo-laptop with a half screen and no backlight. It was nearly impossible to see.

When Judy and I went to Grand Cayman for a getaway, I'd rise early and sit out on our patio. It was still dark, and I could hear the gentle ocean surf less than 50 yards from our rented condo. Under the patio's dim light, I'd bang out all I had absorbed during my ten years as an FBI agent — interviewing techniques, preserving evidence, obtaining and recording confessions, writing reports, dealing with confidential sources . . . the list went on. Once we had assembled it all, we self-published a three-ring, 1,000-page binder entitled the *Fraud Examiners Manual*.

Dr. Gil Geis

Before Don Cressey passed away, he retired fully from the University of California–Santa Barbara. His colleagues invited Judy and me to the nice retirement party they held for him at the college. While there, I met Don's longtime associate, Dr. Gil Geis, of the criminology department at the University of California–Irvine.

Gil is a prolific author. I'd read many of his books, and was honored to be introduced to him. Dr. Geis specialized in the study of white-collar crime. During the party for Cressey, I learned that Gil's stepson lived in Austin and that Geis owned a condo there. I invited him to visit the ACFE headquarters when he was in town, and he took me up on it. After Don died, I was looking for someone to mentor me in the academic world of fraud, and Gil readily volunteered for the task.

There is no other way to describe Dr. Geis: He has a giant intellect and is wonderfully modest about it. He is now approaching his mid-eighties, and his mind is extremely sharp. Gil and I formed a very close bond, and he filled the vacuum when Cressey died. After Steve Albrecht found it necessary to give up his position as president of the ACFE, Dr. Geis stepped into that role for nearly a decade. The ACFE president at that time provided us guidance and direction in the study and research of white-collar crime; he had no operational responsibilities. Gil gave us many wonderful inspirations for innovative approaches to the problem of fraud. Our organization would not have been the same without him.

Commitment to Education

In May 1989, our first training event was a four-and-a-half-day seminar in Austin; we called it the "Fraud Symposium." We had to make financial commitments to the Austin Hyatt, and just guessed at the attendance we needed before we signed papers with the hotel. Encouragingly, the symposium sold out at 125 people. The material we presented was drawn from the *Fraud Examiners Manual*, which was given to all attendees.

Steve Albrecht, Jack Robertson, Jack Bologna, Jim Ratley and I were the instructors. It was a mega-hit despite warnings from doubters, who had said the seminar was too long, and that Austin was off the beaten path. One of those attending was a female postal inspector who, halfway through the session, confessed that she had been sent by her superiors in a more or less clandestine manner to figure out whether we were committing a fraud. We laughed at the notion. Later, she joined the ACFE and got her certification.

Today the U.S. Postal Service and many other agencies formally recognize the CFE credential for hiring and promotional purposes. And the *Fraud Examiners Manual*, given free to attendees at our first event, has now grown to nearly 2,500 pages as the CBOK continues to expand. At the Fraud Symposium, we sent people away happy and convinced that we knew what we were talking about. They told their colleagues, who in turn told theirs. That simple dynamic is a key factor in the ACFE's rapid expansion.

Later in the summer of 1990, we held the First ACFE Annual Fraud Conference in San Diego; 150 people attended. The only reason we picked San Diego was that I liked it. Our keynote speaker for this event was Edwin Gray, who'd been instrumental in uncovering the massive savings and loan frauds of the mid-1980s. During both the first Fraud Symposium and the annual conference, I promised myself I'd learn the name of everyone who attended. Most of them I still know today. But when attendance soared past 1,000, I couldn't manage that memory feat any longer.

Testing, Testing

By November 1989 we had developed the first CFE exam. It was pencil-and-paper-based, and had to be proctored by someone in the area where the examinee lived. Not surprisingly, there weren't many people taking the test, but at least we had one. We kept this up until about 1992, when we converted to the computerized exam we use today.

In 1989 we decided to give an annual award to the applicant with that year's highest score. We named the prize after Morris "Red" Walker, one of our first CFEs, who had died suddenly of a stroke.

Jim and I realized that eventually we'd have to discontinue the grandfathering provision. We did so in late 1995 for domestic applicants and a year or two later for those outside the United States and Canada.

The ACFE's growth was stunning throughout the 1990s, and we were barely able to keep up with it. By the decade's end we had more than 25,000 members. But with success comes competition; it's inevitable.

The American Association of Forensic Experts

In about 1992, an outfit calling itself the American Association of Forensic Experts (AAFE) set up shop. I knew nothing about it until an attendee at one of our seminars said the AAFE was advertising for members, claiming it was "modeled" on the ACFE. I can't recall his name, but he said that the founder of the AAFE, Robert O'Rorke, had created a sham board to connote legitimacy. This attendee had been on the board himself until he found that O'Rorke was using respectable people's names merely to promote himself. The AAFE, according to this fellow, sold credentials known as "Diplomates of the American Association of Forensic Experts" to anyone who applied. I later checked the public records and determined that the company was actually owned by O'Rorke, his minor daughter and aunt — the "board," whose members were listed on his stationery, was for appearances only.

Our own records reflected that O'Rorke had joined the ACFE as a noncertified member, and had ordered a copy of our directory. To detect misuse of our copyrighted membership list, we had inserted the names of three fictitious members and listed for their addresses those of Judy's relatives. Thus, if anyone sent mail to people who existed only in our records, it proved they had used our directory illicitly.

Sure enough, two of these nonexistent people eventually got promotion letters for the AAFE. Since I'd been around the block a few times, I called O'Rorke and recorded our conversation. I didn't immediately confront him about the list. He said he was glad to hear from me, that he was a big admirer of mine and was proud that his fledgling organization was indeed "modeled" on the ACFE.

He wanted me to be on his board, and carefully explained that the position was honorary, paid nothing. In return, I would have the "privilege" of being listed on his stationery. I smiled to myself at the absurdity of it: no authority, no pay, no job duties — just him using my name. I wondered why the other legitimate people on his board, many of whom had prestigious titles, would fall for such a thing. I politely declined his offer, and got to the meat of the conversation.

Did he use the ACFE membership list without authorization to promote his new business? I asked.

O'Rorke hedged but I was persistent. Finally he denied it.

"That's odd," I said, "because I have in front of me a promotion letter of yours that came directly from our directory."

"That name could have come from anywhere," he replied.

Not true, I answered. "The person you sent your advertising to doesn't exist. His name was purposely added to our directory to detect misuse," I countered.

O'Rorke was silent for a time, but didn't admit anything.

About that time, we had launched and published several editions of our newsletter, *The CFE News,* to keep members abreast of current developments at the ACFE. I put a carefully worded two-paragraph piece in the next issue, giving our members a heads up on the AAFE.

O'Rorke promptly filed a federal lawsuit against the ACFE and me for defamation. That turned out to be his mistake. Prior to the commencement of depositions, I called each of his board members, and recorded the conversations. To a man, they confirmed that they had no role whatsoever in the AAFE except for allowing their names to be used on the stationery. A couple of them bad-mouthed O'Rorke, calling him a con artist and saying that they had already resigned from his board in disgust. Luckily the cost of defending ourselves was covered by our general liability policy, and I hired the best lawyers I could.

Depositions began with O'Rorke, who talked out of both sides of his mouth at once. But he did say under oath that he alone reviewed and approved each application. And we got a complete history about his career: small-town cop during college; a professor at two different universities. He claimed he left the second position to start the AAFE. But we later found out that he had been fired from his first position — teaching at a small state college — for plagiarism.

It seems that O'Rorke had accompanied his second wife, a Swede, to Stockholm. When browsing through one of the libraries there, he lifted 11 studies conducted by college professors in northern Europe, and brought them back to the States. His wife translated the works into English, and O'Rorke inserted his name in place of those of the original authors. Then, to gain tenure as a professor, he submitted these scholarly works to his college.

Unfortunately for him, the institution discovered the truth and discharged him. Before leaving, he secured a second teaching job at a small private school in Missouri, which had no knowledge of his history. O'Rorke established the AAFE while there, and used college resources for his own benefit: postage, stationery, and even the labor of his students to stuff promotional envelopes. Ultimately, he was asked to leave that position as well.

At that point, he devoted all his time to the AAFE, which he ran out of a spare bedroom in his house. A college professor told me later that he'd never heard of another academic who was fired from two tenured positions.

O'Rorke was at my deposition when my lawyers introduced about a dozen tape recordings of conversations I'd had with members of his board and with one or two of his disgruntled former employees. O'Rorke had no knowledge that the tapes existed. I watched his reaction carefully as, in recording after recording, his board members stated that O'Rorke's organization was a one-man operation. The color drained from his face as a few of them called him a con artist. The only two depositions were of him and me; he quickly dropped his case for defamation.

O'Rorke was wounded but not mortally. He continued his operation, and eventually changed the name of the AAFE to the American College of Forensic Specialists. Of course, this was no college in the traditional sense. At last count, he offered 13 different "certifications," but his operation remains small, as far as I know.

More Litigation

I was also involved in another lawsuit that dragged on for five years, and eventually cost my insurance company millions of dollars in legal fees. When we established the CFE credential, I attempted to trademark it with the U.S. Patent and Trademark Office. We received a letter in reference to our application stating that "initial designations," as they were called, could not be trademarked.

A couple of years after we began operation, we received a letter from the Society of Financial Examiners (SOFE) claiming trademark rights to its designation, the Certified Financial Examiner (CFE). I'd never heard of the SOFE, but it turned out to be a small outfit headquartered in North Carolina that had used the CFE designation for years before we were formed. Since it also was unable to trademark the designation, it trademarked its training manual, which contained the CFE initials.

On that basis alone, SOFE claimed exclusive use of the designation and demanded that we stop using it. Our lawyers scoffed at the claim and told SOFE to take a hike. From about 1990 to 1992, SOFE sent us several letters, each one sterner than the last. All attempts that we made to get them to go away failed. In late 1992 SOFE filed a federal lawsuit against the ACFE, claiming trademark infringement, and the fight was on. SOFE had about 3,000 members, all of them in charge of examining insurance companies chartered by the various states. Of their members, only about 800 carried the CFE designation.

For nearly three years, lawyers took depositions — including two from me — and examined the financial records of both organizations. SOFE had been around for at least 30 years and had accumulated somewhere in the neighborhood of $400,000 in surplus funds. To stake its claim, SOFE spent every dime it had on legal fees, and borrowed another half-million dollars. SOFE's lawyers sued for all of the money we had grossed — not netted — since the ACFE had gone into business: tens of millions of dollars. Had SOFE prevailed, we'd have been broke, and I would've had to file for personal bankruptcy.

Most civil cases are settled right before trial. I've mused that lawyers don't really make their money going to trial; the big bucks are in getting ready to go to trial. But this case wasn't settled at the courthouse door; it erupted into a full-blown trial that lasted over a week. I was put on the witness stand, where SOFE's lawyers cross-examined me like I was a common thief. It was most uncomfortable. Witnesses were called from both sides. Our star was Isabel Cumming, JD, CFE, the Maryland prosecutor who served on our Board of Regents and had seen the inside of many a courtroom. Isabel wore an elegant red suit, forgoing the traditional black or navy blue, and was eight months' pregnant. She underwent cross-examination with aplomb; the defense attorneys treated her with great deference, and the judge even joked that he was glad she was not a prosecutor in his jurisdiction, as judges were one of her targets.

The child Isabel had the following month was named for me — Joseph Jett. What a great honor. Joey became a world-class skateboarder by the age of 9, beating much older kids and making quite the reputation for himself by earning a full-page story in the Washington Post when he was eight.

After Isabel's testimony, the attorneys summarized the issues. The only people in the courtroom not under oath are the lawyers. They can and do say anything they wish. As I sat at the defense table, my attorney instructed me to look directly at the jury frequently, but to never stare at them or show any emotion.

SOFE's lawyers portrayed me as unscrupulous and dishonest. It took a lot of restraint to avoid getting up and shouting at them, but I remained outwardly calm. The judge's instructions to the jury were complicated and long. They were required to render a verdict on roughly a dozen questions related to trademark infringement.

The courtroom was nearly empty during the jury's deliberations — just me, one of my lawyers and several people from SOFE at the opposite table. It was deathly quiet until I erupted in laughter. Without saying a word, I sat there and laughed. My attorney and the SOFE people perhaps thought I'd lost my mind. The truth, though, is that this kind of behavior goes to the heart of my personality. When under pressure, I don't throw tantrums or sulk; I laugh.

I also laugh a lot when not under pressure; being able to see the absurdity of situations has been a lifesaver for me. Finally, after half a day of deliberation, the six-person jury reached a verdict and returned to their seats. The foreman gave the bailiff a piece of paper, and he in turn passed it to the judge.

My attorneys had told me we had to win on only three certain questions in order to prevail in the suit. We won on all of them. Now we were free to continue using the CFE designation indefinitely. SOFE's lawyers and their clients skulked from the courtroom without saying a word and with their tails planted firmly between their legs.

When the jury left the courtroom, I laughed again; it was absurd. Nearly $2 million in legal fees spent on three initials of the English language. Our insurance company picked up our costs.

Expanding the Common Body of Knowledge

In the early 1990s, we concentrated on expanding the CBOK and updating the CFE exam, which I had written and which had been converted to a computerized test. We had inserted in it numerous internal controls to minimize the possibility of cheating. At that time, to help applicants study for the test, we gave them the *Fraud Examiners Manual* and a list of about eight books for use as study references. Probably about 70 percent of the test came from the manual. But applicants signing up for the test were complaining that it was difficult for them to obtain the study references. Moreover, the number of examinees was light; probably no more than a few hundred a year.

Then Jim had a stroke of genius: putting on one CD every resource needed to pass the exam, as well as a computerized prep course. The final prep course contained over 2,000 questions, answers, and explanations. I wrote about three-fourths of them myself, and eventually we had created a course.

First the applicant would read the *Fraud Examiners Manual*, then start down the list of questions, which were divided into the four areas of our CBOK. If an exam taker answered a question correctly, he or she moved on to the next question. But if the answer was wrong, an explanation of the correct answer popped up, and that question was put back into the mix to be asked again at a later time.

One couldn't complete the prep course without eventually answering all of the questions correctly. That person was then ready to take the computerized exam, which contained some of the same questions but in reverse order from the prep course. This feature kept applicants from simply memorizing answers. The prep course was an instant hit, and the number of examinees rose dramatically.

The Boy Wonder

In early 1990 Barry Minkow wrote me a letter from prison. He was infamous as the "boy wonder" who had committed a $100 million financial statement fraud before the age of 21. His story is fascinating. A high school dropout, Minkow started a carpet cleaning business in his parents' garage at the age of 16. He told me that his main motivation for getting rich was to impress women. I could easily understand that.

But Barry was no businessman. He didn't know how to make money, and started kiting checks to make ends meet. When he was 18, Minkow borrowed money from a bank using fake financial statements and tax returns. When that loan came due, he borrowed from a second bank to pay off the first — again using totally bogus numbers. And when it became time to pay the second loan, he borrowed yet again, providing fake figures to a third bank, and so on.

Within a couple of years, he owed lots of money. Then he hit on the idea of going public with his carpet cleaning enterprise, which was known as ZZZZ Best. As near as he could tell, that was the only way to cover his debt.

But going public requires audited financial statements. For Barry, this wasn't a problem; he simply faked his way through the process by furnishing his auditors with phony supporting documents. Finally, he had enough of the paperwork completed to form a public company, and raise the money he needed to pay his bills. It worked, at least for a time. Because of his youth, Minkow became a media darling, appearing on such shows as *Oprah* and *60 Minutes*, where he bragged incessantly about his business acumen.

But his thirst for publicity led to his undoing. A customer of his carpet-cleaning service noticed Minkow's notoriety and supposed wealth, but couldn't understand why ZZZZ Best wouldn't refund her money on an unsatisfactory job; the company had made one excuse after another. She got the interest of a newspaper reporter who did a thorough investigation of Minkow and his operation. The piece made headlines and was picked up by the powers that be on Wall Street.

The stock of ZZZZ Best went into free fall; the bubble had burst. By the time the smoke cleared, the assets of this supposed multimillion-dollar company were sold for less than $50,000. Instead of taking a plea, Minkow thought his golden tongue would get him through a trial for fraud. Wrong; he was convicted and sentenced to 25 years of hard time.

Minkow had heard through the prison grapevine that I'd previously taped white-collar criminals to use in educational videos. His letter to me, which came out of the blue, said he'd voluntarily tell me his story, providing vivid details of what he'd done and how. I took him up on the offer and arranged through prison officials to spend a half day with him. I hired a video crew in Denver, flew there, and rented a car for the drive to the prison in Littleton. On videotape, Minkow was brilliant. He was one of the most articulate people I'd met. I used the footage as the basis for a training video entitled *Cooking the Books: What Every Accountant Should Know about Fraud.* It too was a best-seller.

Learning from Crooks

Because the prison had been unusually cooperative, I requested and received its permission to interview Minkow by telephone during our Second Annual Fraud Conference, which was held in

Orlando. The session was great; about 300 attendees were there. Barry was hooked up to the public address system so that attendees could clearly hear every word he said.

I asked him questions, and then members of the audience did. He was responsive and candid, and his remarks served as a cautionary tale to the accountants in the audience: Beware of people with his charm.

After the session, I was standing with other attendees at the break discussing Minkow's interview. A guy came up to me, in full view of the others standing around.

With suspicion in his eyes, he said with great conviction, "What do you think you're trying to pull here? Do you think that we're all idiots? That wasn't Barry Minkow. You hired an actor to portray him. There's no way a federal prison would allow you to be hooked up by telephone to a prisoner."

For a moment, we stared at him in silence; then we all broke out in laughter.

Minkow was released after serving 8½ years of a 25-year sentence. It's not uncommon for prisoners to have religious conversions in the joint, and that's what happened to Barry. He went on to become an ordained minister, and now has a small church in San Diego. Minkow also started an organization — apparently for profit — to educate others on how to detect and prevent white-collar crimes. I've been asked many times whether Barry has truly reformed. Who knows? But he loves the limelight and will talk to you forever about his ideas. Because of my background, it's impossible for me to trust people like Minkow. But I wish him well.

The interview with Minkow at the Second Annual Fraud Conference in Orlando started a trend. At every conference since, we've had a white-collar criminal speak. There's no lesson one can learn that's better than hearing from the mouth of an offender what he or she did and how it was done. It's very compelling.

Another speaker we used was Sam Antar. He was CFO of an electronics chain called Crazy Eddie, founded by his brother, Eddie Antar. In the late 1970s, Eddie created the concept of chain electronics stores, a strategy copied by Circuit City (now defunct), Best Buy, and others.

Eddie Antar started small with one retail electronics store, selling televisions and the like. Then he opened other stores financed primarily by borrowing money on the basis of fraudulent financial statements, just as Barry Minkow had done.

And eventually Antar too went public. The Crazy Eddie chain was a family affair. Eddie's father and cousin Sam helped Eddie cook the books — reporting large inventories that didn't exist. The Antars made fools of their independent auditors. During routine inventory observations, Eddie's employees were told to double count and inflate inventory amounts. Workers, at night, would even break into the office used by the auditors at Crazy Eddie's and alter their workpapers.

The chain received income in the form of cash, checks, and credit cards. Eddie skimmed off much of the cash, which he temporarily stored at his house. When he accumulated enough money, he'd hide it on his body and in his luggage, and carry it on a flight to Israel. There he deposited the loot in a bank, and then transferred it to a secret Swiss account only Eddie could access.

In total, Eddie skimmed about $30 million. The scheme was uncovered when Eddie got caught up in a divorce battle with his estranged wife; she spilled the beans. Eddie managed to slip out of the country and was on the lam for three years. But he was arrested in Switzerland while trying to withdraw some of his funds. The authorities had been tipped off and were waiting to nail him. Eddie was extradited to the United States, where he served ten years in prison. His cousin Sam and several other relatives pled guilty to fraud and avoided jail. But Sam, a CPA, had his license suspended.

Like Barry Minkow, Sam became a crusader against white-collar crime and spoke to a rapt audience at one of our annual conferences. We've held them in Boston, New York, Nashville, New Orleans, Chicago, Hollywood, Washington, D.C., Seattle, San Antonio, San Francisco and Las Vegas. The latter has proven immensely popular, and we've been there a number of times. In 2008, we set an attendance record with nearly 2,500 people — the largest event of its kind. So in 19 years, we grew from 150 attendees in San Diego to well over 2,000.

Attending the annual conference is the hardest work I do all year. It's bizarre; everyone there knows who I am, and the only privacy I get is within my hotel room. As soon as I walk out its door, members in the hallway want to stop and chat.

In the early days of conferences, I used to register at the hotel in my own name. No more; one guy called me at about 11:00 PM wanting to know where the ice machine was. But I came to realize this behavior was understandable. I meet these people, and if I'm doing my job, they relate to me. Except for Jim Ratley, I'm also the most visible person there. So it's not surprising that one of our attendees who may have had a couple too many called me instead of the front desk.

But now I always register at these events under an assumed name. It's hard for me to imagine what someone truly famous must have to go through to get some peace and quiet.

15 Minutes of Fame

I'd had mine. I'd previously been interviewed by a reporter from the *Wall Street Journal*. I thought he might be interested in looking at the Barry Minkow footage for an article about accountants and fraud. He watched the video and called me.

"That's interesting," he said. "But what's really interesting to me is how you get guys like him to spill the beans on camera. That's the angle I'd like to pursue if it's okay with you."

It was okay with me. But I never dreamed it would be page one stuff; it was — complete with one of those pen-and-ink drawings of me that the *Journal* is famous for. The article appeared on April Fools' Day. On that occasion, I was on a plane, and the fellow seated next to me was reading the piece. When he saw the drawing, he looked at me carefully, looked back at the artist's rendering, and then examined me again.

"Isn't that you?" he asked.

I pretended I hadn't seen the article, and looked at it while he held the paper.

"Nah," I replied, and shook my head. "That guy is at least 20 pounds heavier than me."

The passenger looked at the drawing again and decided I was right. I didn't tell him the truth, and silently enjoyed a chuckle.

If you appear on page one of the *Journal*, your phone is going to ring. The calls come from people you know and from journalists. I've often marveled when reporters looking for a story find something already written on the subject and essentially repeat it; not too much originality there.

Over the next few days I was deluged with requests for interviews. One came from *Oprah*; I turned it down. Another from *Phil Donahue*; I turned that down too. Then ABC News' *20/20* phoned. At that time, the program was one of the most-watched news shows on television. Eventually I was referred to John Stossel, whose work in the fraud and scam area I respected.

I agreed to appear with Stossel. With ABC's cameras rolling, I interviewed a white-collar criminal in Boston. Then they videotaped a training program of ours where I was an instructor. For drama, I'd even planted a female white-collar criminal in the audience and devised several comments for her to make when she held up her hand.

Then on cue I said, "Ma'am, why do you know so much about white-collar crime?"

"Because I'm a convicted white-collar criminal," she replied.

The audience was stunned when I brought her to the front to address the group. But I had made my point: Many white-collar criminals don't look or act like criminals at all. Stossel and his editors put together a nice piece that made up one full segment of the show.

That would have been tremendous exposure for the ACFE except for one little fact: Stossel never mentioned the ACFE's name. I was furious. Here we had the potential for our association to be exposed to 20 million people. But the only calls I got were from current members and old friends who hadn't seen me in years.

A Key Player

By 1992 the ACFE staff had grown to perhaps 15 or 20 people. Most of them were member service representatives, answering the phone and responding to letters on how to join the ACFE. Other employees took care of accounting, certification, and many other duties necessary to run an organization.

I didn't exactly have an assistant; Kathie Lawrence answered my calls and did my typing. But it was time for me to have an aide. The newspaper ads brought me two serious prospects, a woman named Lorrie and Jeanette LeVie. It was a tough call, but I hired Lorrie because she had previous experience as an executive assistant in an association. Within weeks she had offended nearly all of the employees by throwing her weight around. Lorrie lasted less than a month.

We had hired Jeanette to work in our shipping department, knowing she was seriously overqualified for the job. But when

Lorrie left, I immediately moved Jeanette next to my office and gave her a raise. She has now been with me for over 20 years.

I rarely have to think because Jeanette does it for me. In most instances, she has already figured out what I need before it even occurs to me. Jeanette works wonderfully with the staff and with the many people I stay in touch with.

Nearly everywhere I go, people who know her talk about how great she is — and they're right. It's hard for me to imagine my career without her, and she tells me I won't have to. Several years ago, she earned certification as a CFE, and kept a journal of her studies, which was posted on our Web site for the benefit of others. In early 2009, Jeanette became Vice President – Operations and is an important cog in the ACFE wheel.

Home of the ACFE

Since 1984, I've been in the same office in the same chair with the same desk. The ACFE office is located at 716 West Avenue in Austin, at the corner of Eighth Street. The neighborhood is just west of downtown and is a mixed-use area with both homes and offices.

I bought the building initially when I was in practice with Wells & Associates. It's a three-story Victorian wooden structure built in 1925, and currently houses 13 employees. When I purchased it, there was a sign on the outside announcing it was the Minter-Hughes Building, named by the previous owners for themselves. That wouldn't do.

Someone suggested that it be named the Wells Building. Not only would that have been conceited — even for me — but in the Navy, which shaped much of my life, ships weren't named after the living. So I thought of the idea of calling our place the Gregor Building, after Judy's dad. Since he was a decorated World War II veteran, I obtained duplicates of his many medals, and had them nicely framed. They hang on the first-floor staircase wall. Prior to Jerry Gregor's death, he was able to see the building and was very proud. But not any prouder than I am that he was my father-in-law; he was a great guy.

When I bought the building, it was painted an uninspiring gray color. It occurred to me that it should be Navy blue, the principal color of the ACFE. That entailed having decades of paint scraped to bare wood; I saw no sense in just adding to layers of paint that would bubble, crack, and peel.

If a person spends over 20 years in the same place, he or she has the opportunity to gradually fix it up. With all modesty, the Gregor Building is now breathtaking. The hardwood floors gleam. The place is impeccably maintained, thanks to Laura Collins, who has been with the company for 14 years. Virtually every piece of furniture and art was picked and placed carefully. It wasn't done by an interior decorator; Judy and I did it ourselves. At each ACFE event held in Austin we have an open house. People ooh and ah at it. Probably the Gregor Building, more than anything I own, reflects my personal taste. Many times I've been told that I have a talent for decorating. I tell them I don't have the personality to be a legitimate interior decorator, but I do well. They laugh, I laugh.

Moving Sideways

By the early 1990s, we'd maxed out our space in the Gregor Building. Luckily for me, there was an office complex next door consisting of three small buildings. The owners had defaulted on their loan, and the occupants were paying their rent to the Resolution Trust Company, a government agency established to buy up vast amounts of commercial property as a result of the savings and loan bust that plagued America in the mid- and late 1980s.

These buildings — 10,000 square feet — weren't in good shape, but they sure were convenient. Eventually the ACFE bought the property, for a song really. Prior to granting the loan, the financial institution made us remove all asbestos from the buildings. It seems that asbestos lawsuits were common, and attorneys would sue whoever was connected with it: builders, owners, and even banks who loaned on the property. Removing the asbestos was time consuming and expensive. But even with the hassle and expense, the property was still a great bargain.

We named the buildings after ACFE leaders: the Albrecht Building for Steve Albrecht, our first president; the Geis Building for Gil Geis, our second president; and the Braithwaite Building for John Braithwaite, our first Cressey Award winner, who is a pioneer in criminological research and teaches at Australian National University in Canberra.

Originally, some of the ACFE staff occupied the Albrecht Building. But it's located right on the banks of Shoal Creek, which has a tendency to flood. It did, and the water filled about three feet of the building and stopped just below the computer keyboards. We lost many original files that contained CFE applications and much of our advertising material. Moreover, the dozen or so staffers who were its occupants were displaced for about three months. It was an incredible inconvenience. So we booted out the people who had been renting the Geis Building and relocated our employees there.

We've gradually taken over all three buildings. While it's a bit inconvenient to be scattered, the property has a great benefit: It's now all paid for so we occupy our property rent-free.

But each time the spring rains come, we hold our collective breaths; it's only a matter of time until the Albrecht Building floods again. Currently we have adequate space for fewer than 100 employees. However, if the ACFE continues to grow, we're all going to have to move.

By the mid-1990s, we'd hired three more employees who are vital to our operations. Matt Kinsey, who has a degree in English, went to work in shipping. Matt is a wonderful guy; his first love is music, and his job supports that. He is part of a band called Li'l Captain Travis. Although the band has not been a commercial success, it has a very loyal following and has released several CDs. The original music the band writes and performs is terrific. I've bought all their albums and listen to them frequently. Matt has declined several opportunities for advancement. He's capable of much more than what he's doing, but he's happiest in the low-stress environment of the shipping department, where he remains today. Matt has been with the ACFE well over a decade. His seniority has given him one of six coveted covered parking spaces.

We hired John Warren and John Gill, both lawyers, within six months of each other. Warren was fresh out of Baylor Law School and worked for less than a year practicing law with a big local firm, but he didn't like that profession at all. About the time he came to work for us, I had conceived a large study that would tap our member expertise to find out exactly what kinds of cases they investigated.

The First Taxonomy of Fraud

Although John Warren had no anti-fraud expertise at all, he was extremely bright so I put him in charge of the project. Together, we developed a form that we could send to our members. It asked them to describe in great detail a case that they'd worked on — any case. We received over 2,600 responses chock full of useful information. Warren spent several months sorting the data into a usable fashion, and helped develop what we have come to know as the fraud tree.

I had been taught that there were endless ways to commit fraud, but there aren't. With crimes in the workplace committed by executives and employees (i.e., occupational fraud), we were able to identify three major schemes that could be broken down into 11 sub-schemes that had their own variations.

The important thing was that we finally had a schematic of fraud. No one had done this before. We also asked the respondents about their guess as to the cost of occupational fraud. It's impossible to gauge precisely because all frauds are not discovered, and those that are frequently are not reported. In this first study, the educated guess averaged out to 6 percent of the gross domestic product.

In 1996, with all this information, John Warren and I rolled out the first ACFE *Report to the Nation on Occupational Fraud and Abuse*. Every two years we issue a new report. The schemes haven't changed, but their frequency and the amounts of loss vary each time. Warren is now the ACFE's general counsel and handles our wide-ranging legal matters. He still oversees the *Report to the Nation*, but others on staff, notably Andi McNeal, handle the details.

John Warren also helped me write a book, *Occupational Fraud and Abuse*, based in part on our research. We printed and sold it through the ACFE by our publishing arm, Obsidian. The book sold well in the technical market, and a number of universities bought it to use it in their accounting classes.

John Gill started at the ACFE after several years with a law firm. Like Warren, he did not like the practice of law. Gill was our original general counsel and performed a variety of other duties. But he eventually settled on research, and it's the right job for him. He now is vice-president of education and heads the research department, which consists of 10 or so employees. That department is responsible for every word we write on the detection and deterrence of fraud. Gill's shop also produces updates to the *Fraud Examiners Manual*, the CFE Prep Course, other self-study courses, and the guides for our conferences and seminars.

Both Gill and Warren are now fraud experts and veteran CFEs. Gill is a fine writer, has a great sense of humor, and is quite the oldies guru. If you can think of a song from the 1970s-on, chances are he knows its words and music.

Many other key ACFE staffers have been with us a long time. While I don't mention their names here, it's only for the sake of brevity, not because I don't recognize their importance.

Higher Education

As the ACFE grew, I got very weary of traveling and speech-ifying; I have my 2 million-mile card on American Airlines alone. Gradually others on the staff took over much of the teaching for our organization, and I turned my efforts to higher education and writing.

I'd long observed that accountants got little or no classroom training about fraud. Jack Robertson, who was a professor at the University of Texas at Austin and a member of our original Board of Regents, asked me to guest-lecture in a few of his classes. My presentations were well received. Jack eventually retired from the university, and I was approached by Steve Limberg, chairman of the UT accounting department, to develop and teach a class on fraud examination. I subsequently taught for four years, and it was one of the most popular classes in the Graduate School of Business. When I began, my class was about 65 — very large for graduate school. When I gave it up, there were twice that many students.

Fraud is an interesting topic, and my students thirsted for this knowledge. In 2002 the American Accounting Association — the largest such organization of accounting professors — gave me its "Innovation in Accounting Education" award for the fraud exami-nation class I developed. And John Wiley & Sons approached me about writing a text, which was released as *Principles of Fraud Examination*.

I'd done a bit of homework and determined that out of about 900 colleges with an accounting major, only 19 taught a fraud class. So in 2002 I began the ACFE's Higher Education Initiative. In essence, the ACFE would donate all of the material necessary for an accounting professor to teach a fraud class. By 2008 more than a third of colleges had taken advantage of the offer, and the number grows yearly. Within the next several years a school that doesn't offer a fraud course will be the exception, not the rule. My friend and colleague Mary-Jo Kranacher — a professor at York College and an ACFE Regent Emeritus — has been a major player in encouraging schools to participate.

Principles of Fraud Examination is in its second edition. All the profits from my books as well as the teaching stipends are donated to the ACFE General Scholarship Fund, which provides financial aid to deserving students.

I wouldn't have been able to teach a class without the aid of my loyal employee, Laura Collins. She handled virtually all of the administrative work — taking attendance, grading tests and papers, everything. All I had to do was show up and teach — and, of course, write the material. Since the beginning of the Higher Education Initiative, the ACFE has given away millions of dollars in goods and services to this cause; it's a good thing.

The Cliff Robertson Sentinel Award

So-called whistleblowers frequently suffer a fate worse than death. Most often they're ostracized, vilified, demoted, fired and scorned as "rats." Paradoxically, the discovery of many frauds and other crimes simply wouldn't be possible without them. According to the various editions of the *Report to the Nation on Occupational Fraud and Abuse*, more frauds are uncovered from tips and complaints than all other methods combined.

A classic example of the fate of whistleblowers is legendary screen actor Cliff Robertson, who won best actor in 1977 for his poignant portrayal of a developmentally disabled man in *Charly*. He also was picked earlier by the president himself to star as John F. Kennedy in *PT 109*. But in the same year he won the Academy Award, Robertson discovered that the head of the powerful Columbia Studios, David Begelman, had stolen and forged many large royalty checks payable to Robertson. The actor confronted Begelman and told him that the matter was being turned over to the authorities.

Begelman said to Robertson, "If you do that, you'll never work in Hollywood again."

Undeterred, Robertson saw to it that Begelman was prosecuted. The studio head made good on his promise. Robertson was blacklisted for more than six years and nearly forgotten by the movie industry. But he said he'd do exactly the same thing again.

Personally, I hate the word "whistleblower." It conjures up exactly the image it should not. But regrettably, this term is a fixture in our vocabulary. These people are most often selfless heroes willing to sacrifice for the greater good. It occurred to me that they should be recognized. So I wrote a letter to Cliff Robertson suggesting that we name an award after him and that he should be the first recipient. To my great surprise, he responded.

In 1995 at the ACFE Annual Conference in Chicago, he accepted the Cliff Robertson Sentinel Award with grace and humility. The award carries the inscription "For choosing truth over self." The main criterion is for the recipient to have suffered great harm for doing the right thing. Subsequent recipients have told horror stories of retaliation that boggle the mind. No other such award exists, and it is most fitting that the ACFE was at the forefront of honoring these people.

The Good Life

At one point, Judy and I had lived in the same home in Austin for nearly 20 years, and it was paid for. We began looking around for a weekend place in Bellville, her hometown. That's when we spotted 15 acres for sale at the edge of the nicest subdivision in town. The acreage was beautiful: a creek with running water most of the time, trees ringing the property, city lights and water. It was very affordable then, so we bought it on a whim. As far as I was concerned, we could've pitched a tent there and been happy.

But a couple of years later, we'd drawn plans for what I thought would be our retirement home. It would be magnificent but not large — about 3,000 square feet; after all, there're only the two of us. Since I was a big fan of Gothic architecture, we designed it in that style. And once it was completed, we sold our home in Austin, and Judy moved to our place full time. She named it Castle Creek. I leased a condo very close to the ACFE offices, and spent three or four days a week there. From door to door, the trip is just under two hours.

As time passed and more responsibility for management was given to Jim and Kathie, I spent less time in Austin. In 2005 we hired Toby Bishop to be president and CEO. He'd been a partner with Arthur Andersen in Chicago before the firm collapsed. Toby was a transplanted Englishman who truly loved Chicago. We gave him a three-year contract, which he fulfilled.

Since his heart was in the Windy City, Toby returned there to work for Deloitte. In 2007 I gave up my condo and moved to Castle Creek full time. After Toby left I promoted Jim to president and our CFO, Scott Grossfeld, to CEO. Both have done a magnificent job. Scott recently left to pursue other opportunities and I promoted Jim to CEO. He now holds the dual title and responsibilities of President and CEO.

I get to Austin about once a month so that people who work for us don't forget who I am. With a well-equipped home office, a telephone and computer, there isn't much of a need for me to leave my beloved home. Indeed, days will go by where I don't even venture past the front gate.

My family these days consists mostly of Judy's family, although I have two nieces, Patty and Dianne, and a nephew, Terry. Patty and Dianne are wonderfully adjusted, regardless of the fact that my sister, Sue, was their mother. Terry was the oldest of her children and was raised by a stepfather who was downright mean. As a result, Terry has had problems all of his life. My sister's next child was named Joe, after me. But at a very early age, he developed addictions. First, it was model airplane glue, then alcohol. Eventually drunk and homeless, Joe stepped in front of a train. Whether it was suicide like his mother or a drunken mistake, he was killed instantly.

Judy's family lives in Bellville: her mother, Jenny; her brother, Jerome "Rusty" Gregor, who is five years younger and owns a local gym; Rusty's wife, Carrie, the county clerk; and their two children, Carrsyn and Baylee. Judy is particularly close to her nieces and spends much time with them. Carrie and I have become great friends.

Writing, Writing, Writing

At last count, I'd published 18 books and about 200 articles. I always thought I'd run out of something to say, but that hasn't happened — yet. My article-writing spurt really took off in about 2002. I had arranged for lunch in New York with Colleen Katz, editor-in-chief for the *Journal of Accountancy*, the largest accounting magazine with a circulation of nearly 400,000. Colleen was an elegant lady who'd been the editor of the *Journal* for 20 years. She was also tough as nails, and didn't think much of an idea I had about a regular column in the magazine on fraud. We shook hands and parted; I'd given it my best shot.

But she called several months later, and told me she'd been thinking about my suggestion some more and wanted to give it a try. Colleen made no commitments that it would be a regular feature. She said that would be determined by the reaction to the column.

This first article was entitled "So That's Why They Call It a Pyramid Scheme." It was about "Crazy Eddie" Antar and his financial fraud antics. I later learned that it was the top article for the *Journal* for the year, winning the Lawler Award. I'd go on to publish 48 pieces and win the Lawler Award a second time. Colleen had told me that each time I published an article, it was either the top piece or close to it.

"Joe," Colleen said, "there have been only two other people in the history of the *Journal* who have won the award twice. I can't let you win again so I'm going to establish the *Journal of Accountancy* Hall of Fame and you are going to be the first inductee. That will take you out of the running for future awards; we've got to give someone else a chance."

Colleen and I became good friends. When she retired from the *Journal*, the ACFE hired her as a part-time editor for *Fraud Magazine*.

Another publication, *Internal Auditor Magazine*, has a circulation of about 160,000. I didn't write for them much, but two articles I wrote won the Thurston Award for being the top articles in their magazine too.

I truly love to write, with the possible exception of this volume, my autobiography. To me, writing is enormously difficult but satisfying. And while I'm bragging about my various accolades, let me get two more out of the way.

In 2003 I was elected to the AICPA's Hall of Fame. The American Institute of Certified Public Accountants has 350,000 members, and I have belonged to the organization for nearly 40 years. An unexpected bonus of my membership is that I met its president and CEO, Barry Melancon, over a decade ago in connection with ACFE business; we've become friends.

And in 2010, I was thrilled when York College of the City University of New York conferred on me a doctorate for my work in anti-fraud education. Chief among those I have to thank for this honor is my friend and colleague, Mary-Jo Kranacher, CFE, CPA, chairperson of York College's Accounting and Finance Department. Besides being the ACFE Endowed Professor of Fraud Examination, Mary-Jo is editor-in-chief of *The CPA Journal*, the official publication of the New York State Society of CPAs and a former member of our Board of Regents.

Chapter 8

Looking Back and Looking Ahead

I am an addict. I don't know if I was born that way, but my addictions surfaced early in life and regrettably have helped define me as a person. At the age of 14, I began smoking cigarettes. The habit was considered cool at the time; it surely isn't. My addiction to nicotine began about a year before the Surgeon General declared it a health hazard. Except for a four-year hiatus, I've smoked ever since. It's a good thing that smoking is now socially ostracized; these days it would be easier to admit you are a leper.

But smoking would later prove to be the least of my addictions. Before I went into the FBI, I was addicted to marijuana. And during my times in the Bureau, I got addicted to endorphins from running. I never tried anything stronger than marijuana, such as cocaine or meth, because of one primary reason: My personality is so addictive that I probably would have sold my house and car to buy more.

Because of the problems alcohol caused in my family, I didn't drink much in my earlier days. That changed, very gradually, when I was in my 50s. At first, it was a cocktail or two before or after dinner. Then I progressed to three or four drinks a day. Then six or seven. Finally, I was drinking all day every day — from morning to night. Because I spent most of the time in my home office, it wasn't a situation of me being out on the road causing danger to others. When I went to Austin to visit ACFE headquarters, Judy drove. A few people in the office knew I was drinking; most did not. Judy was concerned with the volume I was consuming, but she was smart enough to know that hounding me was no way to handle the situation.

For more than three years, I consumed at least a fifth of 100-proof vodka a day. I didn't get completely shit-faced on a regular basis, but I sipped constantly. There were several occasions, however, when I was drunk enough to be a hazard to myself.

Once, Judy was out of the house and I was taking a nap or had passed out after heavy drinking. When I awoke, I stood up and promptly fell backward on my head, striking the tile floor. It knocked me out cold. When I came to, I felt something on the back of my neck. It was blood. Still dazed, I called Judy, who came home right away. She took one look at the gash on the back of my noggin and rushed me to the small hospital in Bellville.

Although there are many advantages to living in a rural community, the quality of medical care is not one of them. The emergency room doctor was so old that he had to scoot around the examination table on a wheeled chair.

With his hands shaking, the doctor said, "Good grief, son. That's a bad wound. I'm going to close it right now." So he started driving staples into my skull. About halfway through the procedure, he mumbled, "Oh, I forgot to ask. Would you like to have some local anesthesia?"

Yes, that's correct. He was pounding staples into my head without numbing me. Judy, who was there, later said it nearly made her pass out. Had I been in my right mind, the procedure would probably have been very painful.

Once the old geezer had completed closing the wound, he inspected it carefully. "I don't like how that turned out," he opined. Then he proceeded to remove all of the staples (at least 20 of them) and stitched up the damage.

My personal physician in Austin, Dr. Sidney Robin, took out the stitches about two weeks later. Upon examining me, his first words were "Oh my God! In 20 years of practice, I've never seen anything like this." The poor patch job left a nasty four-inch scar on my cranium that is clearly visible through my thinning hair.

One would think that this experience would have cured me. But no; at different occasions over the next year, I badly cut my head again, requiring further stitches — but not by the old doctor. Then another time, I fell and cracked two ribs. Although my judgment and physical health suffered greatly, my writing strangely did not. Indeed, some of the best stuff I've composed was when I was two or three sheets to the wind. I read somewhere that most of the great Irish writers drank heavily. But that's no excuse; finally, I knew that drinking was getting me nowhere but drunk and hurt.

At one appointment with Dr. Robin, I said that I probably needed to stop drinking in a couple of years or it would eventually kill me. He looked me straight in the eye and said, "Joe, with the amount of alcohol you are consuming, I doubt if you have more than a couple of years — to live."

That was precisely what I needed to hear.

"I'll just quit then," said I.

"No, Joe, don't do that," he admonished. "There's a small but very real chance your body will go into shock from withdrawal and it could be fatal. You need medical detox."

I scoured the Web for the right facility. My first choice was Crossroads Centre in Antigua, established by Eric Clapton. It taught the 12-step program first developed by Alcoholics Anonymous. I studied up on the program and couldn't buy it philosophically. The first step was to admit that you weren't in control of your own life. My attitude was "If I'm not in control of my life, then who is?" So I couldn't adopt even the first step.

I continued my search and found my solution at Passages in Malibu. It was one of the most expensive and exclusive facilities in the country, and I spent 30 days there. I learned a great deal about what motivated me to abuse myself. In sum, I found that success for me came with enormous guilt. Because my family turned out so poorly, every time I accomplished something I felt guilty about it. There's nothing logical about this attitude, but then there is nothing logical about emotions.

The $100,000 I spent for rehab is the best investment I've ever made in my own life. Whatever time I have left on Earth, I want it to be clean and sober.

One might think that my experiences would make me a crusader against alcohol and drugs; it hasn't. In reality, I think that all drugs should be legal for adults who make a free choice. The United States alone has spent nearly $1 trillion on drug interdiction. It has been a total failure. Drugs are more plentiful and of greater potency than ever before.

Most studies conclude that there's only one truly dangerous drug. It isn't pot, crack, crank, meth, heroin, or cocaine; it's alcohol. Booze changes the chemistry in the brain to produce violence in some people. We've all heard of a drunken rampage; no one has heard of a pot rampage. So in our infinite wisdom, we've legalized the only truly dangerous drug while outlawing all the rest.

No, drugs are not the problem; addiction is. For example, some people can have one or two cocktails ad infinitum without ill effects; others can be hopelessly hooked almost from their first alcoholic beverage. When I was young, I was taught that addiction was a character flaw. It isn't. The whole issue is much more complex; many good people — and I might be one of them — are addicts. I'm one drink away from being a drunk. So my solution is to recognize that and stay away from booze, pot, and other mind-altering substances. I don't crave alcohol at all; I've been liberated from it.

Fear of Flying

Prior to the ACFE, I hadn't flown unless I had to, and when I did it scared me to death. When I was an FBI agent, it was the policy to travel armed. It was also the policy to not drink while you were traveling with a weapon on your belt. Because of my extreme fear, I ignored both policies. My pistol was packed in my checked luggage, and I didn't identify myself to the flight crew. Ordinarily I'd have to consume at least three drinks before boarding a flight. Then I'd have as much booze as the flight attendants would allow.

It was a terrible idea but at least the liquor calmed me down. Getting drunk before or on a flight didn't pose much of a problem when I was an agent, but when I got into the private sector it was another story. When I was with the FBI, I didn't usually have to go to work when I got to my destination; I'd check into a hotel and sleep it off. But after the Bureau, it wasn't uncommon for me to work when I arrived. Sometimes it was a meeting with a group; other times I'd be giving a presentation. Being boozed up just wouldn't do.

It occurred to me in about 1985 that if I knew more about how planes worked I wouldn't be so frightened. So for my birthday, Judy bought me a "sky sampler," which consisted of 5 hours of ground school and an equal amount of time in the air with a pilot. I had a wonderful instructor named Paul, a tall lanky young guy building flight time so he could get a position as an airline pilot. Sure enough, the 10 hours in the sky got me over my fear of flying.

By then I was enamored with the idea of getting a private pilot's license. That required at least 20 hours of dual instruction and another 20 hours of solo — in the plane alone. Few students could do it in 40 hours; most took double that. Every pilot remembers the first time he or she soloed. Instructors are smart enough not to tell you in advance when you're ready for that step. But you can sort of tell by your own progress. Sure enough, my time came.

Paul and I landed from a practice flight and he said, "Joe, pull over here to the ramp."

I did.

"Do three touch-and-gos without me," he commanded.

Paul then quickly stepped out of the plane, a Cessna 172, and closed the passenger door. I gulped; I was on my own. When you're in the air, there's no such thing as pulling it over to the curb to catch your breath. Whether you live through the experience is entirely up to you.

I was sweating profusely as I taxied to the runway and asked the tower for permission to depart.

"Eight niner x-ray sierra, you are cleared for takeoff," said the clear voice emanating from my radio.

I pointed the nose of the plane on the runway centerline and, as I was taught, applied full power. I kept one eye on the airspeed and the other on where I was going as the plane accelerated. When it reached 65 knots, I gently pulled on the yoke and simultaneously applied right rudder with my foot to counter the opposite forces generated by the engine's propeller. I was airborne! It was a mix of pride, exhilaration, and fear. But I did my three takeoffs and landings without killing myself. Paul was proud and so was I.

Over the next few weeks, I got in another 10 hours or so of solo flying. Then a near-disaster struck. I was setting up for a landing in Austin and called the tower, as was required.

The controller said, "Eight niner x-ray sierra, follow behind that DC-3." I looked in front of me. No plane. But I rogered anyhow, too shy to ask where the plane was that I was supposed to be following. I lined up on the runway and reduced power.

When I was no more than 10 feet off the pavement, I saw a metallic blur that crossed in front of me from left to right. I came within a few feet of colliding with it; that was the DC-3. It was landing on the crossing runway; the controller meant for me to let the other plane land first and to follow him.

But I didn't understand and had violated one of the principal rules of flying: If you don't know what the controller is saying, ask. When I saw the big plane, I pulled another incredibly bone-headed move — instinctively, I stomped on the brakes. You don't need to know much about flying to figure out that the brakes don't work when you are not in contact with the ground. The prop wash from the DC-3 lifted the left wing of the Cessna, making its other wing almost scrape the runway.

The controller said, a few seconds too late, "Eight niner x-ray sierra, go around!"

I was shaking so badly from the incident that I could barely park the plane. After my post-flight checklist was completed, I locked up the plane and walked away unharmed. It would be nearly 20 years until I flew again. But at least I wasn't afraid of airplanes any more — except when I was at the controls.

Jim Ratley's Hobbies

My next flying adventure occurred in about 2004. Jim Ratley is sort of a hobby-of-the-year kind of guy; this time it was flying. But there were many others before that: scuba diving, guitar playing, fishing, pool; I've really lost track. He doesn't seem to be happy with his hobbies unless he goes all the way and spends a small fortune. When he was scuba diving, he had all of the gear; no rentals for him. He also convinced his wife, who constantly humors him, to go along. Once he and Gloria got certified, Jim pretty much lost interest. Then it was guitar playing. I believe that he had a theory that the more expensive the guitar, the easier it is to master the instrument. So he bought a few and took some lessons.

To quote Jim, "I always wanted to play guitar very bad. And that's how I play."

Next, he went to serious fishing. But he didn't just get a rod and reel; that wouldn't be Jim. He bought complete fishing gear, a boat and trailer, and a mobile home, which he parked on the shores of a rented lot at Lake Fork — a difficult four-hour drive from Austin. That lasted a couple of years before he turned to flying.

Another thing about Jim is that he isn't really happy unless his friends share his passion for whatever hobby he has at the moment. When he started taking flying lessons, Jim kept after me to go up with him and his instructor, a cute little thing named Mary Jane. I finally caved in.

Flying really is much like bike riding; once you learn you don't forget. Within 15 minutes of taking the controls I was doing steep turns, climbs, and descents and even a few stalls. It felt good. Being Jim, renting a plane wouldn't do, so he and another fellow partnered on a Piper Cherokee which he has to this day. Jim even went on to get his instrument rating. The experience in the cockpit, combined with the passage of time since I nearly killed myself 20 years previously, ignited my desire to fly again.

There was a problem, though. The nearest airport to me with an instructor was at Eagle Lake, Texas — nearly an hour from where I live. I sought out a fellow named Lance Easterling, a seasoned veteran in the cockpit, to help me brush up on my skills.

bright metallic blue; the interior was fire engine red. The plane was a total piece of junk. Early one morning I decided to go for some practice flying. The weather was overcast and since I wasn't instrument-rated, I would have to stay low enough to avoid clouds.

The Eagle Lake airport didn't have an automated weather broadcast of barometric pressure, wind direction and speed, and ceiling. I could tell that the wind was calm, but I couldn't judge the ceiling. I decided it was probably high enough to practice takeoffs and landings, so that was my intent.

But the moment I lifted off the runway, I knew I was in trouble: Instantly I was in the clouds. That's a very bad thing for a non-instrument pilot; studies have indicated that pilots without instrument ratings who get caught in the clouds usually last less than two minutes before they lose complete control of the aircraft and go crashing to the ground.

With palms sweating I immediately turned the airplane 180 degrees in the clouds and chopped the power to lose altitude. I could then see the runway, but I was halfway down it. Not wanting to risk another attempt to land, I put the plane on the runway and stomped the brakes hard to avoid running off the end. The left brake locked and I veered off into the dirt, knocking a couple of runway lights out in the process. There was a gully on the side of the runway. I hit that too and the plane nosed down — bending the prop and the nose wheel in the process. I was uninjured and terribly embarrassed; essentially the plane was totaled.

The airport wasn't open yet, but a fellow saw the incident and rushed over to make sure I was okay. I called the plane's owner to report the accident. Rather than being upset, the owner was thrilled.

"I'm so glad to be rid of that piece of crap!" he exclaimed. "It was insured for $80,000 and I wouldn't have gotten half of that for it!"

I guess the guy laughed all the way to the bank; I just slinked away. You would have thought that my near misses would have been an obvious signal that I wasn't meant to fly. But I forged ahead and bought still another airplane — a Piper Cherokee that cruised at about 130 knots.

It wasn't really my kind of plane, but it had one feature that especially attracted me: air conditioning. This vehicle was the Chevrolet of airplanes — inexpensive, dependable, dull. I had it painted, reupholstered and got the panel redone with spiffy new GPS electronics to keep me from getting lost.

Adrenaline Junkie

I spent nearly a year tooling around in my Piper Cherokee when I lost interest in flying. Judy didn't say much, but I knew she preferred that I find a safer hobby — perhaps collecting stamps. But I've always been an adrenaline junkie. That probably was a major factor in my joining the FBI — I just don't like things too safe. And besides, what stories would I have missed telling without my adventures?

After completely tricking out my Piper, I sold it and haven't flown since. I miss it terribly when the skies are "severe clear," as pilots say. But it is an expensive and sometimes dangerous hobby. If I had to really go somewhere, a plane might make sense. Nothing eventful, thank goodness, occurred with my Piper Cherokee. After nearly a year, I sold it out of boredom. But I proved to myself one important thing: I could fly an airplane.

Part of the reason I got burned out on flying was a trip I took with Jim Ratley and Lance Easterling, my flight instructor. We decided to fly in Jim's plane from Texas to an air show in Tampa, Florida.

On the way, we hugged the Gulf Coast where Hurricane Katrina's impact was mind-boggling: mile after mile of complete devastation. Jim, Lance and I took turns flying Jim's plane out and back. If you haven't spent much time in a small plane, let me tell you the noise is deafening. We all wore noise-canceling headsets, which helped greatly.

The trip to Tampa took about nine hours; back it was about eight. By the time we landed both ways, I had a splitting headache from the noise and the pressure of the headsets on my skull.

Once when Jim was flying, he looked in the backseat where I was and said earnestly, "Aren't we having fun?"

I wasn't; I could hardly wait to get there. Straight and level flying with your GPS locked to the autopilot means that you simply sit and watch the instruments. I'd much rather be doing something: climbing, descending, turning, taking off or landing. In a typical cross-country trip, that takes about 1 percent of the time; just not enough action for me.

Part Five

THE GLOBAL FIGHT
AGAINST FRAUD

Chapter 9

Forging Alliances

At last count, the ACFE had 138 chapters in 40 countries. Forty percent of our more than 55,000 members are from outside the United States, and we've established anti-fraud relationships all over the world. While we expect the ACFE to continue growing slowly in North America, our greatest growth potential is in the international arena.

That's something we've put a considerable amount of time and effort into fostering. Not long after founding the ACFE, Jim and I began traveling the world to spread the gospel of fraud detection, deterrence, and prevention.

By the mid-1990s, we'd settled into a pattern. I went east, and he went west. For me it was Canada and Europe — Austria, Bulgaria, Denmark, Germany, Holland, Hungary, Ireland, Luxembourg, Poland and the United Kingdom. For Jim it was Mexico and the

Asia-Pacific region — that meant Australia, China, Indonesia, Japan, Malaysia, New Zealand, the Philippines and Singapore.

Once I jokingly accused him of having his own fan club in New Zealand because he'd been there so often. On one of his trips, he and his lovely wife, Gloria, bungee-jumped off a bridge near Queenstown, where the sport had been invented. Some enterprising fellow on the other side of the gorge videotaped all the jumpers, and then offered to sell them a copy. Jim bought his, and proudly played it for us. On the video, Gloria went first with no hesitation. When it was Jim's turn, he wavered but finally jumped. I laughed hard, but Jim's braver than me; I wouldn't have done it at all.

The Law Enforcement Partnership

Because law enforcement has always been a vital part of the ACFE's mission, we established the ACFE Law Enforcement Partnership in 2005. Participating agencies recognize the CFE credential when they hire and promote personnel. In return, partners are entitled to discounts on ACFE training and other benefits.

In 2007 I hired Alani Mundie to develop and run the program. I'd met Alani through her sister, Liseli, who worked for us while attending college and later went on to a career in the U.S. State Department, where she is today. Alani too had been an ACFE employee shortly after completing her bachelor's degree in political science. Determined to apply her education in the political arena, she joined the staff of a United States congresswoman in Dallas, but later began to miss Austin dearly.

Meanwhile, we had stayed in touch, and Alani eventually returned to the ACFE, where, as International Law Enforcement Liaison, she travels extensively to promote the Partnership, which is growing slowly but steadily. The first four agencies to recognize the CFE credential were the FBI, the Department of

Defense, the U.S. Postal Inspection Service, and the Government Accountability Office.

The Partnership now has 28 members, including the Securities and Exchange Commission, the U.S. Marshals Service — the nation's oldest law enforcement agency — and the Criminal Investigations Division of the IRS, as well as numerous other federal, state and local investigative agencies. Some put large numbers of their staff through the CFE program. Within two years of the SEC joining in 2009, nearly 400 of its employees had earned the credential.

We anticipate the largest domestic growth in membership will be among the Offices of Inspectors General at the federal, state and local levels. We're also working to expand the Partnership internationally. Several times Alani has traveled to Lyon to meet with Interpol and to The Hague to speak with Europol. We're hopeful that both will join the Partnership in the near future. If and when that happens, there's a good chance that numerous European nations would follow their example.

Besides having a strong work ethic, Alani is kind, thoughtful, and shares my dark sense of humor. Having met her family, I know where she got these traits. Her father, John, a lawyer in El Paso, celebrates his birthday one day before mine, although not in the same year. Like Alani and me, he loves to laugh. If he lived nearby, we'd hang out together a lot.

Alani's mother, Lilia, also had wonderful values. Regrettably, she developed cancer, and passed away at only 54. It made me wonder: presuming there is a God above, why does He let bad things happen to good people? Why doesn't He pick on those who deserve it?

Old Days, New Media

Ten years ago, when we wanted to contact a member, we did it by phone or a letter. Now, 80% of our communication is electronic, and we conduct a lot of our training online. Technology has enabled us to develop and educate new audiences — those members who previously wouldn't have been able to attend an ACFE course because it was held too far away or at a time that conflicted with their schedules.

Still, there'll always be strong demand for on-site courses and interaction with the course presenter and other members in attendance. Some people overlook the importance of such networking. So many times in our line of work, the critical factor isn't *what* you know; it's *who* you know that can open a door for you. In our business, knowledge is power — power to be an effective fraud examiner.

Social media — a relatively new use of technology — have revolutionized the way the ACFE communicates with members and how members interact with each other. Our vastly increased use of Facebook, LinkedIn, Twitter, and other such Web sites has enriched our professional community and its dialogue. This kind of interconnectedness has always been desirable. But now, as the ACFE opens more and more chapters around the world, it's indispensable.

Focusing on Members

Members come to us from two sources: from our seminars and, mostly, from referrals by other members. One thing that spurs their enthusiasm is our training, which tens of thousands have attended.

At ACFE seminars and courses, many people tell us, "This is the best training I've ever been to." And members have thanked Jim and me countless times for providing the tools they needed to properly investigate a fraud case. "I can't tell you how much this has helped me," they say. "I had this fraud case dropped in my lap, and I didn't know what to do with it."

To address that need, our training and printed materials provide a methodology that helps a fraud examiner conduct an investigation. In, for example, the Fraud Theory Approach, you first analyze the available data. Next, based on your analysis, you formulate a hypothesis, which you then test. And finally, you refine and amend your hypothesis. Of course, this isn't a silver bullet for solving fraud cases. But tools and techniques like this help fraud examiners conduct better investigations and resolve more cases. And that's what motivates people to join the ACFE and encourage their colleagues to as well. Now, the ACFE can't cure the world's ills. But by applying these methods, our members can track down and bust fraudsters one by one.

Our primary role is to provide a good network where they can get together and exchange information. Recently, we formed a group — the ACFE Advisory Council — to help ensure we provide members with the latest and best fraud-fighting tools and techniques. We encourage participation by members who are subject matter experts in various fields, and we enable them to electronically participate in quarterly member surveys, write or review course materials, provide industry case studies, and assist in professional development activities.

These people are out there in the trenches every day. Based on that experience, they share their views on the future of the ACFE, the direction in which it should be headed, new courses we should offer, and specific problems they're currently encountering in the field, so that we can better design our events, education, and other offerings. In this way, members help the ACFE improve prevention and detection techniques.

Onward

In early 2009, Kathie Green Lawrence retired from the ACFE. We made sure she's financially secure. Now she can spend more time with her grandkids, whom she loves dearly. Kathie spent 32 years with me in some capacity — first in the FBI, then with Wells & Associates, and finally with the ACFE. Working so hard took a personal and emotional toll on her, and she was ready to hang up her spurs. We all owe her a debt of gratitude.

What does the future hold? For the ACFE, a lot. It is still far from its potential, and I derive great satisfaction from knowing it will live on after I'm gone. To ensure continuity, I formed an employee-owned corporation that will take effect upon Jim's and my deaths. Those working at the ACFE now and in the future will inherit it as my legacy.

I also plan to continue my involvement in the ACFE Foundation, a non-profit organization I founded to help support anti-fraud scholarship through tuition assistance and endowments.

Personally, I'm where I want to be, doing what I want to do. Each day is a fresh adventure in which I don't report to anyone or follow a strict schedule.

I'm filled with love for Judy. She's wonderfully patient, and has even grown to like my sixty-fifth birthday present to myself: a small loop ring in my left ear. Why did I get the piercing? Because I was 65, and I could.

I'm taking an on-line novel-writing course and toying with the idea of writing a book full of imagination. It wouldn't matter to me if it sold only ten copies; I'd probably find it enormously fulfilling.

Like other people, I hope the things I've learned in life have made me a better person. Once I became financially independent, I realized how little satisfaction I get from acquiring things and how much I enjoy giving. The best part of my success has been being able to help others in ways that make a measurable difference in their lives.

I haven't yearned for a particularly long life. And considering how I've physically abused myself over many decades, it's a wonder

I'm still here and in good health. The most horrible thought I can conjure up is that of suffering from dementia or being physically dependent on others. If I ever get that way, I'll be ready to find out whether there's a better life on the other side. Maybe I'll be lucky enough to go the same way my Grandpa Will did. One night, at the age of 80-something, he went to bed and didn't wake up.

While I've come to accept my inadequacies, I place a high value on honesty and fair play. As a young FBI agent, I learned that lesson the hard way, and sleep better as a result. It's a good thing, because I've got no patience for distractions. There's much to do, and time's flying.

Acknowledgements

Writing a book — any book — is a daunting process. But writing about yourself might be the most difficult of all. Tim Burgard at John Wiley & Sons, Inc. had been after me for a long time to put my story on paper. I resisted. And then resisted some more. Finally, though, I started filling up this computer screen with words, thanks in no small part to Tim's persistence. From soup to nuts, the process took about two years of starting and stopping. In the early spring of 2010, *Fraud Fighter* was ready to go to print. But I halted it; something just didn't feel right about the book. The manuscript sat fallow. I seriously considered just dumping the whole thing.

Then I had a stroke of inspiration — get Bob Tie involved. I've known Bob for over ten years. Before going out on his own, he was a senior editor for the *Journal of Accountancy,* the largest circulation accounting magazine in the world. I'd published over 50 articles for the *Journal* and he was deeply enmeshed in many (if not most) of them. Any writer worth his salt would admit one thing without hesitation: The author and the editor are full partners in what eventually is published. It is a symbiotic relationship; one can't exist without the other. In my case, this led to multiple writing awards from the magazine. Bob deserves equal credit but it is the custom in his trade that the editor is not even mentioned — an unsung hero, if you will.

I've not met anyone like Mr. Tie. He is a true Renaissance Man. Bob has encyclopedic knowledge on an astonishing range of topics, from history to algebra to music and more. Yes, I take full responsibility for every word in these pages, right or wrong. But you wouldn't be reading any of this if it weren't for Bob Tie.

Index

Index

Index

Index